RELIVI

MAINSTREAM *SPORT*

# RELIVING
# THE DREAM

## THE TRIUMPH AND TEARS OF MANCHESTER UNITED'S
## 1968 EUROPEAN CUP HEROES

## DERICK ALLSOP

MAINSTREAM
PUBLISHING

EDINBURGH AND LONDON

First published in Great Britain in 1998 by
MAINSTREAM PUBLISHING COMPANY (EDINBURGH) LTD
7 Albany Street
Edinburgh EH1 3UG

This edition 1998

ISBN 1 84018 140 0

A catalogue record for this book is available from the British Library

Typeset in Garamond
Printed and bound in Finland by WSOY

# CONTENTS

For Matt, Jimmy and the boys

# ACKNOWLEDGEMENTS

This book has been made possible thanks to the help and forbearance of many people. Not every member of the '68 team was able – or willing – to give unlimited co-operation. Some are less enthusiastic about their manager and club than others, and their candour is appreciated. But all the players have contributed years of inspirational input, for which I am grateful. The players are Alex Stepney, Shay Brennan, Tony Dunne, Pat Crerand, Bill Foulkes, Nobby Stiles, George Best, Brian Kidd, Bobby Charlton, David Sadler, John Aston, Jimmy Rimmer and Denis Law.

I also wish to thank Wilf McGuinness, Tommy Docherty, Martin Edwards, Ron Atkinson, Alex Ferguson, Eusebio, David Coleman, Frank McGhee, John Baumann and the staff at Great Fosters, the staff at Manchester United, Mick Docherty, Peter Slater, the BBC for giving me access to their archive material, Keith Hilton, The Speaking Book Company for permission to quote from their cassette tapes entitled 'Manchester United – The Busby Years', narrated by Pat Crerand and Denis Law, *The Independent*, *The Sunday Telegraph*, David Meek, especially for wading through the proofs, Luis Vasconcelos, Ray Matts, Stan Piecha, Jane Nottage, Jim Hutchison, Jim Mossop, Sue, Natalie and Kate Allsop, and, not least, Bill Campbell and Cathy Mineards of Mainstream for their enthusiasm and support.

# PROLOGUE

A middle-aged man coaxes his bicycle to a halt at the top of the forecourt, dismounts and walks slowly, quietly down the slope towards the great brick bowl that is the stadium. His eyes are fixed on a large bronze figure, and the closer he gets, the slower his stride becomes. It is a respectful, almost awestruck approach. He might be walking down the aisle of a church. At last he stops, as he might before an altar. He has tousled hair, a beard and a rucksack on his back. He stands motionless, his gaze intense, for two or three minutes and then, still slowly, still quietly, turns and wheels his bicycle away.

The bronze figure, standing on a simple bronze plinth, seems to watch the cyclist go back across the forecourt. The statue is of a man in perhaps later middle years. His countenance is benign, the smile gentle, the stance relaxed. He is wearing a blazer which carries the club crest. Under his left arm he holds a football. It captures the image and aura of Sir Matt Busby perfectly.

Above him is a plaque laid out like a football pitch. The words on it read: 'In memory of the officials and players who lost their lives in the Munich air disaster on the 6th February, 1958.' The names of those who perished are spread out on the pitch – Walter Crickmer, Tom Curry, Bert Whalley, Roger Byrne, Geoff Bent, Mark Jones, Eddie Colman, David Pegg, Duncan Edwards, Tommy Taylor, Billy Whelan.

The first three named were officials, the others players, members of the fabled 'Busby Babes', a Manchester United team acknowledged as one of the best ever produced by British football. Busby, their manager, almost died at Munich too. The club were returning from a European Cup tie against Red Star Belgrade, where they had secured a place in the semi-finals. Deprived of so many players, they were unable to progress further that season. But the team, like Busby, recovered, and ten years on accomplished the mission on which their lamented forebears had set out.

For Busby it was the realisation of a dream, and redemption. He had defied the strictures of the Football League to take his players into the European Cup competition, and the loss of so many lives, in particular the young lives, left him carrying a cross of contrition. Winning the European Cup could never bring them back or exorcise the ghosts. But it was the most appropriate and poignant tribute any human could have hoped for. Fittingly, too, Busby's United became the first English club to win European club football's highest honour.

Busby's new team claimed that prize on the balmy evening of 29 May 1968 at Wembley Stadium. They beat Benfica of Portugal 4–1 in a final that went into extra-time. Three goals in a devastating period of seven minutes fulfilled what many of the players considered their destiny. Perhaps even their duty. And now they were legends. Busby, recognised for his achievement with a knighthood, was not merely a football manager but the patriarch of a dynasty and institution unparalleled in the English game.

The emotional forces generated in the wake of the Munich tragedy conveyed the club to an unprecedented position in the consciousness of the nation, and the '60s' team sustained the momentum. They, however, failed to retain the European Cup and it was not until the final months of Busby's life that United won another Championship – and with it the right to compete again for the champions' trophy. Under the stewardship of Alex Ferguson – like Busby, a Scot – United took the English title four times in five seasons between 1993 and 1997, and in the process became the first club in the country to complete the double of Championship and FA Cup twice.

The club's expansion in the '90s has been commensurate with that success. Their Old Trafford stadium holds more than 55,000, all seated – making it the biggest football ground in Britain outside Wembley – and is full for virtually every match. The club, now a plc, is worth more than £400m. Television revenues, sponsorship, merchandising and spin-off ventures of almost every conceivable nature keep the money rolling in daily, not solely on match days.

You wonder what the 'Old Man', as he was affectionately known, makes of it all, peering down from his plinth, for here is the dichotomy. At the far end of the forecourt, beyond the bearded man with the bicycle, a party of children are making their way back to their coach. They are armed with bags full of souvenirs trawled from the megastore. Not one of them turns to look at the statue, or the plaque. If anyone checks the time on the clock hung further along the outside wall of the stadium, the chances are they will not notice that, also, commemorates the Munich air crash. He may be forgiven for feeling he has created a monster rather than a glorious, heroic empire.

But then he will understand. The world keeps turning and he, more than anyone, looked forward. He was the visionary. He gave young men their head and sought new frontiers. Why should youngsters be expected to look over their shoulders, especially when they have bags of David Beckham T-shirts and Ryan Giggs pillowcases? They have their dreams, just as he had.

And therein lies the abiding bond, the common cause. Younger generations of United supporters and players dream of winning the European Cup. They embarked upon the 1997–98 season, the 30th anniversary of that triumphant campaign, still seeking to emulate their illustrious predecessors. Those who have aspired to that and failed will testify that the '68 victory is a monument to the greatness of a manager and his team. It should also be an inspiration to those who now pursue the dream.

The diehard fans glory in their heritage and crave more of the same. They still sing the praises of the patriarch, of 'walking down the Warwick Road to see Matt Busby's aces'. Today Warwick Road is called Sir Matt Busby Way, but they march to the same tune, to the same crusade.

# INTRODUCTION
## by
# GEORGE BEST

When Manchester United won the European Cup in 1968 they not only became the first English club to reach the pinnacle, but also penned the final chapter of perhaps the greatest story in the history of football. If it had been fiction, people would have scoffed and dismissed it as too far-fetched. And yet it happened. It was true, it was real, and no script could have come up with anything like it; no one could have written a human drama to compare with it.

Matt Busby had to rebuild his team after Munich, and just ten years later there he was, holding aloft that massive trophy at Wembley. This was the Holy Grail. To Sir Matt (as he became) it meant everything – and I mean everything. It was his whole life and the pursuit of it almost cost him his life. So many of his great players had lost their lives in the crash. And now the mission had been accomplished. We'd beaten Benfica in seven glorious and unbelievable minutes of extra-time. It was just amazing.

When United crashed at Munich, in 1958, I was a kid in Belfast, and it obviously stunned everybody, football fans in every part of Britain and beyond. And if you hadn't supported Manchester United before, well, they became your second favourites from then on. Everyone took them to their hearts because of the tragedy. And to think that just three years later I'd be at the club! It still seems hard to take in.

It wasn't exactly taboo to talk about Munich at the club, but people just didn't. They didn't have to. It was there in the atmosphere. And soon I found myself part of this great crusade to make United the best in England again, and then the best in Europe. Just getting the club back on its feet again was a huge job in itself, and at the time I don't think anyone involved realised what an enormous task – and what a great achievement – it was. But Sir Matt had his dream and he was determined to turn that dream into reality.

He was one of the greatest managers – if not *the* greatest – of all time. He took his first team to FA Cup success in 1948 and the Championship in 1952, then brought in a totally new team, the magnificent Babes, who won the Championship in '56 and '57. He had to build a third team after Munich and he went about it in such a decisive way. He knew he had to bring in quality players to complement those he had, so he said, 'Hey, I want Denis Law and Paddy Crerand,' and he went and got them. Later he decided he needed a goalkeeper to complete his side, and so he got Alex Stepney. He set his sights, made up his mind that he wanted to get a great side together again and did it.

I came into the side in September 1963, and by then the team had started to turn the corner by winning the FA Cup. We won the League in '65 and again in '67 and were there or thereabouts in everything else, but the 'biggie' was the European Cup. We had a great chance in '66 after a fantastic performance away to Benfica, a match that holds particularly fond memories for me. We demolished them 5–1, I scored a couple of goals and everything really took off for me. Unfortunately, I then got injured and we went out in the semi-final against Partizan Belgrade.

When we got another crack at it, in the '67–'68 season, we were better prepared for it and had the perfect blend of experience and youth. People say the team was over the hill, but it wasn't really. Sure, Bill Foulkes was in his mid-thirties, and Bobby Charlton and Shay Brennan had turned 30, but Brian Kidd was 19 on the day of the final and the rest were in their twenties. John Aston was only 20, I was just 22 and David Sadler was only a few months older. The balance was spot-on.

But then we come back to this incredible script. Both sides had battled for 90 minutes without deciding it. We were locked at 1–1. And then, all of a sudden, it's over. In seven minutes of the first half of extra-time, a spell of sheer magic, the whole competition, the whole season, a whole decade, Sir Matt's whole life, were complete and fulfilled. We scored three goals and Benfica were finished. The European Cup was ours.

The strange thing is I can remember nothing of the build-up to the final or what happened afterwards. A total blank. But the match itself is as vivid as if it were yesterday, every fabulous detail crystal clear: Bobby's header for our first, their equaliser, thumped in by Graca, Alex's fantastic save from Eusebio, my little side-step round the keeper for our second, Kiddo's header, and Bobby's terrific goal to round it off.

We had class and character right through that side, and when it mattered we produced. We made history for the club and the country, and we did it in style. Allow me to introduce you to the heroes of '68.

## 1. Alex Stepney

There were so many great goalkeepers around at that time, particularly English goalkeepers, and as a consequence Alex suffered at international level.

Had there not been people like Gordon Banks and Peter Bonetti to compete against, he would have won a lot more than the one cap he got. But for the club he was a gem. He made it look easy – the mark of a great keeper. He was never flash or flamboyant. He didn't need to be. He had the knack of being in the right place at the right time.

### 2. Shay Brennan

Here's Mr Cool, off the pitch and on it. He was always such a calm, cultured player, who made his debut as a left-winger but found his best position at right-back. No matter how depressed or down you might be, Shay would be sure to pick you up with that great smile on his face. He was so easy-going he was the last person you'd expect to have a heart attack, but typically he bounced back. He's one of my biggest pals and we're even closer now than when we were playing.

### 3. Tony Dunne

People talk about quick players today, but Tony wasn't just quick, he was lightning. The winger would think he was past him and suddenly Tony would be back at him, taking the ball away. He covered so decisively. He was always there. And he had such a terrific temperament. He never got flustered, always remained composed. He was a quiet lad. Others would go off for a game of snooker after training, but Tony would be away to his family. That's the sort of guy he was.

### 4. Pat Crerand

We had a lot of great players at the time and you didn't want any of them to be out of the side, but I always said that if there was one player I didn't like to be injured it was Paddy. He made us play. Long passes, short passes – he delivered them on the spot. We used to take the mick about his lack of pace, but he didn't need it. He made the ball do the work. He was temperamental, but you had to accept that. He was my minder. He's still United-daft, a great bloke and a great pal.

### 5. Bill Foulkes

He was very different from Tony in stature and wouldn't claim to have been as quick, but like Tony he was such a reliable figure in our defence. He was a real stopper and not much got past him, especially in the air. He'd get it and give it. He knew what he could do and didn't try to complicate things. He was a survivor of Munich, so Europe meant such a lot to him. When he finished training he liked to head for the golf course. He was good at that, too.

### 6. Nobby Stiles

Every team needed a Nobby-type player, but there was only one Nobby. He did his job brilliantly wherever he did it – and he could play anywhere. For us he settled into a defensive role alongside Bill, and, of course, he marked Eusebio. I knew what it was like being marked by Nobby, because he did it on me in internationals. He'd apologise at the end but I told him it was okay, he was doing his job. Off the pitch he was different again: a lovely man, and so accident-prone. We called him Clouseau – a walking nightmare!

### 7. George Best

I'd like to think I can look back, all these years on, and feel pretty proud about my contribution to the team. I was top scorer for the club for five consecutive seasons and joint top scorer in the First Division (before there was a Premier League, of course) one year. And I played on the wing! I think I also played my part in the European Cup win, along the way as well as in the final, and that I played the game the way the United fans wanted to see it played.

### 8. Brian Kidd

I remember when he first came into the team, as an 18-year-old, and found himself against Mike England, one of the best centre-halves in the business. Kiddo turned Mike inside out and you knew he was something special. He had great skills for a big lad, and a terrific shot. And can you imagine scoring on your 19th birthday – in a European Cup final? Off the field he was always quieter, but Alex Ferguson realised what an asset he could be as his assistant manager. Alex is full of praise for him.

### 9. Bobby Charlton

'Amazing' and 'incredible' are words that spring to mind. Bobby did it all for club and country, and loved United. Still does. I've never seen a player go past defenders as easily as Bobby did. He'd just glide past them. Then, from 30 yards or more, left foot or right, he'd just hammer it. Such an exciting player. Like Bill, he was a survivor of the crash and went through it all. Big pal of Nobby and Shay, and another family man who liked to get back to his wife and daughters.

### 10. David Sadler

Almost every club in the country wanted Dave when he was playing amateur football in the South, but he opted for United and became a good pal. We were in digs together and roomed together at away matches. He was originally a centre-forward but proved versatile, operating in midfield or central defence, where I felt he was at his best. He had a number of games for England at centre-half. He was a studious, intelligent lad and that showed in his play. Great guy and now runs our old boys' association.

### 11. John Aston

Everybody agrees he was the man of the match in the European Cup final. He absolutely murdered their poor right-back. But unfortunately people just seem to remember his performance that night, when in fact he played a lot of terrific games for us. He was often underestimated because there were so many big-name players in our team, but he never gave less than 100 per cent. His strength was his running and he would be up and down that left flank all day. He grafted non-stop.

### Substitute: Jimmy Rimmer

We were allowed a substitute goalkeeper in those days but poor Jimmy didn't actually get the chance to come on in the final. He was also unlucky that we had Alex at the time because he was another international-class keeper and, like Alex, he played for England. He was still a young lad in '68 and went on to prove his quality with two other big clubs, Arsenal and Aston Villa. He also got a European Cup-winners' medal with Villa, so he did pretty well for himself in the end.

### Denis Law

It would be impossible to talk about all the players we had in those days, but equally I couldn't possibly ignore this fella. He couldn't play in the final because he was in hospital, but he was with us in spirit. He had some mates round for a bevvy or six and I don't think he remembers too much about the match. As a player he was up there with the all-time greats. Electric. He'd snap up any half-chance. As a bloke and as a pal, he's different class. Nobody has a bad word for Denis.

I think it's a measure of the standard we set that three of us won the European Footballer of the Year award: Denis in 1964, Bobby in 1966 and myself in 1968. When you've got three players like that you've got a chance. But we had quality right through the team and we had to have, because to win the European Cup in those days you had to be a bit special. And it was the way we played, with flair and imagination. If the other team got three, we knew we were going to get four or five. We were good and we knew we were good.

This was the way Sir Matt believed the game should be played, and he brought together the players he knew could do it. And he knew how to get the best out of them, how to build their confidence and encourage them to express themselves. He was a great manager and a great man. He was like a second father to me and I was really touched at his funeral when his family told me he regarded me as a son. I like to think his football family did him proud.

# PART I

# ONE MAN AND HIS DREAM

It is inevitable the poorer and harsher environments of the world should spawn hungry fighters and footballers, but the Scottish coalfields exceeded their quota by yielding three of the beautiful game's greatest men and managers. Jock Stein would make Celtic the first British champions of Europe, Bill Shankly would convey Liverpool from the Second Division of the English Football League to the threshold of European supremacy. And yet most observers concur with the view that they and their achievements were probably eclipsed by Matt Busby and his management of Manchester United.

These three extraordinary individuals shared not only their roots but also a contact with football's soul. Their teams were the manifestation of the purist's ethos, their triumph the deliverance of the faithful. Detractors would argue spiritual virtues and principles would not have survived the constraints of more pragmatic later generations. In which case, let us give thanks they lived when they did.

The case for proclaiming Busby's pre-eminence, even in this noble company, is founded on his record over a quarter of a century and a legacy that cannot be measured adequately in titles and trophies. It was convenient to depict him as the manager who inherited a great team that won the FA Cup in 1948, the team that died at Munich in 1958 and the team that won the European Cup in 1968. Life and reality, however, rarely conform to such symmetry.

He did not merely 'inherit' and 'buy' teams, just as he did not have merely three teams. He constantly moulded, developed, revised and refined his teams. The most dramatic and significant unforced changes were made to accommodate the introduction of the 'Busby Babes' in the '50s, but even that fabled side was shuffled and added to before the crash. Busby did spend in order to hasten the club's recovery, yet his line-up against Benfica at Wembley included only two players who had cost transfer fees of any consequence. And Alex Stepney and Pat Crerand had arrived at a combined expense of little more than £100,000.

Busby's teams won also the League Championship in 1952, 1956, 1957, 1965 and 1967, and the FA Cup in 1963. The ground he moved into when it was a bombed-out shell became the finest in English League football and has been improved still further in recent years. In the 1967–68 season the average home attendance was a record 57,549. The club is simply the biggest in the land and one of the biggest in the world. Everywhere the game is played – and you suspect some places where it is not – they know of Manchester United. Matt Busby was the perpetrator of this phenomenon.

Busby was born into a Catholic family in Orbiston, near the town of Bellshill, Lanarkshire, on 26 May 1909. The menfolk of the area worked at the coalface and played football, and young Matt was no different. One activity provided essential income, the other equally necessary escape. He did not, however, seek to shirk his responsibilities. He was six when his father was killed in the First World War and he grew up quickly as a consequence. His maturity became evident in his playing days, when he was a natural captain, and in the way he both settled into and redefined football management.

He played, ironically, for Manchester City, and then Liverpool. He was what was commonly referred to as a 'cultured' wing-half and was much vaunted for his 'reading and understanding' of the game. He won only one full Scotland cap but led his country in a number of wartime internationals. Like many of his contemporaries, he lost much of his playing career to the Second World War, although he might have continued when peace was restored to Europe in 1945.

Instead he accepted an invitation to become manager of Manchester United. It was a career move that appealed to him, and he and his wife Jean liked Manchester. At that time, however, the job did not have the cachet it has now. United had modest status, having spent the inter-war years shuffling between the First and Second Divisions. The club had begun life in 1878 as Newton Heath, founded by employees of the Lancashire and Yorkshire Railway Company as a cricket and football club. They were admitted to the Football League in 1892, losing their first match, against Blackburn Rovers, 4–3. They became Manchester United in 1902, were champions in 1908 and 1911, and FA Cup winners in 1909. By the time Busby took over they were in the shadow of Manchester City, who had Championship and FA Cup success in the '30s. They also had a ground United were to use in the immediate aftermath of the Second World War because enemy bombers had destroyed much of Old Trafford.

The role of the manager, also, was very different from the one with which we are now familiar. Club secretaries and directors assumed it was their right and duty to run affairs, even to the extent of influencing team selection. Working parameters demanded by Busby in 1945 were instrumental in changing the nature and power of management. He insisted on absolute control. He would do it his way or not at all. The club complied and on 19 February 1945 appointed him for five years, at an annual salary of £750.

Busby admitted he had no training for the job, but believed he knew the game and knew players. He felt that losing his father at such a tender age made him sensitive to the vulnerability of young footballers, many of whom lived away from home. The 'Father' of Manchester United was already embracing his new family. The paternal instincts were apparent in his firm but compassionate handling of players. He took the view that if they were made to feel comfortable, wanted and respected, they would respond positively on the field. He encouraged them to be expressive, creative and assertive.

The wider scope of Busby's managerial function necessitated another innovation: the proactive No. 2. He wanted someone closer to ground level. Someone who would work with the players constantly and fire some of his bullets for him. Someone who would growl and cajole, yet teach and nurture with no less care. Someone who would complement yet never seek to undermine him or aspire to his position. If appointing Matt Busby was the single most important decision in the history of Manchester United, sanctioning the recruitment of Jimmy Murphy as his right-hand man might be the second most important.

Murphy, too, had been a wing-half and played for West Bromwich Albion. He was Welsh, played for his country and later managed them on a part-time basis. He was more at ease, however, as a No. 2. Especially Busby's No. 2. A stint as his stand-in after Munich confirmed as much. He turned down many invitations to manage club sides, including one from Juventus. He was content with a low profile, working with his players, honing their raw talent for professional careers. They grew to appreciate his dedication and warmed to him, even those who felt the sharp edge of his tongue. They believed his contribution was not always sufficiently acknowledged. Murphy was 'promoted' to assistant manager in 1955 and in his later years scouted for the club.

The Busby–Murphy partnership established a mode of management aped by some of the sport's most successful figures. Shankly had Bob Paisley; Brian Clough had Peter Taylor. The format worked, and United garnered the benefits after doubtless holding their breath. Busby and Murphy saw no logic in the old maxim that you 'starve a player of the ball in the week and he will be hungry for it on the Saturday'. They trained with the ball, they 'practised' their trade. And eventually they were made almost perfect.

United, redirected and fashioned by Busby, were runners-up in the Championship for three consecutive seasons from 1947, and in 1948, captained by the revered Johnny Carey and playing in blue shirts because of a colour clash with Blackpool, won a classic FA Cup final 4–2. United trailed 2–1 with little more than 20 minutes remaining and Stanley Matthews was reaching out for his winner's medal. But Busby's players, exhorted to keep faith in their practised game, turned the match with three goals.

The Cup was welcomed home to Manchester with a public show of jubilation, yet Busby knew the Championship was the only genuine gauge of the best. Finishing runners-up again in 1951 heightened the frustration – and made the success of the following year all the more precious. It was the club's first title for 41 years.

Equally important were the foundations being laid for the future. United had moved back to Old Trafford in 1949 and Busby believed his players should be bred at home, raised to play the game of his dreams. The first wave of young footballers were already being groomed by the time United won the Championship, and the intake that summer included a boy from Dudley, near Birmingham, called Duncan Edwards. Barely a year later he played, along with Eddie Colman, Billy Whelan, David Pegg and Albert Scanlon, in the first leg of the FA Youth Cup final against Wolverhampton Wanderers at Old Trafford. United won 7–1, and the senior English game was about to succumb to a new, exciting, irresistible force.

Edwards was a real-life comic hero: gifted, strong, modest. He was recognised as a left-half but could play anywhere. In times of need, he would venture forward and plunder match-winning goals. He had a ferocious shot and a presence that intimidated seasoned players. He made his debut for United at 16 and became England's youngest player of the century when he was awarded the first of his 18 caps against Scotland in April 1955 at the age of 18 years and 183 days. Those who knew him and saw him said he towered above all others, the greatest player the club ever produced.

And around him Busby and Murphy assembled a pack of bright cubs. They not only dominated youth football in this country through the '50s but also took over the man's game. The Busby Babes were set free from their pen. The manager may have been mildly embarrassed by the tag, but the alliteration was too good to miss. So was their football. It flowed with the fearless, unrestrained exuberance of youth.

In goal was Ray Wood; at right-back, Bill Foulkes, summoned from the pits of South Lancashire. The left-back and captain was Roger Byrne, a conscientious leader who suffered fools not at all. At right-half was Eddie Colman, a local lad, small and full of mischief and tricks. Mark Jones and Jackie Blanchflower vied for the centre-half's shirt. No one competed for Edwards's place. Busby had to look afield for the centre-forward to lead his attack and paid Barnsley a fee disclosed as £29,999 for Tommy Taylor. Busby felt the burden of a £30,000 transfer might be too much for the lad. His other forwards were Johnny Berry, Whelan, Dennis Viollet, Pegg and Scanlon, the competition further intensified by the likes of Kenny Morgans and the emergence of a youngster from the North-East. The word was he had an even harder shot than Edwards. His name was Bobby Charlton.

The Busby Babes, or the Red Devils, as they were alternatively known, swept to the Championship in the 1955–56 season, beating their closest rivals, Blackpool, by 11 points. This when only two points were awarded for a win. They retained the League trophy and were expected to complete the domestic double in the FA Cup final against Aston Villa, but Peter McParland's infamous challenge on Wood – which reduced United to ten men, one of them an emergency goalkeeper in Blanchflower, for much of the match – proved decisive. United lost 2–1.

In December 1957, Busby paid a world-record fee for a goalkeeper, £23,500, to sign Harry Gregg, an irascible but brave and talented Ulsterman, from Doncaster Rovers. Gregg was recruited to reinforce United's prospects not only at home but also abroad. By then Busby had made his boldest and most momentous move of all.

Chelsea, England's Championship winners in 1955, had been firmly steered away from any fancies of entering a newfangled foreign competition drummed up by the French. The idea was to determine the best team in Europe. Champions of national leagues would compete on a knock-out basis, all the ties up to the final to consist of two legs, home and away. The English Football League, however, dismissed the initiative as an irrelevant fad. The nation that gave the game to the world had no need for such gimmicks. Their clubs had plenty to occupy them in this country. The European Cup was out of bounds.

Busby disagreed and challenged that ruling. He recognised the blossoming of a new game on the Continent, played by artists who caressed the ball and were able to do wondrous things with it. Hungary's humiliation of England at Wembley and in Budapest ought to have been proof enough. Now it was evident in the European Cup, won in 1955–56, its inaugural season, by the Spanish champions Real Madrid. In the final, played in Paris, they beat the host nation's representatives, Reims, 4–3.

The enlightened United manager saw a stage to inspire his team and the country. Here was a competition to fire the imagination and stretch his tyros. Here was a world of romance, mystery, magic, fantasy. New names, new places. A new kind of football. Manchester United would defy the English authorities and enter the European Cup for the 1956–57 season. Busby would pursue a dream to emulate Real Madrid and see his team saluted as the best in Europe.

It is a testament to Busby's managerial acumen that he not only led a later team to European Cup triumph but that he was also coveted and courted by the Spaniards, who offered him 'heaven' at the Bernabeu. He politely but unreservedly declined, explaining he had his heaven at Old Trafford. He had young footballers who played like angels, their wings extended by the demands of a celestial Continental game.

United's impact on the European Cup was instant and spectacular. According to the *Manchester Guardian*'s report, datelined Brussels, 12 September 1956, 'By an Old International', 'Manchester United bore themselves nobly' to beat Anderlecht of Belgium 2–0, with goals by Viollet and Taylor, in the first leg of their preliminary-round tie. The correspondent declared that the resumption of the contest, at Moss Side, should not be missed. It was sound advice. United won that second leg, played at Maine Road because Old Trafford was not equipped with floodlights, 10–0. At a stroke, they had etched their name on the European football map.

Borussia Dortmund – who would feature prominently in United campaigns to come – threatened to erase it in the first round proper. The Germans were defeated 3–2 in Manchester but squandered chances in the return leg, which ended goalless. United were to have another close encounter in their quarter-final with Athletic Bilbao. Their naivety was exposed as they lost the away match 5–3, leaving them with a formidable task at Maine Road. That night of 6 February 1957 remains one of the landmarks in United's European odyssey. They won the leg 3–0 to go through 6–5 on aggregate, and a 65,000 crowd produced an atmosphere probably unprecedented in an English ground. The *Daily Express* reporter Henry Rose, as much a legend at that time as any United player, revealed 'My hands are still trembling as I write' and proclaimed it 'the greatest soccer victory in history'.

Journalists could not only get away with stuff like that in those days, they built reputations on it. United, however, could not get away with another two-goal deficit in the semi-finals. Their opponents were the holders, Real Madrid. The Spaniards won 3–1 in Madrid and two first-half goals in the return leg put the tie beyond recall for United. They did at least salvage self-respect and parity in the second half at Old Trafford, Charlton scoring the equaliser. But Madrid were through to the final again, and beat Fiorentina of Italy 2–0 to retain the Cup.

United regrouped for the following season's competition in bullish mood. They were a year older, more experienced, wiser. More specifically, they were smarter to the ways and wiles of the team that set the standard for the rest of Europe. They would be better prepared for all-comers. Even Real Madrid. United brushed aside Shamrock Rovers 6–0 in Ireland, then found them a more persistent irritant in the second leg and progressed with a 9–2 aggregate win. Three goals at home gave them a comfortable cushion against Dukla Prague, the 1–0 away defeat causing no obstruction to their passage.

Red Star Belgrade were United's quarter-final opponents this time and a 2–1 home win, after conceding the opening goal and inspired by Charlton, sent them to Yugoslavia on a difficult mission. United's planning for the trip involved more than match strategy. They chartered a plane to avoid changing aircraft in London. They took provisions such as eggs and chocolate in case sustenance behind the Iron Curtain proved inadequate, and they sharpened their appetites with a rousing 5–4 League victory at Arsenal. Murphy could not be with United in Belgrade because of commitments with Wales. Injury cost Wilf McGuinness, another promising player, his place in the party and Geoff Bent, a reserve full-back, was preferred to Ronnie Cope.

Their concerns, on and off the pitch, seemed unfounded as they reached half-time leading 3–0. Charlton again galvanised the side. He scored two of the goals, Viollet the other. Sloppiness crept into United's game in the second half and Red Star scrambled an improbable draw, but Busby's players had done just enough to make it to a second semi-final of the European Cup. They enjoyed the evening, Yorkshiremen Jones and Taylor leading a rendition of 'Ilkla Moor Baht 'At'. Later still Colman was up to typical mischief, swapping shoes put outside the hotel rooms to be polished. He was stopped in his tracks when a team-mate warned him he was tampering with the boss's shoes! Here was a group of young men with the world at their feet and not a care to burden them.

The United team that serenaded Belgrade on the afternoon of 5 February 1958 was: Gregg, Foulkes, Byrne, Colman, Jones, Edwards, Morgans, Charlton, Taylor, Viollet, Scanlon.

The following morning the United party headed for home, via a snowy Munich, where the BEA Elizabethan aircraft had to stop for refuelling. Soon the plane was rumbling down the slushy runway in Bavaria, only for take-off to be aborted. The engine sound was not normal but, in the view of Captain James Thain, who was in command although not at the controls of Flight 609, gave no cause for alarm. Such a hiccup was nothing new to these now-regular travellers. Little more than a year earlier they had swept snow from the wings of their plane before returning from Bilbao. A smiling David Pegg was pictured with a brush over his right shoulder after doing his bit.

United's Elizabethan began take-off procedures again, and again came to a halt. This time the passengers were returned to the terminal building and an engineer was called. He suggested the engines could be retuned and the flight resumed the next day, but he affirmed Thain's contention that 'boost surging' was not unusual at high-altitude airports. Staying overnight was not a popular option, so a third take-off attempt was made. This time it was not aborted, but the plane failed to leave the ground. At 3.04 p.m. the Elizabethan and Manchester United FC were decimated.

Two of the survivors were Bill Foulkes and Harry Gregg. Thain was another. He shouted at them to run because there could be an explosion. Foulkes remembers running through the snow with no shoes. Gregg heard the cries of a baby, turned back and re-emerged from the wreckage clutching the infant. In near frenzy, he helped rescue several others before being driven to hospital in a van along with team-mates and their manager. Busby was one of the more seriously injured. Edwards was another. Blanchflower and Berry were badly hurt and never played again. Charlton, Viollet, Scanlon, Morgans and Wood recovered to resume their careers. The full horror hit Foulkes as he checked on the survivors and asked about the rest of his friends, to be told they were dead.

Back in Manchester the first reports were sparse and confusing. Gradually names of survivors filtered through. By the Friday morning the families of those killed were confronting the awful reality. So was the entire city. Children went to school in silent procession, wearing their United scarves. Adults lined the streets to Old Trafford as the coffins were brought home and laid in the gym. All night people arrived to watch, pray, lay their flowers and weep.

The crash had left 21 people dead. (The toll would rise to 23.) They included the coach Bert Whalley, the trainer Tom Curry, the secretary Walter Crickmer, and seven players: Byrne, Colman, Jones, Whelan, Taylor, Pegg and Bent. Also dead were journalists Alf Clarke (*Manchester Evening Chronicle*), Don Davis ('Old International' of the *Manchester Guardian*), Tom Jackson (*Manchester Evening News*), George Follows (*Daily Herald*), Archie Ledbrooke (*Daily Mirror*), Eric Thompson (*Daily Mail*), Frank Swift (*News of the World* and former Manchester City goalkeeper) and Henry Rose.

Fears remained that Busby would not pull through. Twice he was given the last rites at the Rechts der Isar Hospital. Edwards, too, was gravely ill, but he hung on into a second week and surely could not die. Not big, strong, indestructible Duncan. On 21 February, 15 days after the crash, Edwards lost his fight for life. He was 21.

Many years later, another United player celebrated as the most complete footballer in the country, Bryan Robson, asked his manager Ron Atkinson, 'How good was Duncan Edwards?' Atkinson pondered for barely a second and replied, 'About twice as good as you.'

Every year, on 6 February, the *Manchester Evening News* carries in its remembrance column loving messages to the victims of Munich, and especially to Colman, the boy from Salford who proved you did not have to be built like Duncan Edwards to be a great player, or a Busby Babe.

Busby's was a psychological as well as a physical struggle. While the doctors worked on his body, he grappled with his conscience. A sense of guilt was inevitable and almost overbearing. He had taken his boys into Europe despite the opposition of the League. None of this would have happened had he obeyed them. As Chelsea had. He felt he could have nothing more to do with football. Friends and colleagues gradually and gently urged him to reconsider. In his own time. Life had to go on and the club had to go on. They would need him. He would need them. Busby became reconciled by the realisation that his lost boys would want him to go on. They had relished the great European venture as much as he had. They had risen to the challenge of competing against and beating the best. It would still be their crusade. And one day they would win the European Cup.

In Busby's absence Murphy took charge of the team. What team? Just 13 days after the crash United were to play again, in a fifth-round FA Cup tie against Sheffield Wednesday at Old Trafford. Every position on the United team-sheet, laid out in the match programme, was blank. Murphy had to beg, borrow and steal to make up a side that included Gregg, Foulkes, 17-year-olds Alex Dawson and Mark Pearson, and, at outside-left, Shay Brennan.

Almost 60,000 were in the ground, many more thousands locked outside. The great swell of emotion throughout the land closed in on Wednesday's players that night. It was a match they could not win. They must have known that as they stepped out on to the pitch. United were led by their new captain, Foulkes, who won the toss. Was even that in doubt? Brennan, who would complete the journey to Wembley in 1968 with Foulkes, scored the first two goals, one directly from a corner kick, the other drilled in from close range. Dawson completed the 3–0 victory.

United earned a home replay against West Bromwich Albion in the sixth round and, with the considerable help of another survivor of the crash, Charlton, who set up the only goal for Colin Webster, went through to the semi-finals. They had to negotiate a further replay, against Fulham, Charlton scoring three times in the two matches, and incredibly they were in the final.

Alas, the fairytale ended there. Even with Busby back to look on and inspire, Charlton could not weave his spell over Bolton Wanderers. As in the previous year, United were undone by a challenge on their goalkeeper that would not be tolerated in the modern game. Nat Lofthouse barged the ball in, leaving Gregg prostrate and groggy for some time. The Lion of Vienna scored both goals in Bolton's 2–0 win.

The sympathy that had ushered United through their domestic programme was conspicuously absent when they took up the European Cup torch. They recovered splendidly after going behind in the first leg of their semi-final against Milan at Old Trafford. Viollet, another survivor, equalised and Ernie Taylor converted a penalty. In Italy, however, the reception from their opponents and supporters was overtly hostile. Missiles were thrown at the team coach. Unnerved or not, United, deprived of Charlton's services because he was on England duty, were outclassed and lost 4–0. The return journey overland was long and sobering. Real Madrid, who went on to win the final again, were more gracious, offering United the trophy in tribute to those who had died. United, appreciative as they were, felt they had to decline.

Now the real task of rebuilding began. Busby could not wait for another generation of Babes to come through *en bloc* and could not, in any case, guarantee to produce the likes of the Babes ever again. A club renowned for its tight purse strings would have to spend, and Busby had an ally in a new director, Louis Edwards, a rotund, affable businessman who would succeed Harold Hardman as chairman in 1965. Albert Quixall, who had captained Sheffield Wednesday in United's first match after Munich, went to Old Trafford early in the 1958–59 season for a British record fee of £45,000. United were runners-up in the Championship, but this was a false dawn. More strengthening was required. Maurice Setters, Noel Cantwell and David Herd were recruited. Cantwell became captain.

In the summer of 1962 Busby pulled off his most ambitious, delicate and expensive transfer, signing Denis Law from the Italian club Torino for £116,000. The Scot became an idol overnight and was soon to be acknowledged by the fans as their King. Now United had two great players, even if Charlton had been switched from inside-forward to outside-left. On 6 February 1963, Pat Crerand, the Celtic wing-half, came on board. United completed the season narrowly avoiding relegation and winning the FA

Cup. The anxieties of the preceding months were cast aside by a performance at last evoking memories of the great days. Law turned on to Crerand's pass to beat Gordon Banks and give United the lead against Leicester. The two Scots were magnificent. Scottish-born Herd scored the other two in United's 3–1 win.

Busby had his first trophy since before the crash and a passport back into Europe, albeit for the Cup-Winners' Cup. United flexed their muscles and skills with a 7–2 aggregate win against the Dutch team Willem II, Law scoring a hat-trick in the home leg. In the second round they met the holders, Tottenham Hotspur. They lost 2–0 away but retaliated 4–1 at home, Herd and Charlton each scoring twice.

When United won 4–1, with a hat-trick from Law, in the home leg against Sporting Lisbon, the semi-finals beckoned. Instead came humiliation. To Busby's unbridled fury, they capitulated 5–0 in the Portuguese capital. There was no sign of the benign expression or gentle smile this night. Factions within the camp blamed the manager for his 'play your usual game' creed. The team left themselves exposed and were consequently punished. There had been a discernible undercurrent of discontent. Cliques were threatening to split the family. The 'home' players blamed the 'outsiders'.

Busby and his aides were conscious that this was a matter they had to address, and their course was eased by the graduation of a new class at their academy. Among them was a wisp of a lad from Belfast who, at the age of 17, had his first experience of European football in the ill-starred tie against Sporting Lisbon. George Best, more than any other player, would avenge that 5–0 embarrassment. Busby now had three great players, a pyramid on which to build his dreams. The rest would have their qualities and be essential to the structure, and all would be loyal to the cause.

United were runners-up in the Championship that season to a new power in the English game, Bill Shankly's Liverpool. Early the following season Quixall departed, to be followed by Setters. Cantwell, the club captain, played only two League games. Brennan settled at right-back, Tony Dunne at left-back. Foulkes was established at centre-half. Pat Dunne was in goal. Nobby Stiles, local boy and United fan, found a regular place. John Connelly arrived from Burnley to play on the right wing. Charlton, Herd and Law formed the awesome inside trio.

This time United's rivals for the title were yet another emerging force, Don Revie's Leeds United. Busby's team had the edge going into the last week of the campaign and, with two goals from a patched-up Denis Law, beat Arsenal 3–1 at Old Trafford in their penultimate match. Leeds had to win at Birmingham in their final fixture that Monday evening to send United to Aston Villa, 48 hours later, on tenterhooks. Developments at St

Andrews were relayed north and Birmingham's 3–0 lead prompted premature celebrations. By the time Leeds drew level tension had gripped the United crowd. To an eruption of relief and joyous invasion of the Old Trafford pitch, Birmingham held on for a 3–3 draw. Busby had another champion team.

He also had an Inter-Cities Fairs Cup (forerunner of the UEFA Cup) semi-final against Ferencvaros of Hungary to encounter. United had overcome Djurgarden (Sweden), Borussia Dortmund (that club again), Everton and Racing Club Strasbourg (France) to reach the last four. The tie went to a play-off after a 3–3 aggregate draw; United lost the toss for the right to stage it and were defeated 2–1.

A return to the European Cup provided more than ample consolation. United eased into their stride, beating the Finns Helsinki JK 9–2 on aggregate in the preliminary round and ASK Vorwaerts of East Germany 5–1 in the first round to earn a meeting with one of the most feared clubs on the Continent, Benfica. The Portuguese had made four appearances in the final, winning the trophy twice. They were a side of gifted, exciting individuals, none more gifted or exciting than the 'Black Panther' from Mozambique, Eusebio. His lithe body and languid style belied explosive pace and ferocious power in his shot. He demonstrated his potential at Old Trafford, and although United scraped a 3–2 win, the portents for the second leg in Lisbon were not good.

As United were driven from their hotel in Estoril to the Stadium of Light that warm March evening in 1966, they were taunted by the natives brandishing open hands, the five digits reminding their visitors of the score the last time they had been in town and presumably what they should expect this time. The previous visit, after all, had been to Sporting. Now they were at the mercy of mighty Benfica, a team unbeaten in 19 home games in European competition. United's nerves were further tested by a delay to the kick-off as Eusebio was presented with his European Footballer of the Year award. Denis Law, recipient the year before, dutifully posed for pictures, shaking hands with his successor.

Chants of 'Ben-fi-ca, Ben-fi-ca' boomed from the steep gallery as the Italian referee, Concetto Lo Bello, at last summoned the teams to action. The lesson of '64 heeded, Busby ordered a strategy of containment for the first 20 minutes, hoping to frustrate the opposition and silence the 80,000 crowd. That objective was accomplished, although not in the manner the boss had instructed. United were three up in 14 minutes. The Eagles had been grounded; the contest was over. The mocking hands proved prophetic, United eventually winning 5–1.

It was one of the most astonishing performances and results in the history of the European Cup, and the pivotal figure was 19-year-old Best. He headed the first goal after six minutes, darted through Benfica's bewitched defence to despatch the second after 12, and tormented them throughout. Connelly scored the third, and after Brennan's miscue presented the Portuguese with a goal early in the second half, Crerand and Charlton completed the magnificent atonement.

In the mayhem that followed, Charlton had his shirt ripped from his back and United's trainer, Jack Crompton, goalkeeper in the 1948 FA Cup-winning team, was struck to the ground by an irate fan. But nothing could leave a blemish on this perfect night. It was almost midnight as the wires hummed across Europe news of this vibrant, imaginative display by United, given its extra dimension by the effervescent Best. He was called 'O Beatle' by the Portuguese, which became 'El Beatle' in the English press. In Portuguese or Spanish, he was the symbol of an age as well as a team.

United were through to the semi-finals, as they had been in 1957 and 1958. The draw, pairing them with the unexceptional Partizan Belgrade, reinforced their belief they would go on to win the Cup. That confidence may have turned to carelessness come the first leg in Belgrade, yet they were probably too dependent on Best. Busby played the winger despite a troublesome knee and the gamble failed. The Irishman created a chance which Law, a player also hindered by knee problems, should have converted, but contributed little else. Busby, flanked by Murphy and Crompton, watched from the bench in dismay as his wonder boy went down clutching his knee. It was his last match of the campaign and United had to try to overturn a two-goal deficit in the home leg without him.

An own goal, palmed in by Partizan's goalkeeper Soskic, was all United could dredge from the game, and Crerand's dismissal, along with his Yugoslav sparring partner, compounded Old Trafford's despair. *The Sun* newspaper declared, 'End of a Busby Dream.' Even within the camp they feared as much. The manager was down and although the players offered words of encouragement, that they would win the Championship the following season and then the European Cup, it was mere rhetoric. All conviction had been drained.

United had failed to qualify for Europe in 1966–67 but that, along with their summary elimination from the League Cup and rare early demise in the FA Cup, enabled them to focus on the Championship. Busby solved a lingering goalkeeping problem by signing Alex Stepney from Chelsea and his stars lit the road to the title. They completed the triumphal march with a characteristically flamboyant victory, 6–1 away to West Ham United, a side that included three of England's World Cup-winners, Bobby Moore, Geoff Hurst and Martin Peters.

Busby and his players were back on the trail of the dream after all and, but for that priority, might not have yielded their domestic dominion to neighbours City. Much was made of the 'ageing' side, but youngsters David Sadler and John Aston now featured regularly, and there was a new Kidd on the block. Brian Kidd, an 18-year-old local boy, was a forward with skill, strength and thunder in his left boot.

United's European programme began with a regulation loosener, Law and Sadler scoring two apiece in the 4–0 home win against Hibernians Valletta of Malta, although the goalless return leg caused unscheduled discomfiture. A 0–0 draw away to Sarajevo was distinctly more satisfying, even if they had to ride their luck. United were, it seemed, getting the hang of this two-legged European game. Goals by Aston and Best gave them a 2–1 entry to the quarter-finals, after an ill-tempered encounter. Kidd followed up an own goal with a late strike to provide United with a 2–0 advantage for the trip to Katowice in Poland and the return against Gornik Zabrze. There they defied the icy bite of winter as well as a sustained onslaught and came in from the cold with a 2–1 aggregate success. They had reached the semi-finals of the European Cup for the fourth time.

Whatever role fate or destiny might have played at this stage, it was appropriate they should now face Real Madrid, the first club to eliminate them from the competition back in 1957, their inspiration and their friends, Busby having secured diplomatic relations by organising a series of friendly games between the clubs in the interim. The Spaniards had claimed the European Cup for a sixth time two years earlier and, although they had descended some way from their zenith of 1960, they remained a valid challenge for aspiring champions.

For all United's endeavour, and the exhortation of their most vociferous followers on the Stretford End, they had only a 1–0 lead, courtesy of Best's left-foot whiplash following Aston's cut-back, from the first leg at Old Trafford. The Bernabeu loomed: large, awesome, intimidating. The auguries before the game were not encouraging. Law failed a fitness test on his knee and was resigned to surgery. United appeared in need of a miracle rather than an operation as Madrid swaggered into a 3–1 half-time lead, Zoco's own goal proffering an apparent morsel of consolation.

From somewhere (the lap of the gods?) they found the resolve to make a match of it and Best's header presented Sadler with the chance to bundle in a second. Best then appeared in more familiar guise, taking the ball to the line and pulling it back for a supporting forward. Except that the support arrived in the least familiar guise: Bill Foulkes. The 36-year-old centre-half, survivor of Munich, dogged of late by injury, was driven by some unfathomable urge to execute the decisive flourish. United had drawn 3–3 and won 4–3 on aggregate.

As the players made their way to the team coach after the match, Stiles, having left the dangerous Amancio his calling card, was hit on the head with a beer bottle. He dabbed the trickle of blood with his fingers but was quietly shepherded on board by Busby. Now was not the time to make a fuss or do anything to spoil this. Now was the time for glorious reflection. Just ten years on from Munich, Busby was leading his team into the final of the European Cup, against Benfica, at Wembley. The dream was there to be lived. Who said it was not destiny?

# PART II

# DAY OF DESTINY

Great Fosters is the sort of place you would have in mind for that special occasion: a historic, dignified haven, all polished oak and ornate ceilings, peaceful gardens and water. The publicity material says the Grade 1 listed building 'was once a royal hunting lodge in the heart of Windsor Forest and for nearly four centuries the stately Elizabethan home of many notable families'. Since 1930, when it became a hotel, it has provided food and shelter for such distinguished travellers as Charlie Chaplin, Orson Wells, Vivien Leigh, Nijinsky – the dancer, that is – and the Emperor Haile Selassie of Ethiopia. Anyone who happened to be here in this corner of Surrey towards the end of May 1968 may have recognised the guests as the management and players of Manchester United.

This is where Matt Busby chose to prepare his charges for their special occasion. Here he would fine-tune them, mentally perhaps more than physically, for the European Cup final. Wembley was a relatively short journey away yet might have been in another world. The players relaxed, cocooned as they were from pressure and much of the hype. They recall the soothing atmosphere of the old brick building, even if there is no sign of the suits of armour one of them talks about. The long walk down the field that Bill Foulkes recollects would now be brought to an abrupt end by the M25.

Thirty years on there are inevitable changes. Facilities have been updated, converted and modified to cater for conferences and weddings. But the antiques, log fires, Jacobean chimney pieces and mullions are sacrosanct. The players would doubtless recognise the topiary garden, the moat, the Japanese bridge and the rose garden. On the wall of a corridor hangs a montage of press cuttings. At the top is a picture of Bing Crosby, the hotel behind him. A smaller picture shows the Manchester United team, with the European Cup, and an understated caption which explains they stayed here.

The local paper, the *Surrey Herald*, made rather more of the visit in their edition of Friday 31 May. Under the headline 'United stars stay at Egham hotel', the story revealed that half a dozen members of the party began match day by celebrating Mass in the chapel of the Salesian College, Chertsey. The paper identified the worshippers as the assistant manager Jimmy Murphy, physiotherapist Ted Dalton, an old boy of the college, and players Pat Crerand, Nobby Stiles, Brian Kidd and Francis Burns.

Crerand is pictured with excited pupils on the school lawn and Stiles apparently told a *Staines and Egham News* reporter, 'We find praying helps to ease our minds before a big game.' The headmaster, Fr Edward O'Shea, said, 'It is a great privilege to have you here on the greatest day in the club's history.' Crerand took away a ball to be autographed by the United and Benfica players.

The article went on to disclose that on the Tuesday morning, the day before the match, the party had 'split up into twos and threes. Some strolled in the bright sunshine, and others caught taxis into Egham, where they visited some of the shops. Some visited Eric Williams's menswear shop in the High Street. On the day of the match Bobby Charlton was having a cup of morning tea in the hotel when our reporter asked him how he felt. "Great," he replied, "and the hotel's just right – very pleasant."' Charlton was pictured taking the air, and signing autographs. The intrepid reporter also caught up with the manager. 'Matt Busby said, "We're in pleasant surroundings which are just right for relaxing before the match." After watching the Derby on television the players boarded a coach for Wembley, where they later realised their manager's lifetime ambition by winning the European Cup.'

The manager of the hotel at the time, John Baumann, is still here, as general manager and director. Coincidentally, he retires just before the 30th anniversary of United's European Cup win. He is dapper, his hair and beard grey. He is softly spoken and apologises he does not remember more than he does of those few days, 30 years ago.

> I remember young girls gathering at the front entrance to see George Best. We were asked to keep it away from the press but these things get out. I can remember a birthday party. [Brian Kidd was 19 on the day of the final.] I don't think they'd been before and I don't know why they chose here. I believe they were here two nights but we do not have the register from that time.
>
> I was very proud because I met Sir Matt Busby in the corridor on the evening before the occasion and he said, 'Are you going to watch the final?' I said, 'No, I'm afraid we haven't got any tickets.' He said, 'Don't worry about that, I'll get you a couple of tickets,' and he produced two tickets. I

went with my brother and there we were, sitting in the most marvellous seats, in the middle of the stands at Wembley. I remember Bobby Moore and all sorts of England players at the time were watching. It was quite fantastic.

At the time we were using different accommodation. We were using what we now use for staff quarters, over on the other side. I remember Alex Stepney being there. But Sir Matt was in one of the suites upstairs in the main hotel here. I believe most of them liked their breakfast in bed. My wife says she can recall they were allowed only tomato juice and steak for dinner. She says they had tea and papers in their rooms. She took the papers to them herself and collected their signatures for her brother. When she came to reception she asked this person if he was connected with Manchester United. He said, 'Not really, I'm just the one who looks pretty and doesn't do very much.' She later found out he was the trainer [Jack Crompton].

The grounds went back much further then, about a third as far again, and the avenue of the lime trees extended back there where the M25 now runs. And, of course, in those days it was much more peaceful. We also had a bit of extra space at the front, which the council foreshortened some years ago. But they would certainly recognise the place. It's not really changed externally. We would have had a swimming pool and tennis court. We've added a games room in the conference centre, and a sauna.

David Coleman was here doing interviews for his television programme. He interviewed the players, and me, in the Anne Boleyn Room. I asked him if he could just make mention of the fact they were staying at Great Fosters. He said, 'We're not supposed to do that, but I'll see what I can manage.' He did manage it. Just a very short mention, that they were staying at the hotel in Egham. It was after that a lot of local people came to the front entrance. George Best was the one all the girls came to see. There was a lot of screaming. There were also a lot of police here, and they had a job to make clearance for the coach to depart to the match. Manchester United didn't stay here the night of the match, and to my knowledge they didn't stay here again.

David Coleman, a former Stockport County youth player and athlete of some repute, has 'majored' in the two sports during a distinguished career as BBC commentator and presenter. Many viewers suspected he had leanings towards United and he tracked them all the way to Wembley that season. The club patently regarded him as a talisman. He explains,

> Louis Edwards and the directors had a superstition about me because they'd never lost when I commentated. I did all the rounds up to the final but Ken Wolstenholme was contracted to do the final, so Louis rang up the BBC's head of sport, Bryan Cowgill, and asked him to put me on the match. Bryan didn't believe it was Louis Edwards, asked him for his number and rang him back. That satisfied him it was Louis, but he had to explain there was nothing he could do about the commentary.
>
> I did have a special affection for United and they helped me as much as they could that season. I had difficulty getting to Katowice for the Gornik game because I'd been asked to speak at an Olympic fund-raising dinner on the Monday and couldn't travel with the team. When I finally got there at six o'clock on the Wednesday morning I bumped into Louis, getting out of a taxi. He said I should have told him and they could have helped in some way. Then, as he went to his bed, he said, 'Don't tell Matt.' It was as if he was a player and didn't want the boss to know he'd been out late. It was snowing and bitterly cold there. I did the match wearing a balaclava. There was no policing of industrial emissions there in those days and I remember the snow turning black.
>
> I travelled with United to Madrid, went on the team coach and had the special privilege of access to the dressing room. I remember, when Bill Foulkes scored and I said on the commentary 'Foulkes, 3–3', suddenly thinking, 'Oh my God, I've got the wrong player,' because he never crossed the halfway line! I was sitting in the team bus next to Paddy Crerand after the match when we heard this crash of glass. Somebody had dropped a bottle from one of the tiers at the Bernabeu on to Nobby Stiles's head. Paddy said coolly, 'It's a good job it's only his head. It might have done some serious damage.'
>
> On the day of the final I was linking our programme from the lawn of the team's hotel. It was Derby day and the

players were put to bed in the afternoon, but they were leaning out of their windows asking what was happening. I'd interviewed the players the day before for the programme. Each did a piece about the match. They were in good spirits. Kiddo, who grew up not far from Nobby, was regaling us with stories about the Stiles family business. They were funeral directors.

The mood of the party heading for Wembley was anything but funereal. The accompanying cheers and waves rekindled the sense of national pride England had generated two years earlier when they won the World Cup at the same venue. Outside the stadium supporters sauntered, mingled and sat in the warm sunshine that early evening of 29 May. A group of Benfica fans were engaged in good-humoured banter with their English counterparts. The Portuguese had arrived in a van of some vintage, decorated for the occasion with the names of the players, daubed in white. Charlton, whose goals had defeated Portugal in the semi-final of the World Cup, was spelt out in capital letters. Stiles, too, was singled out for special recognition. He was billed as 'The Bad One'. The little man had terrorised Eusebio during their international encounter here and was planning more of the same. United would be content to play, effectively, ten against ten.

As the players strolled on to the turf at Wembley for the ritual 'feel of the pitch', Kidd was greeted with a chorus of 'Happy birthday to you'. When they came out again, both teams in change strips because of a colour clash, United all in blue, Benfica all in white, the great bowl reverberated to the thunderous reception. Scarcely a face in the 100,000 crowd was visible through the giant mosaic of flags and banners. This was now the people's dream, as well as Busby's, and Benfica must have felt the pitch becoming heavier even as they filed towards the halfway line for the pre-match formalities.

The teams were:

*Benfica*: Henrique, Adolfo, Humberto, Jacinto, Cruz, Graca, Coluna, Augusto, Torres, Eusebio, Simoes.

*Manchester United*: Stepney, Brennan, Dunne, Crerand, Foulkes, Stiles, Best, Kidd, Charlton, Sadler, Aston.

The referee, Concetto Lo Bello of Italy, was as familiar to the players as they were to each other. He had officiated at the Stadium of Light when United won 5-1.

Charlton had taken over the captaincy from Law, who was recovering in hospital after a cartilage operation, and much as the Scot might have been missed, it was perhaps appropriate the privilege should have been the

Englishman's on this night. Having lost the toss to Coluna, the Benfica skipper, appearing in his 50th European game, it was Charlton who kicked off and directed the opening move which established a pattern for the match. Aston accelerated and Benfica had to resort to foul means to stop him. Often the butt of United fans' scorn, the winger was almost irresistible. It was the performance of his life.

Sadler, too, gave a glimpse of what was to come, his stretch proving insufficient to turn in Crerand's free-kick. Eusebio skipped past Stiles with rather more conviction and thumped the bar with his right-foot shot. Best had a half-chance and Sadler again stretched in vain for Kidd's header after Aston had surged away from the hapless Adolfo. Kidd had a shot blocked before Sadler squandered another opportunity. He scuffed his left-foot shot wide with Henrique at his mercy following a return pass from Kidd. Sadler slammed the turf with the palms of his hands in frustration. Busby, sitting on the bench, Murphy and Crompton to his right, lit a cigarette. So did McGuinness, now also a member of his coaching staff, sitting behind with Burns and the substitute goalkeeper, Jimmy Rimmer.

The award of a free-kick to Benfica just outside the area earned Lo Bello a close-up of Stiles's notorious fangs. Eusebio's low shot defied the wall but not Stepney's safe hands. Eusebio incurred the boos of the crowd and the wrath of Stiles after tumbling under his challenge. In truth, he was chopped, and in today's game Stiles would have been booked. Thirty years ago he protested Eusebio had conned the referee and bizarrely mocked the great man's fall to the ground. The free-kick was awarded but Stiles's theatrical antics evidently amused Lo Bello and Coluna. It was not enough, however, to assuage the United fans, their drone at half-time reflecting a dismay their side had not capitalised on that early superiority.

Best was similarly unimpressed at being fouled soon after the resumption of play, indicating his marker had a mental problem. An unlikely head was to present Benfica with more serious trouble after 53 minutes. Sadler, out on the left, checked on to his right foot and atoned for his first-half profligacy with a chip towards the near post, which Charlton headed on and beyond the reach of Henrique.

While Wolstenholme, assisted spasmodically by the meticulous enunciation of the former United player and England manager Walter Winterbottom, provided the words to the BBC's pictures, Alan Clarke and a promising broadcaster called Peter Jones were entrusted with the corporation's radio commentary:

> It's there, a great goal by Bobby Charlton, from the head as
> well, and the cross, a beautifully placed one, by David Sadler.

And so Manchester United in the lead by one goal to nil,
eight minutes into the second half.

Best popped the ball into Benfica's net, but the officials had signalled for
offside. The Irishman burst clear again, this time to have his path blocked
by Henrique outside the area. Best responded with something from his
mesmerising repertoire, twisting past three defenders and bringing
Henrique to an excellent save. Sadler seized on the rebound, only for his
shot to hit the goalkeeper's legs and balloon over.

United's dominance appeared to lull them into a false sense of security
and Eusebio, with Coluna's support, nearly punished them. Stiles berated
his collegues in the usual way. Whether or not they took heed, their lead
was cancelled out after 79 minutes. Augusto, Torres and Graca were
involved in the move which melted away the left side of United's defence.
Augusto eventually flighted the ball, Torres beat Foulkes in the air and
headed down in the direction of Eusebio, who was covered by Stiles. The
ball evaded both and was met by Graca, arriving unhindered, to score with
a first-time right-foot shot.

Suddenly Benfica were the team moving forward with confidence,
United anxiously seeking to regroup. Eusebio played a one-two with Torres
but could not unsettle Stepney. Then, with normal time almost up, he was
released to confront the goalkeeper again. Charlton was muscled off the ball
on the edge of Benfica's area and Graca's swift counter exposed United.
Stiles was instinctively lured to Graca, who played the ball forward into the
path of Eusebio. He had a clear passage between Foulkes and Dunne, and
although both defenders converged on him, United's fate was in Stepney's
hands. Eusebio, at speed, took one touch with his right foot and, from just
inside the area, thrashed at the ball with his left. Stepney, all in green,
stationed seven yards off his line, was thrown back three yards and on to the
ground by the force of the shot, yet climbed back to his feet still clutching
the ball. Eusebio, following through, pawed Stepney, then applauded him
in a lavish gesture of appreciation. Stepney merely kept his eye on the target
for his throw-out, barely acknowledging Eusebio.

> Anxious eyes on the watch now. Three minutes of full time
> to play. Benfica 1, Manchester United 1. Nodded away by
> Benfica to Charlton. Can Charlton get a shot in? No he can't.
> And so Benfica come racing away, and it's up to Eusebio, up
> through the middle. He's clear now, can he shoot? He does,
> and Stepney saves it, a great save by Stepney, and Eusebio
> goes right up to him and pats him on the back there. A great

> save by Stepney because Eusebio was clear, and he's
> applauding goalkeeper Alex Stepney for that save.

The European Cup final required extra-time for only the second time and United were the team more relieved still to be in the contest. Busby and his bench men came on to administer massage and faith. Charlton had his socks rolled down in extra-time. Best and Stiles followed suit. They also rolled up their sleeves, literally and metaphorically, as darkness at last descended. It now seems strange they wore long sleeves on such a warm evening.

Barely three minutes into the first extra period, Stepney gathered a throw-in from Dunne and rolled the ball to Brennan, only for it to be knocked back to him. Now he opted for the direct approach, hoofing it upfield. Kidd won the header, flicking it on for Best to dispute with the last defender, Jacinto. Best got to the ball a vital split second ahead of Jacinto, who was reduced to a forlorn fly kick as Best slipped the ball through his flimsy resistance. Henrique advanced towards the edge of his area but this time Best was in command of the situation. His right foot dragged the ball to the left, away from the stranded keeper, and his left foot guided it gently towards the beckoning goal. For a tantalising moment it seemed that Humberto might track back in time, or even that Henrique might recover his ground and salvage his cause. But their combined efforts were to no avail, Henrique's despairing lunge carrying him into the back of the net, close to the nestling ball.

> Stepney comes out this time, kicks it right-footed, high inside the Benfica half, a chance here for George Best. George Best is through, he goes round Henrique, he must score, George Best must score. George Best has scored. George Best has put Manchester United into the lead. Bobby Charlton sinks to his knees, Nobby Stiles does a cartwheel. United are in the lead again, two goals to one, two and a half minutes into the first period of extra-time . . . and the red and white banners really are reeling now away to our right.

A minute later Aston's pace won a corner on the left. Charlton arced in the kick and Sadler won the ball in the air. Kidd headed it towards goal, and although Henrique saved, the birthday boy nodded the rebound back over him. Aston, having expended so much energy destroying Benfica, could not face another gallop to join the celebrations wheeling around Kidd on the other wing.

It's Charlton, the man who does everything, to take the corner . . . Here it comes, right footed, swirling in the lights, inside the penalty area, a chance there for United . . . and it's there . . . and Brian Kidd celebrates his 19th birthday in the grand manner, by scoring the third goal for Manchester United in the fourth minute of extra-time.

United were rampant, Benfica in disarray. Best's deflected cross bounced off the top of the bar, and from the terraces and stands they sang, 'We'll be running round Wembley with the Cup.' Wolstenholme told his television audience, 'Undoubtedly the Manchester United fans are outshouting and outsinging the England fans in the World Cup final.' By way of underlining the fact that this was no ordinary spectacle, Charlton was penalised for a foul on Eusebio and suggested his old adversary was diving. His case was backed up by Stiles, of course. Eusebio restored himself to a vertical position and struck the long-range kick into United's defensive wall.

United had no such difficulty breaching Benfica's defences. Brennan played the ball up to Kidd, who laid it off to Charlton and, in the blink of an eye, spun out to the right to receive the return. The youngster sucked in Cruz, hurdled his desperate tackle, hared down the wing and, with his weaker right foot, stroked the ball into the stride of the advancing Charlton. The captain unhesitatingly, and unerringly, looped his shot into the far corner.

Bobby Charlton makes it four for Manchester United and does that characteristic little throw salute of the arm, a little jump in the air, and a battery of photographers come on. Bobby Charlton, for my money, certainly in my time, the greatest of them all, scores with ease and confidence. But some splendid running by Brian Kidd, who went round Cruz, no trouble at all, gave it to Charlton, and Charlton hammered it home for number four, and his own second here tonight. United 4–1 up, nine and a half minutes into the first period of extra-time.

Kidd almost added to his account but Eusebio mustered a semblance of retaliation, his header exercising Stepney. Dunne was hurt in the challenge and Eusebio's sporting gesture, staying with the full-back until play was stopped and help summoned, won him warm applause. But then it is easy to be gracious when you are 4–1 up and the job is done.

Aston, too, might have pondered on the fickle nature of football fans as he received treatment on the touchline after being assaulted by Henrique in a position where he might have anticipated a tackle from the right-back. 'John-ny Aston, John-ny Aston,' cried those who had barracked him on not-so-good days. On this night of nights, however, he had been a revelation, and his father, John Aston senior, a member of the 1948 FA Cup and 1952 Championship-winning sides, then a member of Busby's staff, watched with pride and satisfaction.

Eusebio remained dangerously defiant to the end, and Stepney remained his Nemesis, holding on to a scorching shot, unleashed with virtually no backlift. Charlton, still working, fetching and carrying, was back in his area to head clear. Best decided it was party time, audaciously flicking up the ball before lobbing it into the area. Now the songsters gave us, 'Goodbye Benfica, goodbye.' A couple of fans ran on to the pitch in premature celebration and Wolstenholme resisted any temptation to recycle his 'they think it's all over' classic. But then, just two years on, it was not yet a classic.

By the last throes Stiles had become sportsmanlike, acknowledging Eusebio had outwitted him to create another shooting opportunity. Even he found it easy to be gracious when the shot soared off target. His job was done.

The referee's final blow of the whistle confirmed that Manchester United, the first English club to enter the European Cup and the first to reach the final, were now the first to win it. Busby was not chasing rainbows after all. His was a dream to be lived. Now he strode out on to the pitch to share the joy with his players. He was followed by his entourage, including a wildly grinning McGuinness, who unashamedly directed his excited applause at the manager. McGuinness was not alone in absorbing the personal meaning of this crusade.

Busby's eyes searched out Charlton from the growing confusion of bodies at the centre of the pitch and they embraced in a moment that required no caption. One by one, the rest hugged their boss. Tony Dunne gave him a playful tap on the back of the head. Torres, hovering for his chance, then moved in and asked Charlton to exchange shirts. The Englishman apologetically explained he couldn't, or not yet, anyway. There was something he had to go and get first. He found a fresh spring as he negotiated the steps and combed his wispy hair with his hand.

> Bobby Charlton, coming up to the royal box, below us now, to receive the Cup on a night of nights here at Wembley. There's a big roar of the crowd as he shakes hands. Bobby Charlton, lifting the Cup high above his head. A wonderful scene here at Wembley, the banners away to our left here, the red and white, waving. And to our right, too, because this is certainly a great night.

In fact, it was as much as Charlton could do to raise that gigantic piece of silverware chest-high. His colleagues wore exhausted expressions. Viewed now, they seemed surprisingly subdued. Perhaps they felt an obligation to observe some perceived, dignified protocol. Many things have changed in 30 years. More likely, a psychological burden, intensified over the years, had taken its toll. Kidd, the 19-year-old, was less inhibited. He smiled happily, naturally, and kissed his medal. They put on a celebratory show for their delirious, besotted fans, but for some this was an ordeal too far. The fun for them would begin the day after, when they took the European Cup back to Manchester. The satisfaction, private or public, would be with them for the rest of their days.

Eusebio received more appreciation as he again retreated, the vanquished hero. During the 1966 World Cup finals he had seduced the nation with his majestic football, his fabulous goals – he was the tournament's top scorer – and his angelic demeanour, only to be eliminated by Charlton's two goals. And then this. *Déjà vu*. Like Charlton, he is now an ambassador for his club, country and game. He was given a rapturous reception as a guest at Old Trafford in 1997. Looking back, however, he is not fawning or patronising. Portugal's greatest player says, 'I have a good relationship with United, as I do with football people in many, many parts of the world. We all know the great players United had in 1968 and for them it was a home match. Stepney made a good save from me but I was not really fit. I had a fractured knee. We played with injuries like that. It was nice for Matt Busby to win the European Cup, but I was not happy that night.'

David Coleman was back in the United camp after the match and recalls,

> I remember the boys taking the mick out of Bobby for scoring with his head. They were a very together club and team, from Matt all the way through, although the person who looked after Bobby and a lot of those players was Jimmy Murphy. We were going to link up to the hospital where Denis Law was and speak to him, but we got a message back from a nun, who said, 'He's too emotional to talk to you.' Denis had had some pals round and he told me later he was actually sloshed. They'd fed him with McEwan's.
>
> The teams and guests went to a central London hotel [The Russell, in Bloomsbury] afterwards and my wife and I were invited to the private party. I remember travelling along the M4 at eight o'clock in the morning to get back and get the kids to school, but I don't remember too much about the night before. For Matt's 80th birthday he was given a party

by the ex-players' association and he invited me as one of his
own guests, along with the likes of Denis Compton, Tom
Finney and Cliff Morgan. We were all made honorary
members of the association.

The newspapers devoured the story of the dream that came true. 'WHAT A
GREAT DAY FOR BUSBY,' the broadsheet *Daily Express* of 30 May splashed across
its front page. In a ghosted piece he said, 'At last, at last! We have done it. It is
Manchester United's European Cup, my dearest longing for the club. It is the
greatest moment of my life.' Accompanying the words was a cartoon by Roy
Ullyett, capturing the 'end of an 11-year dream'. Busby, in striped pyjamas, is
sitting up in bed, smiling, his left hand clasping the European Cup, which is
sitting on his bedside cabinet. He is saying, 'I woke up and it was REALLY
THERE!' General de Gaulle's possible resignation as president of France was
reduced to a short single-column story. United's betting fraternity may have
noticed, at the foot of the page, the report of Sir Ivor's win in the Derby.

But this was a day to acclaim another win. *The Guardian* took up on the
common theme. 'Busby dream comes true at long last,' the front page
heralded. *The Sun* proclaimed, 'Busby's marvels win like a dream.' A picture
of Busby holding the Cup aloft with apparently greater ease than his captain
had dominated page one of *The Mirror*. The paper declared, 'MATT'S MADE
IT!' and carried his quote: 'It's bloody marvellous . . . I'm the proudest man
in England.' Frank McGhee introduced his match report in *The Mirror*
with 'Manchester United are the new kings of Europe'. Elsewhere there was
a picture of the 'emotional' Law, entering into the spirit of the occasion as
he watched on television, and the first snaps of revellers in Trafalgar Square.
There would be more party pictures from the homecoming, said to have
been witnessed by 250,000 in Manchester's streets and Albert Square. Ten
days later Busby, already a freeman of his adoptive city, was knighted.

McGhee, like Coleman, had covered the long and steep ascent to the
summit. Not only that season but for many seasons. Also like Coleman, he
was comfortable in Busby's company. The Old Man, as we shall hear, perfected
the art of making every media man feel good, but McGhee belonged to a
generation of media men that was trusted by managers and players, in an age
before the uncaging of Fleet Street's 'Beastie boys'.

Retired from full-time work but still penning match reports for *The
Observer*, McGhee remembers how it used to be:

> I don't think anyone in the press today is as close to Alex
> Ferguson as I was to Matt. Or, for that matter, to Don Revie
> and Bill Shankly. Managers and players just don't trust the press

these days, and you can understand why. I remember talking to Tom Finney in the 1958 World Cup and he was moaning about Derek Kevan. He said he felt he should expect to pass to an England colleague who could stop the ball. He knew I wouldn't turn him over, but if an England international criticised another player now he'd wake up sweating it might be in *The Mirror* as 'Player slams England team-mate'.

A lot of the problem is caused by the disparity in earnings now. At the end of an England tour in my day the press would have a collection, a tenner a head, to give the players a party. You just couldn't imagine that now. Players and press generally had a much better relationship. I got on well with the United lads. I'm still pals with Denis and Paddy. I still get a Christmas card from Bobby and his wife, Norma. The present players may have as good a relationship with each other, but I can't imagine them having the sort of relationship with the press that the '60s side had.

I had a soft spot for Matt but guarded against showing too much sympathy for the team. I was as critical of them as anyone, but it was impossible not to have an affection for them after Munich. A tide of emotion carried almost everyone along. But there was also an anti-United contingent and a backlash against them.

I think psychologically they'd got the final won going into it. They were, after all, effectively at home at Wembley. They had to do it that year. Matt had had enough. He didn't want the responsibility any more. He was hanging on for it. The team could have been shored up, but the question was, 'Who was going to do it?' Giving the job to Wilf McGuinness was the wrong route. Revie might have done it. It needed someone prepared to emerge from Matt's shadows.

That was the challenge for those who followed Busby, and the thorny problem for the club. Despite McGhee's view, shared by a number of the players, that the Old Man, now in his 60th year, had had enough, Busby concluded that ghosted article in *The Express* of 30 May 1968 with the pledge: 'It must not be the end. It must only be part of the beginning.' He did indeed go on, for another year, and then came back for still more. But in reality this was the end. The end of an epoch as well as a dream and a crusade.

# PART III

# THE PLAYERS

## 1. ALEX STEPNEY

Born: Mitcham, Surrey, 18-9-42
Debut: v Manchester City (h), 17-9-66
United career: Football League – 433 appearances, 2 goals;
FA Cup – 44, 0; Football League Cup – 35, 0; Europe – 23, 0.
Total – 535, 2.

At the start of the 1966–67 season the team fashioned to realise Matt Busby's European dream remained incomplete. He had his great artists, all in their pomp: sublime, beguiling, awesome. The rest of the cast, not merely supporting players but skilled and essential performers, were in place also. All, that is, except the goalkeeper. The decline of Harry Gregg, survivor and hero of Munich, had left a void still inadequately filled. David Gaskell, potentially outstanding, in reality undependable, had been tried and discarded. Pat Dunne, potentially dependable, was never likely to be outstanding. Busby recognised it was time to address the weakness in his line-up.

He looked to Chelsea, managed by Tommy Docherty and bizarrely, though conveniently, blessed with two of England's best goalkeepers. Peter Bonetti, already recognised as perhaps second only to Gordon Banks, had been joined at Stamford Bridge by an emerging talent in Alex Stepney, signed from Millwall. Busby sensed Chelsea could not indulge themselves in an embarrassment of riches indefinitely and offered a solution. He would have taken Bonetti; he was content to take Stepney.

Stepney arrived in the mainstream English game through the non-league side door. He distinguished himself sufficiently with his famous local team, Tooting and Mitcham, to attract the attention of Millwall. He graduated with distinction and became a member of the Chelsea academy in the summer of 1966. He stayed with the club less than five months. He would stay with United for 13 years.

Stepney gave United the missing ingredient. He would not, perhaps, rank among the all-time greats, but without him Busby's dream might have remained precisely that. Such was the significance of his contribution. He went about his job with a calm self-belief that had not been apparent for some disconcerting time behind United's defence. He had what the game refers to as 'good hands'. He was capable of breathtaking saves, yet never prone to displays of gratuitous flamboyance, even if he converted two penalties in the 1973–74 season. He had his lapses of concentration and, in his later years, his vulnerability inevitably became more costly. In his prime, however, he was an excellent goalkeeper, a principal character of United's halcyon period.

\* \* \*

He was known to his team-mates as 'Big Al' but now seems a figure of modest stature, almost dwarfed by the young giants who represent the modern breed of goalkeeper. As the outfield players are put through their training paces by the club's new manager, Stepney exercises the goalkeepers. This is his role, a specialised job for a man equipped to provide the special requirements. But this hero of United's European Cup success had long since ceased to ply his trade at Old Trafford. He had even drifted out of the game after shuttling between America and Altrincham. He had a pub, worked as a transport manager at Trafford Park and then helped run a van-hire company in Rochdale before an opportunity to scout for Southampton in the North-West presented him with a way back.

Alan Ball, the then Southampton manager, decided Stepney had a more specific role to play, coaching his goalkeepers, but that would have meant moving home. No sooner had the dilemma arisen than Ball was on his way to Manchester City, and Stepney was invited to join him. Work on the doorstep. Now he needed not a second thought. To his relief, Frank Clark, put in charge at City after the departure of Ball, asked him to continue at the club. So here he is, this bright, crisp, winter's morning, stretching his charges left and right, high and low, with catching practice at Platt Lane, Manchester City's training ground.

Upstairs in the restaurant at the club's modern complex, he sits down to a late lunch and shares his memories of a playing career that found fulfilment across the city, memories that flow the moment he turns on the tap.

> I'll never forget anything of it from the time I joined United, because I'd signed for Chelsea in the May and the

arrangement was, I was assured, that Peter Bonetti was leaving. That was the opinion of not only Tommy Docherty but also Joe Mears, the chairman, and I wanted that made quite clear before I signed. I wanted first-team football. I'd just won three England Under-23 caps in the Third Division, with Millwall.

Unfortunately, Joe Mears died that summer and the new chairman wanted Peter Bonetti to stay, which obviously caused a problem. Then Peter got injured after about six games of the new season and I played in the game against Southampton. We won, I think, 3–0, and on the Monday morning Tommy Doc called Peter and me in and said, 'I'm in a ridiculous situation. I'm going to have to play you in alternate games.' We both looked at each other and looked at him, and he said, 'Right, Peter, you're fit now so you play on Wednesday, and Alex, you'll play here on Saturday.' So that was it, and off we went training.

After training (ironically at Mitcham) it was, I think, Frank Blunstone who told me the boss wanted me back at the ground. So I went back to Stamford Bridge, not knowing what was happening, and Tommy Doc says, 'I've got a surprise for you. Get in the car.' He took me to the White House Hotel, near Euston Station. I asked him what was happening and he just said, 'Wait and see.'

And then the revolving doors started moving and in walked Sir Matt, with his trilby and his pipe, with Jimmy Murphy trailing behind, carrying a case. Within half an hour I was a Manchester United player. It was a wonderful time to come to the club. The team was at its peak. But it was also the way the whole thing was done that impressed me. Matt introduced himself and said, 'Look, Alex, I'm going to go with Tom in my room; Jimmy, you take Alex in your room.' Just for ten minutes. And, of course, Jimmy just reeled off all the names at the club, your Laws, your Bests, your Charltons, and then in came Matt and they changed over. He said, 'I want you. You'll play in my first team.' It just didn't sink in, but I was a United player straightaway. Unbelievable.

There was something about the atmosphere at the club and it came from Sir Matt. He was one of those guys . . . directly you met him, he was your grandfather. It was as if

you'd known him all your life. When I was house-hunting he
showed us round. Wonderful. He had class and the respect
was there straightaway.

Stepney had the self-assurance to assume a familiarity not all of his team-
mates shared with Busby. For others the great man remained a distant if
unusually benign figure, a man to be in awe of. He was, after all, the
manager. But Stepney, like Paddy Crerand and, later, Willie Morgan, was
more at ease with Busby, able to socialise and play golf with him. The other
two were Busby's countrymen. He was a Londoner and Londoners were
perceived as pushy. Perhaps that was it. Or perhaps, arriving from outside
at this stage, he carried none of the emotional and psychological baggage
that burdened some of the longer-serving players. Stepney confirms, 'I
never felt out of it or in any way that I didn't belong.'

His new colleagues welcomed that self-confidence and fed off it. They
won their second League Championship in three seasons with greater
conviction and Busby paid public tribute to the decisive role played by his
goalkeeper. That declaration served also as a reminder that he considered his
own judgement as sound as ever. There was universal accord on the point.
Stepney was acknowledged as a wise investment, and now United had
another chance to deliver that elusive trophy. Stepney recalls,

> I think there was a feeling in 1967–68 that this was the last
> chance of the European Cup. We had won the
> Championship and won it well, and we were still up there.
> But how many more chances do you get? I felt our hardest
> game was Sarajevo. Gornik was hard, but not as hard as in
> Sarajevo. And then, of course, came the semi-final, against
> Real Madrid, although I thought that was the final, really. It
> was as well we won it, because we were sort of left in the
> lurch as far as the League was concerned and Manchester
> City won that.
>
> It was Matt again who did it in Madrid. When we were
> 3–1 down at half-time we just sat in the dressing room in
> silence. Everybody was down and Matt really didn't say
> anything – until the whistle went to go out for the second
> half. He just said, 'Hold on, it's only 3–2, you know? You're
> only a goal behind. Go out and play.' Everyone had forgotten
> about the great goal George had scored at Old Trafford. And
> then we got a goal and were back. They probably went the
> other way.

I don't think we were in any danger of being too confident for the final, because after we won the League in '67 we went on a world tour and we played Benfica in Los Angeles. They beat us 3–1 and caused us a lot of trouble in the game, and that put us in good stead for the final. There was something to prove. We wanted revenge.

This day of judgement began in an environment just a few miles from Stepney's home, yet it might as well have been on a different planet. The splendour of the team hotel, Great Fosters, at Egham, Surrey, provided a measure of how far the boy from Mitcham had come.

It was a really olde worlde hotel. Wonderful grounds. And every room was different. There were four-posters and there were suits of armour and it was a place where you could just stroll around and occupy yourself. Very historic. I watched the Derby on television but otherwise just walked around and it helped me take my mind off the final. I came from Surrey but I didn't even know the place existed.

It was a very hot summer's day. It was so humid. I've got a picture of me holding the Cup and my shirt and shorts are absolutely drenched. I'd been given a taste of the Wembley atmosphere the week before by Sir Alf Ramsey. He gave me my only England game against Sweden, although I was sub 20 times. He didn't say it was to help me in the final, but knowing Alf he might well have thought, 'Why not?'

Before the final it was much the same as a normal game. The same rituals, the same people making most of the noise. I never got changed until half an hour before the game. Bestie would come in ten minutes before the game. We all had our ways. We never went out and warmed up in those days. Paddy had plenty to say and Bobby, being the captain, would go round talking to the players. Nobby was another talker. We also had Wilf McGuinness, a good talker, geeing everybody up. Basically, though, we were left to do our own thing. We had that feeling we were part of Matt's jigsaw. We played the way he wanted us to play. We were in that team because there was something about us that he liked. That night we had that feeling we were definitely going to win. There was never any doubt.

I thought the first half of the game was boring. It seemed

so, anyway. Yet we had lots of chances, which you realise when you see it again. And Eusebio hit the bar, and he got one through the wall. I got that and it settled me. The goal they got was always going to be a danger: Torres in the air, knocking it down. We knew all about Eusebio, of course, but we had a belief in Nobby. I don't think Nobby would get away today with a lot of what he did, but there were a lot of things then, like barging keepers, you can't do now.

The only time he got away from Nobby was just before the end of normal time and it was 1–1. Wembley's pitch at that time was notorious for slowing up the ball. It was before the Horse of the Year Show ruined the pitch. When Simoes, I think it was, hit that through ball I thought it was mine, so I came off my line. And the bloody thing slowed up, and now I'm in no-man's land. I then went back because I thought Eusebio was going to chip me. If he had done, I was beaten. So I went back just a couple of yards. Then he just set to hit it and that gave me the moment to come forward, and fortunately he hit it straight at me. But he did hit it. I've still got an inverted Mitre stamped on my chest! I was able to stand there, holding the ball, thinking 'Thank you'. I think that save stands out in people's minds because of the time in the game. If it had been three minutes after the start instead of three minutes before the end nobody would have remembered it.

If it does not challenge Banks's save from Pele in the 1970 World Cup finals as 'the greatest', it was undeniably more important. And almost as vivid in the memory as the ball clasped in Stepney's midriff is his apparent cold indifference to Eusebio's gracious acknowledgement. Stepney now explains,

It goes back to Millwall, and I was very fortunate to play for them. I was taught, when I got the ball, to concentrate on what I had to do, my next move. I didn't come into the pro game until I was 20 and had a good three-year apprenticeship as an amateur with Tooting and Mitcham. I was told not to worry about anyone around me, to get on with my game, because they can cheat you. I'm not saying he was trying to cheat me, knock it out of my hand or whatever, but my concern was 'come on, let's get away'. I knew there was very little time left and we had to hold out. I don't think they ever pushed us after that.

After the 90 minutes we all sat down and had Johnny Aston and Jack Crompton coming round, rubbing our legs, and then it was just 'keep playing, keep playing'. Funny part about the second goal is that I threw the ball to Tony Dunne, he played it back to me. I threw it to Shay Brennan, he played it back to me. So then I kicked it, Brian Kidd flicked it on and George went round the keeper. Shay Brennan reckons he started that move! On the day, Johnny Aston had an unbelievable game. That was incredible for him. If you are going to have a game like that, then that was the one to have it in.

Bobby, Nobby, David and I were in the England party leaving the following morning for a friendly in Germany and then going on to Italy for the Nations Cup, and Alf had said we weren't allowed to go out after the final. In fact, Nobby, David and I, with our wives, finished up in Danny La Rue's after the official function at the Russell Hotel. Bobby was sick and didn't even go to the banquet, and Paddy Crerand was the same.

Of course I was aware of what it meant to Matt and Bobby and Billy. It's one of those where you will always be asked, 'Where were you when United's plane crashed at Munich?' I was still at school, and after school I walked home and heard the news. I used to work for the local corner shop and go round with the greengrocery on a bike. I remember riding round and at every house I came to, I'd ask what was the latest news.

It's amazing when you look back over your career how things turn out and what coincidences crop up. When I signed for Millwall in 1963, the manager gave me two tickets for the Cup final. I'd never been to a Cup final in my life, but I went to Wembley that year. And, of course, I saw Manchester United beat Leicester City. Who would have believed I'd end up playing for Manchester United in a European Cup final there?

I can only say I've been very fortunate in the sense that I played in a team that had three European Footballers of the Year, all forwards, all in the same team. Think about that. Unbelievable. But we all fitted Busby's jigsaw. Defensively we

were tight, strong. We had Nobby, a good reader. We had Pat
and Bobby, breaking out from midfield. But then Matt
always used to say, when you win the ball, just make sure you
give it to them, and those three great players always ran into
space.

The others were underrated, though, definitely. Tony
Dunne, for instance, was the best left-back I ever played
with. Denis Irwin reminds me so much of him. Quick,
dependable, gets on with it. Very quiet. Arthur Albiston,
who came into the team in the 1977 FA Cup final, was
similar as well. United have always had someone steady
there, someone who's never really in the limelight but done
it. The club have basically had three left-backs over a 30-year
span.

Matt won lots of recognition for his achievements, and
rightly so. He was given the freedom of Manchester, he was
knighted and he had all sorts of other tributes. But he wasn't
a young man any more and I think he was understandably
feeling the pressures, so the next year he let it go to Wilf
McGuinness, and Wilf changed it to his way of thinking,
which he was completely entitled to do. But Wilf was
unfortunate. He got to semi-finals and with a bit of luck
would have won something. But it just didn't happen for
him.

The early years of Stepney's career with United catapulted him to the
pinnacle of the game. For the most part, his middle and later years at Old
Trafford conveyed him on an emotional roller-coaster of a ride that was
never boring, if, alas, never as successful. The euphemistic 'transitional
period' seemed unending, Busby briefly returning to the helm before Frank
O'Farrell came and went. Tommy Docherty took the club down to the
Second Division, instantly returned them to the First, and although
Stepney and United were surprisingly defeated by Second Division
Southampton in the 1976 FA Cup final, they beat Liverpool the following
year. Within months, however, Docherty was sacked, and Dave Sexton was
Stepney's last manager at United. Stepney recalls,

> We started well under Frank O'Farrell and went to the top,
> but after Christmas it all went wrong and we never did
> anything. That was really the end of the team. Tommy Doc
> came, Denis left, Bobby retired, Nobby left for Middles-

brough, David Sadler left. I was still around, but the European Cup team was no more.

But we'd done it. It's a completely different game today. The game has obviously improved. Everything does, records get broken. I just feel when I watch the games now that the team spirit isn't the same. They are very much more individualistic today. They do it their own way, they do their own thing. It just doesn't seem the same. Forget the hugging and kissing. We had great individuals, but we worked and played as a team. We had the experience of playing at the highest level. This team hasn't done it. They've got a fourth go at the Champions League and they should have a chance.

I don't go up to Old Trafford now. If I wanted tickets I could get them, but I don't think there's the same feeling there now. I still mix with the lads. David Sadler has his get-togethers and works really hard at it. He's a diamond, David. Always been the same. It's unbelievable most of the lads are still in the area. I think that says a lot about the bond and the team spirit.

The area has held Stepney as it has held most of the '68 team, but his children have pursued their own sporting interests. His two sons went to a rugby-playing school and found contentment in the oval-ball game. One of them became head greenkeeper at Ashton-on-Mersey Golf Club. His daughter, from his second marriage, cares more for horses than football or any other game.

Stepney, however, remains a football man and his enforced exile from the game hurt and frustrated him.

I tried to get back into the game when I came back from America but couldn't. The game didn't really want goalkeeping coaches or anything like that, and I think they paid the price for that and realised it. When I played you could say we had 12 or 13 English goalkeepers who could play for any country in the world. Where are they now? Then you could reel off the likes of Bonetti, Banks, Montgomery, Corrigan, myself, Rimmer. All class keepers.

The difference in the make-up of the lads now is that they haven't been given the structure to be top class, but I think we are changing that and doing something about it. I'm enjoying doing my bit and enjoying being with City. I've no problems working here. I'm not the first to have crossed the city. It's a very friendly club and I've been well received by everyone. It doesn't bother me or anyone that I'm an ex-United player now with City. My interest now is City and doing the best I can for them. There's so much potential here and I'd like to help them get back to the top – and if that's at United's expense, so be it.

# 2. SHAY BRENNAN

Born: Manchester, 6-5-37
Debut: v Sheffield Wednesday (h), FA Cup Fifth Round, 19-2-58
United career: Football League – 291 (1) appearances, 3 goals;
FA Cup – 36, 3; Football League Cup – 4, 0; Europe – 24, 0.
Total – 355 (1), 6.

The lean, dark Mancunian of Irish stock was not one of those in the Munich air crash, yet emotionally, perhaps even spiritually, he was subjected to that brutal ordeal and came through the other side as much as if he had found himself in the snow and debris that bleak afternoon of 1958. He had been back at home, but there was no sanctuary for Seamus Brennan or any of the players and members of staff not aboard that ill-fated flight. Those killed and injured were his work-mates, friends and more. He was in awe of Duncan Edwards and did not compare himself with many of the others.

In the days, weeks and years that followed, however, he would become an important and much-loved figure in the rebirth of Manchester United, this modest though mischievous full-back cum wing-half cum inside-forward cum unlikely outside-left stepping from the shadows to score the club's first two goals post-Munich and later sharing the ultimate fulfilment of Wembley. He discovered his niche at right-back and developed into one of the most stylish practitioners of that unglamorous craft. He represented the Republic of Ireland on 19 occasions.

But as important to club and country as his intelligent defending was his contribution to team spirit. Almost to a man, the United team of the '60s would vote Brennan their most popular colleague. He masked his humility and vulnerability, if not an inferiority complex, behind his *joie de vivre*. He might have been the original loveable rogue. Like Best he enjoyed drinking, and if that meant breaking a curfew, then so be it. Unlike Best, his comrade in arms, he was not a superstar and it never became such a drama, never headline material. His appetite for betting was just as voracious. And yet everything he did he smeared with his infectious smile and unfading charm, and the others adored him for it.

There were tears, too, not least when he learnt he was no longer wanted by United. The boss steered him towards a coaching/managerial career in Ireland, but Brennan was smart enough to realise he was not cut out for the job. He involved himself in a courier service in Waterford, and when the Big Ref in the sky showed him the yellow card of a heart attack, he moved over and allowed his second wife, Liz, to run the business. United responded with a benefit in Dublin. Now he contentedly occupies himself on the golf course and relishes his trips back to the bosom of his football family.

\* \* \*

He ambles through the foyer of the Midland Hotel, or whatever the modern name for it is. To Shay Brennan it is still the Midland, United's hotel in the heart of Manchester, a place to soothe the soul and rekindle the memories. He is here this time for United's European Cup semi-final, second leg, against Borussia Dortmund in 1997. He had arrived the previous day and spent a long evening exploring old haunts and reviving old acquaintanceships.

Now, this mid-morning of match day, he has the air and appearance of an affiliated member of the Rat Pack: slightly haggard in a distinguished kind of way, good looks fighting a spirited battle with the good life. The hairstyle is still circa 1968, though greying, the shirt open-necked. Outside a typical Mancunian reception sends a group of Dortmund fans, eager to accept civic hospitality and party in Albert Square, scurrying beyond reach of a pernicious shower. Inside the refurbished hotel, Shay Brennan is unhurried. It was, he explains, an extremely convivial evening. 'Went to the Circus, on Portland Street. Get all sorts of people in there. We had a good time. Too good.' Make his tea.

The Wythenshawe accent has withstood the Irish influences, although he takes the opportunity to stress he comes from genuine Republic stock and was entitled to represent the country. 'Now it's enough if your father drinks Guinness. No, honestly, tea will be fine.'

The bond with United was equally strong. Brennan recalls,

> I loved Manchester United when I was a boy. Johnny Carey,
> Johnny Berry . . . I idolised them. When they came back with

the Cup, in '48, I ran after the bus along Princess Parkway. There were thousands of people lining the road. But the great team was the one that died at Munich, the Babes, and when I went on the groundstaff, at 15, I trained with those great players – Roger Byrne, Eddie Colman, Duncan Edwards. We'd have to do the chores, clean the dressing room, clean the boots. I signed professional at 17 but, I have to be honest, I would never have got into the Manchester United first team but for the accident.

Duncan was the best player United ever had. Jimmy Murphy was in charge of our Youth Cup side and brought Duncan in from the first team and told the rest of us to play our normal game. Of course, when we were 1–0 down at half-time he told us to look for Duncan – and, sure enough, Duncan scored twice and we won the game. As Jimmy used to say, he was like a man playing with boys, even though he was only a boy himself.

A couple of weeks after the accident we had our first match, an FA Cup tie against Sheffield Wednesday at Old Trafford. Jimmy had taken us to the Norbreck Hotel in Blackpool, and a lot was being bandied about as to who would be in the team. A few, like Harry Gregg, Bill Foulkes and Ian Greaves, were certainties. But my name was never mentioned, so the night before the game I went out with a friend and we had a few drinks. Next morning, Jimmy told me I was in the team. At outside-left. I'd been playing inside-forward in the reserves. I didn't have time to think about it. I phoned my father at work, and my brothers, but I can't remember much more about that day.

I remember the match. I scored two goals and I was the worst player on the park. The first goal was lucky, a corner. All I wanted to do was make it look decent and reach. But the wind caught it and it went into the back of the net. And all of a sudden you're a hero, because you've scored a goal. I've played 100 times better games for United at full-back or wing-half and never got a mention.

We finished up winning 3–0 and Wednesday could never have won that match. United could have fielded a team of women, because nobody would have beaten us that night. The ground was packed and the crowd that was locked out didn't go away. They just listened to the cheers. The world wanted

Manchester United to win. The sympathy we had was incredible.

The FA Cup eluded United that season, as did the European Cup, but a new team and new friendships would flourish, as Brennan remembers.

Wilf McGuinness and I were very close. He and I were best men for each other at our weddings. He was very unlucky, getting injured and having to retire from playing. Nobby and Bobby were the ones I'd play cards with. We had crib challenges. I roomed with Bobby around the time of the European Cup final. There were one or two cliques over the years, but I could get on and mix with all the lads.

Bestie I first remember on the groundstaff, and he was always pleasant, always smiling. You'd tell some of the apprentices to go and get a tracksuit or something and they'd kind of sneer, 'Who does he think he is?' But Bestie always had a smile and was likeable. I liked to drink, but I didn't lead him astray. George was a nice fella then and he is now. Every time he comes to Ireland I go and meet him. Even now, when maybe they wouldn't recognise me any more, they'd recognise George all right. I've seen him at airports, being late for his flight because he's been stuck signing autographs and having his photograph taken. He's always been good to his father. He used to fly him over for home matches. He always had a word, a little joke for people. But the papers didn't write that sort of thing.

I used to be thankful every match I wasn't the full-back marking him. You would have to foul him to stop him. You'd have to pull him or kick him. You couldn't play him fairly and expect to get the better of him. He'd be through you. He was good on both sides and had so much confidence. He knew he was going to beat you. Sometimes the boss would switch it round in training, the reserves' forwards for ours, and I'd do a marking job on Bestie. You'd get the ball and think you'd got plenty of time, and he'd be after you. He was such a good tackler. He could have played midfield after the wing and strolled it. He could create so much space for himself, from nothing.

Bobby was serious about his game and when the boss made him captain he took it very seriously. He always gave

101 per cent. He'd be up and down when you didn't really need him to do that. But that's how he was. He wanted to play and he was such an honest player. His asset was on the ball. He would come two yards off you to get the ball. You'd think, 'I want it, let me have a go.' But Bobby, and Bestie and Paddy, they were the ones who could use it. That's why it was easy for us at the back. We always had three or four players who wanted the ball off us. We were always spoilt for choice.

Bobby, of course, had come through it all and what a great player he was for the club. I remember, after the maximum wage was abolished, that Bobby was paid five pounds more than me. Five pounds? He should have been on three times as much as me. He was recognised all round the world. I remember he stopped the traffic once in Italy. The crowd were all chanting, 'Charlton, Charlton' when they saw him on our coach. United were never known as the best payers, but everyone wanted to play for them. Even Jimmy Greaves and Bobby Moore asked Bobby if there was any chance of joining us when they were on England trips together. Mind you, we had crowd bonuses, for over 25,000. We got gates of 60,000-plus.

Even when Paddy was having a bad time he would still want the ball. He was a great passer of the ball, but some days he'd be off and give it away. Denis would shout to him, 'Don't forget, Paddy, we're playing in red.' Denis was a great mickey-taker, and, of course, he was another great player and, like Paddy, a great character. It was never boring with those two.

Nothing and no one frightened Paddy. I remember a trip behind the Iron Curtain when it was all very strict and we had all sorts of forms to fill in. Paddy filled in his: 'Name: Bond. Occupation: Spy.' He didn't care. And he was always getting up late. The coach would have to go and pick him up at his home. I'd have to get his cornflakes and boiled eggs for breakfast to get him going. What a character.

So was Nobby, but in a different way. We used to call him Inspector Clouseau. He was accident-prone. He'd lean over for the toast and get butter on his sleeve. He'd regularly walk into glass doors. He'd have blood on his collar after shaving and he'd spill beer down his tie. He once got to his car and thought he'd lost his keys, so he got a taxi home for the spare ones, came back again and discovered the original keys in the ignition and the car unlocked. We used to play cards for forfeits, and on the way back from a trip Nobby had to carry Bobby's duty free. He dropped it, the bottle of whisky broke and it went all over Bobby's cinecamera. He could also get nasty and angry, especially when David Herd used to wind him up. But what a player. He was brilliant for us, and England. He and Billy were great together. One little, one big and both so hard. If you brushed alongside them it would hurt you. They wouldn't do it deliberately, it was just the way they were. Hard.

It makes me laugh when I hear all the talk about how much quicker the game is now and how much quicker the players are. Well, if there's any full-back today as quick as Tony Dunne they should put him in the Olympics. There's nobody faster than Tony. I don't think I was slow, either. And Denis, over 20 yards, was electric. And all this about time on the ball. Try playing against Leeds, Norman Hunter and all, and expect time on the ball!

Before Johnny Giles left us for Leeds he and Nobby [brothers-in-law] were always taking the mickey and I was on the end of their fun. I was a bad header of the ball. I admit it. We were being beaten somewhere and they shouted at me to go up for a corner: 'Go on, Bomber, go up.' After that I was 'Bomber'. It just stuck.

But I like to think I played my part. I wasn't a great tackler or passer but I suppose I could read the game and I kept it simple. At a place like Manchester United you're always in fear of losing your place and sometimes I did. When I was dropped I felt it more for my father, who'd get ribbed by his work-mates. The best footballing full-back we had at United was Frank Kopel. In the reserves, he could do anything. I'd watch him in games and think, 'Once he gets in the first team he'll keep me out.' But he just went. Whether it was the atmosphere, I don't know. There are lots of kids who look great players at 15 and then just go.

The task of nurturing that raw talent lay with Busby and Murphy.

Jimmy would frighten you in practice matches. He'd play with you and shout at you. He'd say, 'You want to start worrying when I don't shout at you.' But a great man and a great coach.

The boss did it in a quieter way. If you were having a bad time he would never come in and slate you. Every player knows when he's having a bad time. He'd say, 'Defensively we're not doing this.' He wouldn't upset you personally by saying 'You're not doing this'. But you knew. And you'd play for him. Some managers go effing and blinding at players, and I don't think I could have handled that. He knew how to handle players. Professionally, he knew what he was doing. I was lucky to play not only with great players but for the best manager in the game.

The boss knew everything. He knew his players. I broke the curfew a few times at the Norbreck – down the fire escape and off to Brian London's club. There were a lot of nasty people around who used to phone in and I was reported a couple of times. Jimmy Murphy once took a call from somebody who said I was drunk in Wythenshawe. I'd missed the bus but I'd only had one drink. That was the sort of thing that used to happen.

The boss would tell us we had to behave like professionals. We used to drink at a pub called the Brown Bull, but although the boss knew everything he'd get names mixed up and he said, 'I've been hearing reports about you drinking at this Black Cow.' He knew we'd been there till two or three o'clock in the morning sometimes, and he made sure it didn't get out of control. He knew how to handle it.

He knew I liked a bet and if I was going through a bit of a bad spell the boss would say to me, 'Are you gambling again?' I'd say, 'No . . . well, a little bit.' He'd know. I couldn't kid him. Sandy, his son, was a mate, a good lad. It was a great family. Jimmy's family were lovely, as well. The players became, in a way, part of the family.

The father may have been all-knowing, but there was a feeling that Busby's commitment to a cavalier game unsullied by tactics and pragmatism rendered him incapable of handling the changing trends. Brennan concedes there is evidence to that effect. He recollects,

The worst day of his life after Munich was in the Cup-Winners' Cup in 1964, when we were beaten 5–0 away to

Sporting Lisbon after winning 4–1 at Old Trafford. We felt we were through after that first leg and that's how we played. Dave Gaskell reckoned they looked dangerous every time their keeper got the ball. We had a three-goal lead but the boss wanted us to win the game. He always wanted to show off Manchester United, whereas most teams would have shut up shop, as Fergie did with United away to Porto in 1997. If we got one goal he'd never say, 'We'll keep that.' He'd always go for another and want us to win in style.

Ironically, it was United's unnatural instinct to try and protect a one-goal advantage that almost proved their undoing in the European Cup final. Brennan enjoyed the first part of a win double in the afternoon.

I watched the Derby with Nobby. I backed the winner, Sir Ivor, and ended the day with a nice double. I watched the game on television in full for the first time only four or five years ago and didn't realise it was such a good game. I didn't realise how many chances they had. I thought they only had one apart from the goal. We missed lots. It was a great game of football.

I'd always thought Eusebio hit that late shot with his right foot. He actually hit it with his left foot. Simoes never really got a mention, so I take that as a compliment. Johnny Aston should have retired after that game. He had a magnificent game. They knew all about Bestie and watched him closely, but nothing about Johnny, and he revelled in the space. I wouldn't have liked to have played against him that night. Nobody could have topped that.

I remember sitting with Bobby in the stand at Wembley after the game. He wasn't well. It was all very emotional for him, I think. He had to get away from all the fuss. They were already taking the seats out for something else. Maybe it was the Horse of the Year Show. We had the official reception at the Russell and then I remember going to Danny La Rue's club with Nobby and his wife. I had breakfast before I went to bed.

There is a school of thought, to which a number of the '68 side subscribe, that they were unfortunate not to retain the trophy. The contention is they were cheated out of a crucial goal in the second leg of the semi-final, against Milan, at Old Trafford. Brennan issues an unequivocal challenge to the theory: 'That talk is wrong. I don't think we were unlucky at all, not over the two legs. We lost 2–0 over there but we were murdered. They missed two or three sitters.'

Brennan's career at Old Trafford ended a year after United relinquished the European Cup. Busby had handed over team affairs to Wilf McGuinness, Brennan's friend. His best man. He hoped and had begun to believe they would work another season together. He felt as if his life had shattered with the illusion.

> I thought I was going to be kept on. We were going on tour in the summer and I'd been measured for my suit. I took that as meaning I was going to get another year's contract. I was late for training that morning and sneaked into the gym, pretending I'd been doing weights. Jimmy Murphy came out – and I'd got friendly with Jimmy over the years – and he told me they were letting Denis go. I was shocked but at the same time relieved, because I thought if he was telling me about Denis he would have told me if I was going. Then Jimmy Ryan and Don Givens were sent for. Next thing, I was sent for.
>
> It was the boss who told me, not Wilf. And he was a bit emotional, a bit upset. And then I just filled up. I told the lads and I think they were upset. Then I went back to the ground to tell the women there. Jimmy was there and he had just heard. He didn't know. We were both upset. I think he felt he'd been squeezed out a bit by then, even though he was still assistant manager. Jimmy wouldn't have taken over as manager. He was a great coach, great working with players, but I don't think he wanted to be manager. I was never bitter towards Wilf, and we're still pals. Now we have a chuckle about it. I tell people he's the man who sacked me.
>
> The boss advised me to take a pension [twenty pounds a week] rather than a testimonial. I think Nobby got a pension, as well. I was gambling and it was good advice. He thought if I got a testimonial I'd blow it, so I should have a pension for the rest of my life. I suppose he was right; I would have blown it. He was trying to help me.
>
> After United I didn't want to go anywhere out of the First Division. I'd seen players leave, go lower down the League and never be the same. The boss advised me again. He

thought I could be a manager and Waterford, a good team in Ireland – we beat them the previous year in the European Cup – came for me as a player-manager. He advised me to take it and learn the trade. So I went over, but I didn't really enjoy it.

I wasn't a manager-type person. I was caught between the players and the directors. The chairman was a friend of mine and he listened to me, but mostly the directors talked a load of rubbish. I didn't like dealing with the press, either. When the press rang I'd tell one of the lads to say I was in the shower. At a sportswriters' dinner one of the reporters said, 'You might not be the best manager in the country, but you must be the cleanest.' I packed up before I was sacked. My good friend told me they were going to.

I met Liz, my second wife, at that time and we had the idea to set up a courier business, shifting parcels. It's gone all right. I had a heart attack and a big by-pass so Liz runs it. I'm settled in Ireland and it's only an hour away. We have two daughters and I also have two daughters from my first marriage. I enjoy my golf now. I'll never be a good golfer, but the exercise is good. And I still enjoy a drink – too much, I think. I'll have a Caffrey's now. Will you have one?

His friend Best has admitted to a similar liking, but Brennan can at least satisfy himself he played out his peak years.

George never gave himself a chance to prove he was *the* best. He went in his prime, and that's the tragic part. He talked to me about his lifestyle. He'd agree it had to stop – then carry on. That was George.

It's good to see him and all the other lads when I can. I can't get to all the association dos but come over when I can. It's not only the likes of Bobby and Denis I like to see again, it's also the reserves who were there, all great lads. When we have our get-togethers and remember the old days, we don't talk about the football as much as the nights out. What I miss is not the actual game but the training, the five-a-sides, the fun, the banter. The lads.

We have this daft thing going. When I walk into a room and the lads are there, Paddy starts off the applause. If the others don't join in I walk out. I'll go to a function where

Denis or Bobby is the chief guest and the MC will say, 'We've got one of the greatest players of all time . . . did this . . . did that . . .' And I stand up. I can get a laugh and get away with that. It's the way I am.

When I go back to Old Trafford I go to see Mrs Burgess, the lady in the players' lounge. She used to look after the kitchen and after training we'd go to the kitchen and have a cup of tea. I like to see the people from way back and I'm cheeky enough to go back, whereas someone like Tony Dunne, who was always a bit quieter, doesn't find it so easy. I think Alex got refused one time.

From what I see of the present team, mainly on TV, I don't know whether they are good enough to win the European Cup. We were a great team. Defensively they are about the same, but we had three great players. There aren't three like Charlton, Law and Best in the present United team. England, Scotland and Ireland don't have three great players like those between them. Those three are the main difference. Beckham is certainly no Bobby and I don't take seriously Schmeichel's comments that this team would thrash the '68 team.

Bear in mind that England had won the World Cup two years earlier. Today England, Scotland, Ireland and Wales together wouldn't win the World Cup. There's a big difference now. United have definitely been the best team in England over a number of years, but whether they are good enough to win the European Cup is another matter. I feel terrible going on about our 'three great players' when we also had Johnny Aston, Brian Kidd and David Sadler, all tremendous forwards. But because they were playing alongside three world-class players, they have tended to be overlooked.

United's 1997 European campaign ended a few hours later, but you suspect Shay Brennan made the most of the evening nonetheless.

# 3. TONY DUNNE

Born: Dublin, 24-7-41
Debut: v Burnley (a), 15-10-60
United career: Football League – 414 appearances, 2 goals;
FA Cup – 54 (1), 0; Football League Cup – 21, 0; Europe – 40, 0.
Total – 529 (1), 2.

United's other Republic of Ireland full-back hailed from Dublin and followed a well-charted course across the water to Old Trafford. Although he was already an established player in Irish football, he is remembered as a shy, self-effacing young man, nothing like that rascal Brennan, from Manchester. Also unlike Brennan, he established himself in the team in the early '60s and remained a fixture for more than a decade. Busby paid Shelbourne United £3,000, plus an appearance-related bonus, for his services. It was one of the great yet understated deals of his stewardship.

Busby, the other United players and scores of frustrated opponents over the years gave Dunne rave reviews. Some called him a model pro. That was almost demeaning. Some reckoned he was the best left-back in the world. That was more like it. A small figure with Beatles-style dark hair, he was as quick as a whippet and had the sharp but fair bite of a tackle to match. Busby, as we shall hear, relied heavily on his pace in defence. Later, as overlapping full-backs became *de rigueur*, Dunne was able to deploy a natural resource as an offensive weapon also. He played at right-back in United's 1963 FA-Cup-winning side but eventually became the regular left-back.

He left the club still the unassuming little Irishman, but harbouring a sense of injustice and betrayal over his testimonial match. He found sanctuary and a new lease of life at Bolton Wanderers, where the management and atmosphere evidently facilitated such discovery on a regular basis. He retained his fitness, his appetite and, crucially, his speed to play on for another five seasons in the Football League before running down the clock in America.

His coaching/management ambitions proved less enduring. He hoped to find a niche at Bolton but things did not go to plan. He went to Norway and enjoyed some success, although he did not enjoy part-time football. He tried scouting but the role did not fit – or perhaps he did not fit the role. Either way, it was the end of the football dream. Reality dawned in golf, albeit in a humble form. He now runs a driving range in Altrincham.

\* \* \*

Follow the signs to Altrincham Municipal Golf Club and Old Hall, sweep up the drive . . . and start looking again. Even now, he is apparently cast as the quiet, self-effacing little Irishman. Not for Tony Dunne the grand stage, the limelight or the ready acclaim. He is tucked away in the wings, down a muddy track across the cobbles and in a crevice of an old barn. A handsome, converted barn, mind. But there is nothing elegant about his workshop. He leans through a hatch to hand over a basket of yellow golf balls and a customer heads out into the bright winter sunshine as it grapples with overnight frost.

Dunne's face is round, beaming like the morning sun; familiar, welcoming. A silver tinge is recolouring its frame but the hair is still Beatles-style. That, too, is somehow welcoming. He leads the way into his office, a tiny room behind the 'shop front'. Pictures of cars offer a defiant gesture to the starkness. On a typewriter sits a black and white photograph of the 1968 European Cup-winning team. Dunne, wearing a Manchester United anorak, nestles in an old garden chair – and begins to confound the typecasting of a quiet, self-effacing little Irishman. He talks, willingly, candidly, often passionately, sometimes sadly, about his life with United and beyond.

> I was not really a United fan as a boy. Just a football fan. Like most of the lads in Ireland, I got all my football information from the radio, on a Saturday. But I did happen to go and see United play Shamrock Rovers in the European Cup. Shamrock Rovers were a very good team at the time. And, of course, Manchester United had Billy Whelan playing for them, who was marvellous – and Irish. But, unfortunate as it is to say it, the crash was the thing that made Manchester

United such a worldwide name and has so much to do with the aura of the club. History is so often wrapped up around sad occasions.

I had no real hesitation in going to United but it was like going into a blind alley for us from Ireland. We all wondered whether we were good enough. That's what frightened us. We didn't see ourselves with players like they had. They were just names, heroes. Back home you played in the street and said, 'I'm Billy Whelan today'. But you couldn't imagine this happening. My mother calmly put it in perspective. She said, 'Well, you can always come back home.'

You were conscious they were something you weren't part of. You were in awe of people there because they were there when the crash happened, and they came out of the crash and performed again. So you tended to think they were always that much better than you, more knowledgeable, more respected. It was intimidating at times. I always felt the European Cup was in honour of the people who had died in the crash, because you felt they would possibly have achieved it. They were a great team and I think that was the feeling in the town and country. I think that was the feeling of the people who followed, including those who were dismissed, because it's a very ruthless game. The European Cup had to be won for those who had died.

Matt Busby really thought only of two things: the League and the European Cup. The European Cup was an obsession for him. No doubt about it. He always said he felt duty-bound or honour-bound to do it for the people who had died in the crash. He must have had nightmares about it, as must Bobby Charlton and Billy Foulkes. I don't think he felt guilty, but I think there was a feeling in him that he wanted to finish the thing he had set out to do, to fulfil the mission. He was a fairly religious man and, on the night the European Cup was won, he would have felt there were a lot of happy faces up there, looking down.

When he had succeeded I don't think he could jump out of his seat quick enough. I don't think he felt such an obligation to the people who'd done it. Billy Foulkes had carried on and done it, and Bobby Charlton obviously had. Wonderful player, and played a great part in winning it. But there were a lot of people who had disappeared and gone their separate ways, some through injuries, and probably felt like outsiders because they were never really accepted. The people who'd done it weren't really the most important people for him.

I never talked to Bill or Bobby about the crash. I was too much in awe of people like that to ask questions. I looked at them as professionals, ready-made professionals, and I was always trying to be a professional. I never had this wonderful touch that Bobby Charlton had, this wonderful movement. In Ireland we practised playing and kicking the ball in the road, and a lot of kids had skill. But when you come to Manchester United and see the likes of Bobby Charlton . . .

Dunne arrived at Old Trafford during an uneasy time for the club and management. The sympathy that cradled United through the immediate post-Munich period had gone. Players came and went. Some clashed with other players, some with the management. Dunne kept quiet, stayed and played his way into the team.

Matt Busby actually came for me earlier in the 1959–60 season but left me to play for Shelbourne because they had a chance of winning the Cup, and we did win it. I headed straight over and went with the youth team to a tournament in Switzerland. We won the Cup and I made my senior debut that year. It was a difficult time for United. People were still supporting them and they'd had so much success over the years, but I think they were only coming because they felt obliged to. Matt Busby and Jimmy Murphy and all the backroom staff were trying to get it going again, trying to bring through young players and trying to bring in the right players from outside.

Maurice Setters was one of those who came and went. Great character. Used to stand there with those big shoulders and give anybody a piece of his mind. I remember he gave another lad from Ireland, Eamon Dunphy, a rollicking. Eamon was a cocky little devil. For a little Irish fella it was strange, because normally they were very quiet and got on with it, but he was always that way. Once you knew Maurice he was a really wonderful character. I think he must now look back and rue certain things he did. He was a brilliant defender but suffered through trying to do things he wasn't so good at. He could tackle, jump, head. He was a really strong, aggressive player. A winner. But he tried to do clever things in tight situations that the best players wouldn't try to do, and once his mind was made up, that was it with Maurice. And as a defender that can create problems. But he should never really have left United because his ability as a defender was top class.

Matt Busby's players had to play a certain way. He didn't ask a good forward to defend. He asked a good defender to defend and keep the good forward supplied. Matt wasn't a great tactician, but he was a psychologist. Everything was a jigsaw to him. He believed in his people. He believed he could have his people out there and they would perform. If they couldn't perform he would get somebody that would perform.

As a jigsaw, every piece was a complementary factor. If Bobby Charlton was behind me and got into trouble, I would get a rollicking. If I went ahead of Bobby and was trying to cross it, Bobby would get the rollicking. He'd say if he wanted somebody crossing the ball he wanted Bobby doing it, and if he wanted somebody to defend he wanted Tony doing it.

He knew your ability. He knew I was very quick so he tried to make me the last man. He knew I was not so sure of myself. I did extra training to make myself better and he knew it. He knew his people. He knew how to talk to people. He knew how to give you a rise – half of what you were going to ask for and you'd come away thinking he'd done you a favour. You'd go in to ask for ten pounds and he was always there in his big chair, and you'd always sit in a low chair. And as soon as you went in he'd say, 'You've had a good season, you're playing well, I'm thinking of giving you a rise. As a matter of fact, I've got it in your pay packet this week, five pounds. How's your mum and dad? What have you come to see me for?' Well, what answer is there to that? He used psychology very well.

He not only knew his players but he also knew the players he wanted to play, so much so I would say it was a fault of his. He didn't like to change the players. He'd rather have you play with injuries than take a chance. He'd make you feel bad about missing a game. He'd whisper in your ear, 'Where were you on Saturday?' I'd say, 'What do you mean, where was I on Saturday?' He'd say, 'The fella who played for you gave their fella too much room, he didn't put himself in position, he didn't make himself last man. Tony Dunne would have. Can't wait to see Tony Dunne this week.'

You felt he was the schoolteacher. It seemed as though he was in control of your life. I'd come from Ireland and had never seen anybody like him. He'd been in the crash; he'd survived the crash; I mean, I thought he was like King Kong. I couldn't say – as I couldn't to my teacher at school – boo to him. I would never even tell him my thoughts. I thought whatever he thought was enough. Nobody really answered him back.

He might have been a good psychologist but he was dreadful with the names of opposition players, always getting them mixed up. He'd have centre-halves playing centre-forward. Nobody laughed, but everybody had a smirk on their face. No matter whether he got their names wrong, the thing was he had total confidence in you to beat them. He'd say, 'Tony, you know he's quick, you know what you've got to do. Just make sure you're the last man, because the fella in the middle is a bit quick, so just work on that for me.' And yet he could remember the names of people he dealt with. If there were 25 reporters in a room he knew each one's name. How could people think anything but nice things about him?

The atmosphere he created in the dressing room was such that if anybody was to shout, you would have had five heart attacks. It was just like that. He walked in, took off his hat, gave his bits and pieces, put his hat back on and said, 'Right lads, let's go out and play.' If you'd played badly up to half-time he'd come in and say, 'If you don't work as hard as these your ability will never come out. If you don't you'll come off the field beaten. I'm telling you now, before it happens.'

So they were all simple instructions, though not so simple to put into practice. But when you've listened to somebody like him telling you, then you think it's all possible. Whatever he says is possible. And anything that falls below is a failure on your part, not on his. His standards are right up there, and he's talking like it's expected. 'You're the best team in the world, but if you don't go out and work, what do you expect?'

As Dunne and others testify, Busby was not renowned as a tactician. The very idea of adopting a modern system of play was anathema to him. An uncomfortable experience reaffirmed his conviction. As Dunne recalls,

> He didn't like the League Cup. He didn't want to play in it. The FA Cup was a nice day out, but for him the best teams played for the League Championship and the European Cup. So we played at Blackpool in the League Cup and he said, 'We're going to try one of them systems everybody's doing. It seems to be the thing to do.' So we played 4–3–3. I think we were five down at half-time.

The flow of words is interrupted by Dunne's sudden fit of laughter. Eventually he is able to resume.

> We came in and he said, 'You can forget this sort of stuff. These systems don't work. Let's get back to normal.' We certainly didn't win the game but he made the point. He couldn't care less if we won or lost because the League Cup meant nothing to him. He tried this system but didn't go into any elaborate preparation and training for it, and afterwards, of course, he dismissed it totally because it didn't work.

Busby's psychological magic potion still had to counter Dunne's inherent meekness. The belief and sense of destiny that swept his colleagues into the European Cup final failed to penetrate the quiet, self-effacing little Irishman.

> I didn't think it inevitable we would win the European Cup. In important games the tension would be incredible. He would try to take the fear out of you. 'Why should you worry? He's frightened to death.' But that never took the fear away from me. He had that belief in you, but then when you made a mistake you were thinking, 'Oh, no.' It didn't give me confidence.
>
> Confident players are people like George Best. George didn't seem to worry. He took it slightly differently from anyone else. Early on I didn't think he was confident because he was quiet and shuffled along. But there wasn't another player in any game who really stood out as being confident

the way he did. They all had little things, little routines before a game. Some fell asleep, others would be jumping up and down.

Bobby was nervous. I'm sure he felt like me at times and his ability was 100 per cent more than mine. I always thought Bobby felt Manchester United more than anybody. He felt it if the crowds weren't up because the club might be losing money. That's how he felt for it. He was probably the best player England had at the time. Made for international football. And on the field he ran for 90 minutes. The enthusiasm! He would get frustrated because he always wanted to win. He wanted the club to rise, and I think that stemmed from the crash. He took an awful lot of things on himself. But he was quite a nervous man and if he could be nervous it was no problem for me to be nervous.

I didn't really enjoy the night of the final. There was too much at stake for me to enjoy it. I felt we were in control of the game but we had to put in a lot of hard work. When you're nervous before the game your mind focuses totally and you try to do it to 100 per cent perfection. That's what you're looking for because you feel that's what you've got to give The Man. Anything you do wrong is a little chink in your armour.

The fear is to come off having failed him. You've been geared for this. Everybody says you're a great team, and this is what you have to win. And we can win it. We are good enough to win it. But in football it's Sod's Law; it doesn't always work that way. You need the luck. We felt quite comfortable but it's no good you feeling comfortable in a game, because while you're doing well somebody else mightn't be and he will need your help.

We had a good team, a good footballing team. I had John Aston in front of me and he had a field day. So the more I could get it to John the better. He had sussed that the full-back was a bit square so if the ball was pushed past him he'd give him trouble. He was brilliant. Exciting for people to watch. But we didn't quite kill them off. We made an awful lot of chances and didn't put them away. And we knew they were a good team, and a good team can come back. We were uptight all the time.

At the end of the 90 minutes I was knackered. I had

cramp; my legs were absolutely tied up. Alex Stepney was pulling my feet. I was in terrible pain. But Matt came on, rubbed my legs and said, 'You're ready now. Let's get it together. We've had no luck.' That was it. There was no pain that could hurt you as much as seeing him if you'd lost. Because he was miserable. He had this face, like a dog. He'd put on his hat and say, 'All right, lads, it didn't happen for us tonight. See you. Enjoy yourselves.' And you felt like cutting your throat. You didn't want that to happen.

When we got to four, with just a few minutes to go, I thought, 'Come on, get it over with.' They shouldn't have been able to come back from that, but I wanted it over with. I was too tired to enjoy it. When he blew the whistle I thought, 'Thank God that's over.' It was a relief. We'd got to win it, and yet when we did it was a terrible anti-climax for me. I'm sure it was for other players too. Sometimes you win a game and think, 'yeah!' Not that. It's the winning of the thing. It's the crash, the history. You felt like you were going down a tunnel, and every time you lost you felt like a flop. But to win the European Cup, that was going to take a great deal of pressure off you. Because now you were there, and you know when you're there once you can be there again quite easily. Because you're good enough and suddenly the flowers are blossoming. You're now the top team and it's taken this great weight off your back and you've won it at last.

And at the end you're half running around and your legs are killing you. You see Busby coming towards you and you're walking through people and you're just not there. You're going through the motions of people talking to you, you're looking at them blank, you're saying things but it's as if your mouth's not moving. And I'm thinking I could just do with being with my wife and father, who was over from Ireland on the boat with his mates. I was frightened of doing anything disrespectful but I just wanted to be with them, listen to them singing, have a few pints with them, probably fall down drunk and they'd put me to bed. They'd accept me more doing that than trying to dress up to the 'image' for the official banquet.

I wasn't too good there. Quite a few of us couldn't get above it. Sitting with the wife, I must have been bad company. The beer didn't taste right. It didn't seem to be the pint it should have been. You didn't want to excuse yourself and go to bed. I brought my father and I knew where he wanted to be, with his mates, drinking. I woke up at six or seven o'clock in the morning, went to his room and he wasn't there. He was outside with his mates. They'd come round for him. They'd been up all night drinking. He'd missed that. If I'd had a few pints, then bed, I would have enjoyed it 100 per cent more.

Why I had that feeling, I don't know. Because I'd played in all sorts of games, and nothing like that had ever happened. I could see the supporters were enjoying every minute, and quite rightly, and I was thinking, 'I'd love to be like that. I'll have my day.' And I did, a couple of weeks later. Really loved it. But the night itself is not something I can look back on and say I loved every minute of.

I loved the winning of it because it was so important to me. I would have thought – and I'm sure a lot of us would have thought – we were failures if we hadn't won. And what would have happened I don't know. It wasn't a situation where I was worried about my position, because the manager thought an awful lot of me. It's just that everything was geared to it. I thought we would have won it a couple of years before. I thought we would have beaten Partizan because we were streets ahead of them, but we were a little naive. We'd wanted to win it too much and got carried away. The great thing about the team I played in was that it never played any differently, only if teams forced us to.

The team Dunne played in was blessed with the presence of the 'Holy Trinity', but much as Dunne bowed to their supernatural talents, he was comforted in the knowledge they had human feelings.

For a start, the important thing for me was to be in a team that was winning, but I always believed they could only feel as good as the rest of us could. Unlike the night of the European Cup final, I could enjoy the drink and the feeling after a game. If somebody said George was great, somebody else might say what about Bobby or what about Denis? But in the '60s we also had the likes of John Connelly and David Herd. They were exciting, top-class forwards. They were the ones who had to suffer. Also in the team we had Nobby Stiles, an England international, but he really only got recognised for his notoriety. Paddy Crerand was slower than anybody you've ever seen, but his skill wouldn't be out of place today when you have a touch and can pass a ball like him. Glenn Hoddle, who would have been a wonderful Manchester United player, probably had more about him than Paddy, but Paddy had the same ability to knock the ball high and low. Paddy and those others didn't really get a mention. People like me.

But Manchester United was built on the Stretford End, and all those who stood there were knowledgeable people. They'd seen great players before. And when you ran on the field they clapped and sang your name. And you knew that when you did something good they would appreciate it. 'Make Tony Dunne King of Ireland,' they demanded. I mean, they can say what they like about anybody else, but they are talking about *you* as the best. They make you feel like King Kong. They can only sing the same things to George. To play for them was unbelievable.

The realisation of the European dream was, Dunne knew, the beginning of the end of Busby's reign. And now the club had a problem.

It was impossible to follow Matt, in so much as he was who he was and what he was. But I thought Noel Cantwell could have done the job. He had a wonderful brain as a footballer and he and Matt seemed to get on smashing from what I saw. I think Noel went out to learn his trade, he knew Manchester United and I think he was ready. Why it didn't happen I don't know, because I would never have asked.

I thought Wilf was unfortunate. He may have done it but it wasn't the right time. Some players let him down and there was a great upheaval. I think it was the first time you could get to Matt. I wasn't the type to get to him. Others were and some played golf with him. As a manager he could deal with people. He was very astute, disciplined. People couldn't just knock on his door and walk in. But I think his door was open to certain people later, and I think people were looking for faults. They were saying, 'He's not doing this right.' But I did think the man I knew as Matt Busby would have closed the door. I think he'd changed. He'd won it, he'd done it. It was over. But he still wanted the acclaim.

And, really, it could have been so simple, with Matt as general manager and Wilf as his assistant. Wilf trains us all week, then Matt Busby walks in, takes his hat off and says, 'Wilf's told you how we should do it. You know you have to work. Get out and do it. Have a good day.' Puts on his hat and walks out again. And nothing would have changed. But he didn't. He left the door open, for people to talk to him. I would say he possibly didn't help Wilf, he hindered him. And he came back, and we won more games under him. Then Frank O'Farrell came and he went back to the way he was with Wilf.

By then the club needed changing. It needed someone to come in and acknowledge that Matt was a legend and listen to him, but make it clear the club would continue as Manchester United and that he was the manager. I got the feeling sometimes – and I hate to say it – that Matt was happy with failure, because that brought him back into it. I think he still liked to be part of the gloss, and then when the gloss shifted he liked to come into the fold again. I think he gloried a little bit in coming back. By the time Fergie brought success to United it had gone past him. His life had been football. His best pals weren't around him. There were no Jimmy Murphys.

For all he did and all he built, even he didn't open the door for old players to come back. But then that was possibly understandable because he didn't really need them and probably didn't want anyone to chip off a little bit of the shine that still shone. Maybe that's life. He built the empire and one would forgive him all these little things . . .

Dunne's emotions have been stretched these past minutes and now he hesitates. The hurt inflicted more than two decades ago is seeping from beneath a lingering, but fragile, sense of loyalty. He cannot tell all, but he cannot tell nothing. In doing so, he feels, he achieves an acceptable balance and kind of puts the record straight.

We fell out but that's something I wouldn't like to talk about. I wouldn't say I loved him. I was in awe of him. If he told me to climb a wall I'd climb the wall. I didn't play as many internationals as I would have liked because he wouldn't let me. He said he couldn't have me playing for Ireland because he couldn't have me injured. So I missed an awful lot of internationals simply because I thought he was right. And he was always on my back. He said I was the best full-back in the world. Very complimentary. He didn't have to say these things. He gave me days off. I had so much respect for him. Everything he said was right.

When the other players were getting all the headlines in the papers he'd say, 'You don't have to worry, you were the best player on the park. I know it and the fans know it.' He always used to tap me on the shoulder and say, 'Remember, I'll be there for you when you need me. I'm the man that's going to look after you.' And that used to embarrass me. And he'd say, 'How's your mum and dad? Are you bringing them over next week? How's the kids? Is the house all right? Windows need doing? Get Les [Olive, the club secretary].' And he'd say, 'I'll look after you.' In the end, I know he didn't. I probably built him too high. It was a great period of my life. I loved it. And he probably gave me the worst night of my life. Him and the club. It was my testimonial.

Dunne declined to elaborate but his grievance is familiar to his colleagues and others connected to United. He felt Busby reneged on an arrangement over his testimonial match, at a time when Denis Law's had to be accommodated also. It is understood Dunne made £7,500 from his game, £1,500 of which was consumed by expenses.

The wind of change, now generated by Tommy Docherty, blew Dunne out of Old Trafford at the end of the 1972–73 season. 'I didn't think I had to go. I thought I was quite capable. I could have gone to London when I left United but it was Jimmy Murphy who said to me, "Go to Bolton, I know they want you." So Bolton was the place and we went up to the First Division. Ian Greaves was a great manager, had a great way of playing.'

Dunne attempted to fashion a coaching career at Burnden Park but admits he was 'perhaps too aggressive and wanted to get at players'. The shy, self-effacing little Irishman?

I left thinking I might get another job. But that was the '80s and the game went dead. I went coaching in Norway. Had a good little team. Third in the League, and they also made it to the semi-final of the Cup, first time in their history. But you train three times a week, and do nothing else.

So I went scouting, and what happens is you go in the guest room after the game and I felt as though everybody in there was after the manager's job. I thought there had to be something else. I can't do this week in, week out. So I was doing some coaching with the schools when a fella at Trafford Council told me they were going to build a driving range. Then he said they couldn't afford it, and would I be interested? I saw it as an opportunity. There was nothing in football, so why not? It wasn't like now. It's Sky that's pulled it up again. Makes it look beautiful. And it's driving a lot of footballers off the streets, giving them jobs.

Now, though, the clubs are businesses with different objectives. It seems strange to talk about Manchester United as a business. It was a club when I was there. One time you could be nipping in there, round the back, to the tea lady and have a cup of tea. You could get Bill Shankly in there, old players in there. It was a place, and a football club. But now you need passport numbers.

I'm not really interested in going to watch them now. They're a very good team. Ron Atkinson had a wonderful team. I used to pop down and see them. But there's this feeling you have to ask for people to go with, rather than being invited. Some people can go and it's not a problem. I'm not like that. They're good, don't get me wrong. I get tickets. I write the cheque and the stamped addressed envelope and they send back the tickets. But you feel that's all you get. And you don't like to tell people because you feel it's more a knock-back on you than them.

I feel there's a terrible divide at Manchester United now. It's nothing to do with the manager, players or the people who work there. It's just that it's now this company. It's moved into a different time since Matt Busby. There were unfortunate times with Tommy Doc, and I would have to say he deserved to be sacked. You can't do things like that in the club. [Docherty left his wife for the wife of the club's physiotherapist, Laurie Brown.] Louis Edwards was a super chairman, a lovely man, and I felt there was something not quite right after he died.

Martin Edwards took over and now it's a business, and

businesses can dismiss anything, can't they? The players of the past are recognised by everybody, but there are different recognitions in life. One is where you can walk into a place that you were part of and part of your life was there, a wonderful part. I'm lucky to be a part of the history, a member of the first English team to win the European Cup, the only holder of Irish, English and European Cup-winning medals. But I would have to say I sometimes feel like a window cleaner there.

I have a feeling that if they could close the chapter on that period they would. I think Brian Kidd and Alex Ferguson would welcome you with open arms. How do you get to them? Where do you go? There's no door you can walk in as an ex-player. There's no seat. Every player's bum on a seat costs that company money, and where's the loyalty in business? I've done it, past my time. It doesn't really bother me because life goes on and I do other things. But you're aware of it. We have the old boys' dates and it's lovely seeing some of the older lads, even though I'm not a great 'harper-backer'. I'm lucky to have played for United in that period, and then with that wonderful Bolton team. But if I went down to Bolton Wanderers tomorrow I'd be as welcome as anything.

Manchester United plc may not have Dunne's approval, but Alex Ferguson has.

Fergie's done an absolutely fantastic job. He's a great manager and must be a great manager to play for. He's looked after them and pulled them into the fold. They're playing a winning game and as at all times it's about confidence. They really have it buzzing. I don't know what it's like there now because I don't go, but it can't really be the same without the Stretford End. That gave it something.

You're always going to get comparisons between the past and present and there's one now, with Bobby Charlton and this young lad [presumably he means David Beckham]. I think the young lad will be under more pressure than Bobby because Bobby would accept anything. I think comparisons between Bobby and the lad today can't be taken seriously. Bobby Charlton used to get the ball and dribble past people.

He used to drop his shoulder, he used to glide, then he'd whack it. And the leather balls were very difficult to hit. Now they are very light. If you are a good striker of the ball today and you are a clever little fella you can shift the ball sideways for a shot on goal and you can become a great player. Or maybe I'm wrong!

I think the present team can win the European Cup because it comes down to a one-off situation. Once you're in there, you're good enough to win it. They've got lovely stability at the back, and they've got players who can play.

But are they as good as his team? He thinks long and hard before responding.

There were so many in my team who could score goals, even before Kiddo came along. As a matter of fact, Kiddo looked like he would be better than Bestie. If he'd been a little bit quicker he could have been anything. We had quality players who played to the pattern. Busby would obviously have wanted Denis in the European Cup final team, although it wouldn't have made any difference because on the night we were wonderful. Four goals – you can't do any better than that.

But the forward line I always think back to was before '68. That was something. Connelly, Herd, Charlton, Law, Best – where do you go from that? It was the forward line we played at Benfica, in '66, when we won 5–1. They were all cut-throat merchants. They'd cut your throat to get their goals and didn't think anything of it.

Business is cut-throat at any level, but Dunne professes himself content with his lot, and here he is never far from the family embrace.

My son, Anthony, works with me. I've got two daughters, three grandchildren – marvellous. And the good lady. Thirty-six years we've been married. The job can be hard work, but if business is up it's the best job in the world.

An awful lot of people who come here want to talk football. Not just Manchester United supporters. They're Manchester City supporters, Everton supporters, all sorts. They all care about football. But there's a bit more animosity in football today. In my day you didn't want City to go down. You hoped your team was doing better than them, but just a few slots. And it's a big town. I think it's very sad City are down.

At least his customers recognise him, then?

Some do, some don't. Some say, 'Are you . . .?' I say, 'I used to be.'

# 4. PAT CRERAND

Born: Glasgow, 19-2-39
Debut: v Blackpool (h), 23-2-63
United career: Football League – 304 appearances, 10 goals;
FA Cup – 43, 4; Football League Cup – 4, 0; Europe – 41, 1.
Total – 392, 15.

The Holy Trinity will forever be exalted above all others, but the popular maxim of the time was that when Pat Crerand played well, Manchester United played well. That was some burden to shoulder, but then little intimidated Crerand. His defiance was as conspicuous as his visionary football. He was a paradox: at once a slow, ungainly-looking player, indifferent in the air, scored relatively few goals for a midfield man and had a dangerously short fuse – and an orchestrator of the most refined, classic football.

Crerand was granted his mantle of responsibility for United's fortunes after the 1963 FA Cup final. He had overcome a difficult first few months with a team that seemed as likely to be relegated to the Second Division as win a trophy. However, as the severity of that infamous winter abated and United worked their way through the backlog of fixtures, they arrived at a delayed final with their First Division status preserved and their minds cleared. Here was a Manchester United team playing with rediscovered joy and self-belief, and at the hub was Crerand, given licence to exploit his rare passing technique. United won 3–1 to complete their first post-Munich success, and the Crerand connection was forged.

The roles of wing-halves and inside-forwards were being redefined and Crerand, although a robust tackler and fearsome competitor, excelled when able to give free rein to his creative and expressive attributes. So it was that Busby released him from more defensive duties and provided him with the perfect foil in the combative Nobby Stiles. Their complementary functions – the battler and the passer – would produce the heartbeat for the '60s revival.

Crerand's competitive instinct was a product of necessity. He was raised in Glasgow's notorious Gorbals district from Irish stock and developed not only a sense of self-preservation but also a social conscience. He would declare an ambition to be Prime Minister and few doubt he would have made an unforgettable impact. He has never been reluctant to proffer an opinion or expound a theory. And always he would deliver his dictum with passion and conviction.

The orator in Crerand would blossom as a media pundit, but in those formative years he had to play as well as talk a good game in order to garner any street cred. The shipyards offered the most secure passage in life for the youth of the area, yet young Patrick Timothy was intent on steering a course in football. He went to school early in the morning so that he could play football before classes started, and took every other opportunity to exercise those fledgling skills.

The word on the street was that Crerand had a chance and, to his astonishment, intelligence to that effect reached one of the Old Firm clubs. The Catholic one, of course. He signed for Celtic along with the player who would captain Britain's first European Cup winners, a year before Crerand and United lifted the trophy. Unlike Billy McNeill, Crerand has little to show for his Celtic days, only a Scottish Cup runners-up medal in 1961. He was to find fulfilment south of the border.

Before he left Celtic, however, he represented the Scottish League against the Italian League, whose side included compatriot Denis Law. In the summer of 1962 United rescued Law from his Italian purgatory and the then British record transfer fee of £116,000 proved a bargain. Law made a further repayment by recommending Crerand to United. Matt Busby was torn between Jim Baxter and Crerand but, although Law rated the former the more gifted player, he felt the latter's more durable game would better serve the club in the long run. So, in February 1963, Crerand went to Old Trafford in a £56,000 transfer, making his debut against Blackpool. It was another of Busby's outstanding deals.

Three months later Crerand had an FA Cup-winner's medal, followed by Championship medals in 1965 and 1967, and then his European Cup prize. A total of 16 full caps represents scant recognition of his ability, although he had to contend with strong competition and perhaps a lingering prejudice. Crerand's opponents had to contend not only with his velvet touch but also with the iron fist and, as with Law, the fighting impulse was a mixed blessing. Again in common with Law, however, the volatile temperament was a symptom of burning commitment.

Crerand carried that enthusiasm and determination into a coaching job at Old Trafford before his ill-starred appointment as assistant to manager Tommy Docherty. The Celt cocktail proved too potent for one club and Crerand joined the exodus of the '68 team. He was given the manager's chair at Northampton Town but found it too uncomfortable. He left the game to try his luck in the pub trade and public relations and, after causing a characteristic stir as a television panellist, made a niche for himself on local radio as a professional United fan.

* * *

It is a few minutes before kick-off at Old Trafford and most members of the working media are settled into their seats in the press box, which is positioned in the heart of the old main stand, albeit a little to the right of the halfway line. To the left is the directors' box and on the other three sides the paying customers, ensuring a sample of the great theatre's atmosphere. One or two latecomers bustle up the stairs, among them the familiar figure of Wilf McGuinness, bald of head, wide of smile and expansive of pleasantries all the way to his United Radio commentary position.

Another familiar figure and another former United player has yet to bustle his way to another radio commentary position and his colleague from Piccadilly 1152 glances anxiously towards the bottom of the box. His expert summariser is at least in sight and the commentator need not be concerned. He should know by now that this is part of the pre-match ritual. The chances are it will be re-enacted at half-time and at the end. Paddy Crerand is trapped in conversation with a gaggle of punters who have lain in wait. He appears a consenting captive, one hand scribbling an autograph, the other seemingly being wrenched from its socket by an over-zealous admirer as he engages the self-appointed exclusive audience in excited banter.

The referee's final check with his fellow officials is the sign to break free. One more round of laughs and the beaming, self-satisfied faces turn to view the action. Crerand, also sporting a glowing countenance, bounds up the steps at a remarkable rate of knots. 'You were never as quick as that on the pitch, Paddy,' some wag at the back shouts. Was that Wilf? Anyway, it strikes a chord and everyone enjoys the crack. And Paddy long since ceased to take offence at jokes about his tardy pace. It almost became his trademark.

But what he lacked in speed he managed to make up for with other qualities, among them enthusiasm. It is instantly apparent that the passing years have done nothing to dull that. In fact, he has changed comparatively little since he was shuffling around down there in the middle, confounding visiting defences with a perfectly measured, threaded pass into the path of Law or Best or Kidd. He is still lean and, yes, you imagine he could still be mean.

The old combative edge comes across in his comments. He is fiercely loyal to United, effusive in his praise of the home team, scathing in his condemnation of the referee when a borderline decision goes the way of the away team. The fire and aggression go down well with the listeners. This is vintage Crerand. It's what they want to hear.

Crerand is part of the family, always has been. He was estranged after falling out with Docherty but his heart was always here. He was one of Matt's boys, hand-picked to do a specific job, and he responded. He was comfortable with Matt. Another Scot, another Catholic. He had unshakeable self-belief and the patter to match his swagger. He was engaging, if at times too opinionated, and Matt felt he brought spirit to his family.

Busby, ever mindful of creating a homely, welcoming first impression (remember Stepney's experience?), took Law and his wife along with him when he met Crerand at the airport. Crerand would be further impressed by the patriarch's personal interest in his growing family. The club was almost an extension of the players' family life.

Crerand says of Busby, 'We had great respect for him. He was loved by all his players. He was fair and honest. You knew exactly where you stood with him. There was never any in-between with him. He was a very good-living man, very religious, never used bad language, never anything crude, and he didn't let his players do anything that wasn't right, either.'

It was five years to the day after Munich when Crerand joined United, and he was sensitive to the trauma Busby had endured in losing so many of his 'Babes'. Crerand reflects, 'It must be very difficult when you grow up with all those kids and know their families, and suddenly all those kids are killed. It must have been horrendous for him.'

The welcome at United may have been warm, but the reception from English football was distinctly chilly. The League and Cup programme had been thrown into chaos by the worst freeze since 1947 and clubs were seeking desperately needed match practice in more clement climes. United went to Ireland and gave their new wing-half the chance to acclimatise. It would, however, take more than friendly exercise to eradicate the malaise that threatened to drag them down to the Second Division. Even the brilliance of Denis Law might not have been enough to spare them that ignominy.

Crerand would have wished for an easier introduction to the English game. His imagination was stifled as he was deputed to help United battle their way out of trouble. Somehow they did, finishing an inglorious but safe 19th in the First Division table. Somehow, too, they managed to avoid the tricky draws along Wembley way, squeezing through the congested schedule almost before Crerand could find his feet.

At Wembley, however, he stood firm and imperious. The pressures of fending off relegation removed, United revelled in their new-found freedom, and no one more so than Crerand. The underdogs outplayed Leicester City, the 3–1 scoreline scarcely reflecting their superiority. United were on the up again, and Crerand had established himself as an integral force in their ascent.

Championship successes gave the boy from the Gorbals a view of the game's loftiest peaks. He first glimpsed the summit after United's momentous 5–1 win away to Benfica. Crerand feared he had undermined the cause by smashing a mirror in the dressing room while playing with a ball before the game, but any superstitions were swept away by the majesty of United's football. The Scot was sufficiently becalmed to register his only European goal.

> I really thought we were going to make it all the way after that. I can't believe we didn't. That night in Lisbon was our best ever. I'd seen Real Madrid beat Eintracht Frankfurt 7–3 in the 1960 European Cup final at Hampden Park and they were absolutely magnificent. And I think our performance at Benfica was up there with that. We produced a lot of fabulous football over the years, but that 5–1, on Benfica's home ground, that was something else. Especially after our 5–0 hammering by Sporting Lisbon two years earlier, when Matt said our performance was an insult to the people of Manchester.
>
> We should have gone on from that win in '66 and won the Cup, but we had injury problems. George missed the second leg against Partizan and it all went wrong for us. But we should have had it that year. We all knew that.

Crerand, sent off in the second leg against Partizan, and his team-mates focused still more clearly on their objective two years later. He savoured the build-up to the finals, the journey to Wembley and the atmosphere of the great occasion, but wondered whether they might be punished for squandering opportunities.

We missed a lot of chances and should have sewn it up well before they equalised. When it was 1–1 I was sure George's goal wasn't going in. From where I was, it looked as if their keeper's dive was going to keep the ball out.

It was unusual in that the teams knew each other so well. The Portuguese, as they always are, were all very friendly and extremely sporting, particularly the captain, Coluna. At one point he kicked the bottom of my boot in a tackle. He was down to my pace – and worse – from then on. After the game we tried to break with Wembley tradition by getting Matt to come up and accept the trophy, but he refused. He was never a showman. If Munich was the low point of his career, then this was the highest. He was like a little kid of five years on Christmas morning. Like Bobby, I was ill at the end.

There are still some poignant memories. Of going to the all-night banquet at the Russell Hotel, and seeing Duncan Edwards's parents and Eddie Colman's parents. All the parents of the Munich victims were invited. I didn't know what to say to them and there were a lot of tears. It was very sad. I kept thinking that if he had been alive, Duncan would have been playing instead of me.

The more feisty side of Crerand's character can obscure a sensitive, perceptive, compassionate nature. He willingly shouldered the responsibility of being Best's 'minder' and dismisses much of the adverse publicity about the Irishman as 'newspaper talk'. But he also recognises, with obvious sadness, the self-induced element in the decline of a genius.

The biggest thing that damaged George was that he lost his fitness, and the way he lived didn't help. I think he lost a bit of appetite when he stopped playing with the players he'd been brought up with. George today would admit that he himself was the problem, not the club or anything like that. The problem Matt had was that he couldn't go home with George. If you are a single lad you don't sit in the house every night, do you?

Crerand accepted Best as a house guest in an attempt to curb the instincts for extra-curricular activity, but the forces of time would not be repelled. Although Crerand is adamant that United were unjustly dumped out of the semi-final of the European Cup in 1969, signs of their demise loomed large and ominous.

The club felt Crerand had a role to occupy beyond his playing days and he duly joined the coaching staff in the summer of 1971. He survived the 'Night of the Long Knives' that accounted for Frank O'Farrell, Malcolm Musgrove and John Aston senior, and became assistant manager to Tommy Docherty. It would be described as a 'marriage made in hell' and, sure enough, it did not last. Busby, the club patriarch, was distinctly more enthusiastic about the appointment than the new team boss.

Crerand departed, having come to the conclusion he had stayed around too long anyway. In 1976–77 he had a six-month spell as manager of Northampton Town, which did little to rekindle the spirit. He changed direction as a public relations officer for a Manchester engineering company and followed a traditional route for an ex-footballer as a licensee, in Altrincham. To a new generation of United followers, however, he is the unrestrained, caustic, outspoken, ever-devoted champion of the club on Piccadilly 1152.

'Fergie's done a magnificent job,' he tells his audience a thousand times. And at the end of the match against Crystal Palace, which United have won with two first-half goals, he sustains the high-intensity chatter with his listeners, bouncing back excited questions with his forthright comments. Suddenly he whips off his headphones to bellow a suitably abusive message to a current United player, Gary Pallister, who appears to be having some difficulty negotiating the seats in the centre of the stand after conducting an interview. The amiable big defender smilingly shares the joke and resumes his precarious course.

Crerand returns to his listeners, secure in the knowledge the flow of his words will never be constrained. 'His tongue was always faster than his legs,' some wag at the back reckons. Was that Wilf?

# 5.  BILL FOULKES

Born: St Helens, 5-1-32
Debut: v Liverpool (a), 13-12-52
United career: Football League – 563 (3) appearances, 7 goals;
FA Cup – 61, 0; Football League Cup – 3, 0;  Europe – 52, 2.
Total – 679 (3), 9.

Even the most elaborate tapestry needs a wall to hang on. Manchester United had Bill Foulkes. Solid, dependable, durable – all those labels were stuck on him. But his was not merely a physical presence and support. His was a psychological, perhaps even spiritual vinculum with the cause that rose again from the ashes of Munich. He and Harry Gregg were the only survivors of the crash who carried the torch into the FA Cup tie against Sheffield Wednesday. Foulkes was the captain. He was still there at Wembley in 1968, and although the captaincy, and so much more, had passed to Bobby Charlton, Foulkes alone had made the full journey.

He had none of Charlton's elegance or skills, yet such was his importance to the crusade that he defied injury, at Busby's behest, to play in the second leg of the semi-final at the Bernabeu – where he emerged the hero in an improbable guise – and the final. For all Busby's devotion to the game of the angels, he demanded of his centre-half an earthy, no-nonsense resilience, and if that meant peppering the punters in row Z then so be it. Foulkes was just the man for the job.

In his earlier days he was a right-back, though no less compromising and no more indulgent. He came from the pits – yes, many have suggested he was mined – of South Lancashire, born in the rugby league town of St Helens. His father and grandfather played for that famous club. Only when he was picked for England did he feel confident he could hold his own with the Babes and make a career in football. He played through United's pre-

Munich Championships, FA Cup and European campaigns and was the obvious choice to lead the team after the crash. More conspicuous personalities would ease him out of the skipper's role, but he remained the guardian and protector, a John Wayne-type figure who enabled the others to rest easier simply by his being around.

He won four Championship medals and an FA Cup-winner's medal before accomplishing his own mission in the European Cup. He played on with United for another two years, by which time he had made 682 appearances for the club, and then joined the coaching staff. He subsequently had coaching posts in America and Norway, and more recently forged connections with Japanese football, in managerial and then in scouting and consultancy capacities.

* * *

He now qualifies for a pension, but he still cuts an impressive figure. The slight gait and grey hair cannot disguise the familiar cowboy image. The old gunslinger is in his city civvies, immaculately turned out in blazer, collar and tie. He strides not into some main-street saloon, but the United museum café, and the greeting is genuine rather than sycophantic. He offers to pay for two coffees but the man behind the counter will have none of it. This customer contributed more than most to the creation of the United empire, an Old Trafford now comprising executive lounges, restaurants, bars and stores. No member of the '68 side has seen greater change. This softly spoken, gentle man recollects his early days at Old Trafford.

> I came here as a boy, although I worked in the pits until I was 23. I had three years playing in the first team and working full-time in the coal mines. I became assistant to the under-manager, quite a good job and well paid. I did quite a bit of overtime, as well. I didn't really want to turn pro because I was getting twice as much money from the Coal Board as I was getting here. To be honest, I never thought I could really make it because there were so many great players here. I didn't think I'd be good enough. But Matt said if you want to be a professional you've got to be a full-timer. Then I was picked for England and he said, 'Don't you think you should sign full-time now?' I played against Northern Ireland, at right-back. We won 2–0 and Billy Wright congratulated me on how well I'd played. So I said 'okay' and signed.
>
> I was getting married and pointed out to Matt that in the

mines I was exempt from National Service. He said they'd take care of that, as they did for Mark Jones and David Pegg. So I got married and within two weeks I was on my way down to Aldershot for two years' National Service! It was arranged I'd have three days a week at the Officers' Training School down there and the rest of the time here. But I couldn't always get the passes I needed, so I had to go in disguise – big overcoat, trilby hat and briefcase – to get past the MPs. That was actually the CO's advice. He said it would get me through and it worked every time. Nobody ever stopped me on the station.

That little subterfuge captured the spirit of the time. Foulkes and his colleagues were adventurers and achievers, carefree, gifted young troubadours who took their show around the land and then beyond, beguiling their audiences and mesmerising their opponents. Munich claimed more than the lives of eight friends and team-mates. It claimed some of that spirit forever, leaving in its place a demon that will not be exorcised. The voice softer still, he recalls the team of 1958.

The Munich team was such a great team. Brilliant players, young players. You realise even more now that we had so many world-class players. The team that died would have been, I think, European champions that year and maybe for many years to come because they were that good and they were still growing, still learning. You could see the confidence in the team.

I never really spoke to Bobby or Harry about the crash afterwards. The only thing I discussed with Harry was about how he nearly took Jackie Blanchflower's arm off with a tourniquet! But about the crash, no. I think we all prefer to keep our thoughts to ourselves. I've suffered badly from it because I do a lot of travelling and it affects me when I fly even now. Even before I fly.

I don't think Bobby enjoyed his football as much after Munich and that applies to me, as well. I remember in particular playing away in Estudiantes, in the World Club Championship, and after it I felt I never wanted to play again. I mean, I didn't want that sort of stuff after the career I'd had. Before Munich it was a different game and there was a different atmosphere in the team. We were all young together, growing up together, and didn't realise the talent and the stature of some of the players.

It was very emotional leading the team out for the first time after the crash, against Sheffield Wednesday. I would hate to go through it again. I felt a bit sorry for Sheffield Wednesday. Albert Quixall, who was Wednesday's captain, was shaking with emotion. He was nearly crying. The team we put out was a mixture of kids and over-the-hills and whatever, but we still came through. I think it was mainly due to the crowd and the emotion. How could Sheffield Wednesday have won that game?

The emotion could not sustain United's momentum all the way to FA success that year, and Busby had to negotiate one of his most difficult and perhaps defining periods, on the field and in the dressing room, before his reshaped team reached Wembley again in 1963. They disposed of Leicester City with the kind of panache that was to become their trademark in the seasons ahead. Foulkes recalls that time with lingering alarm.

In '63 we could very easily have gone down. We got a draw at City with a dubious goal scored by me! But it kept us ahead and we didn't go down. There were arguments in the camp around that time, Matt acted and it wasn't long before Noel Cantwell and Maurice Setters left the club. It was a critical period for Matt, to have to sort that out, a test of his strength. But he was a strong man and a great manager. He appeared to be a very nice man, genial, a sort of father figure, and he lulled people into thinking that about him. But there was another side to him. He was a Gemini. He was two different characters. He could be ruthless, tough, and at times he had to be.

I remember a pre-season jaunt in Austria. We played two or three games there. One of them was against an Austrian national XI and I was left out because of a calf injury and sat on the bench. There was quite a big crowd but it was very quiet on the bench. They weren't happy with what was going on. We were being beaten four or five-one. But Matt was very calm. Harry did something and Matt said, cool as anything – you could feel the ice coming from him – 'That's the last game you'll play for this club.' He cut off Johnny Morris in a similar way. When he decided, good God. That's the way he was.

He collared me and threw the leather at me a couple of times. When I was on the staff, semi-player but reserve-team coach, I saw Brian Kidd at a dinner at the Piccadilly Hotel one Christmas time. Players weren't supposed to be there and, of course, as soon as he saw me he was away, or so I thought. My wife and one or two others saw him again. I came in as usual the following morning, very early, getting ready for training. Matt stepped out of the shadows and said, 'Why didn't you tell me about Brian Kidd?' I didn't know what the hell to do or say. I said I had seen him but I thought he'd gone home. He said, 'Don't do that again. I rely on you.' That gives you an insight into him. He was a tough man, a hard man. He wasn't a softie. But he was also a nice man, a considerate man, a family man. You always knew, though, that there was the other side.

Tales of splits in the camp and over-zealous training games are part of the United lore, but Foulkes, another fundamentally nice man known to have had a harder side – he has even been called a bully – is adamant there was no rift between him and Gregg.

I was always pretty strong-minded. I knew what I could do and I knew how to do it. I was known as a strong, physical player, but I was fair. I tried to be, anyway. Yes, there would be one or two set-tos, but that happens at every club. This talk of Harry Gregg and me not getting on is absolute rubbish. Harry and I are good friends and always have been. I heard about the story so I tackled Harry about it at a dinner we had in Ireland. He said he was going to ask me the same thing. We had arguments, we could belt each other to hell, but then it was forgotten. That's football. But there was no undercurrent or anything like that.

The Championship successes of 1965 and 1967 confirmed a unity of purpose as well as abundant talent within the camp. Deep into that 1967–68 European Cup campaign, however, Foulkes feared the dream was beyond realisation.

We should have won it in '66 and two years on I thought our chance had gone. The team we had in '66 and '67 was a great side, but we had injuries just at the wrong times, with Best and Law and David Herd. Then, in '68, we had injuries again. Denis was having more problems and, remember, he had done a fantastic job for the club. As soon as he came in he was unbelievable. I had a knee ligament injury that season and, to be honest, I thought it had finished me. I refused to play in Gornik and Matt was very annoyed. David Sadler played and was great, but we lost 1–0. Then Matt took a gamble, bringing me back for the second leg against Real Madrid.

I hadn't played for about four months because of my knee, but he played me in the last League game, against Sunderland. He gave me a test in a practice game and put Alan Gowling against me. Alan knocked me around a bit and I came through it, but my knee blew up. I had the fluid aspirated off the knee and played against Sunderland. We were still in with a chance of winning the Championship but City won and we drew 1–1. I wasn't tested, really, which was just as well. I could hardly walk. Again I had my knee aspirated and played in Madrid with it strapped very tightly.

Nobby Stiles and Tony Dunne were absolutely brilliant. They covered me. All I had to do was stand there. But it was a big gamble. We were just 1–0 up from the first leg, when George scored. There was no explanation as to why I was playing, he just said I was playing. And then, of course, I scored that goal, which was incredible. I can't explain it, and nobody else can explain it.

But also like everybody else, he recollects it vividly.

At half-time we were a bit despondent because they had murdered us. They were brilliant. But at 3–1 they were only a goal up on aggregate and if we pulled that back it would mean a replay in Lisbon. As Matt reminded us, we'd beaten Benfica 5–1 there and we would stay at Estoril again. We didn't need the replay. First David scored, though I don't think he knew much about it. The ball hit him on the shoulder or somewhere and just went in the net.

Then I remember Nobby shouting to me, 'Where the hell are you going?' Now I couldn't give Nobby enough credit for the way he covered for me that night, in front of me and behind me. I just got on the end of everything in the air and hit everything. Anyway, he was shouting at me because Pat Crerand had picked the ball up for a throw-in on the right and was looking for someone to give it to. At that stage of the game everybody, including Madrid, had frozen. George was marked very tightly and nobody seemed to make a move, so I made this run and shouted to Paddy. He looked and decided against it, and threw it to George.

My idea of making a run was to pull one of their players off George and it worked. George went down the line, beat two or three players, looked up and, of course, I was the only player in the box. He had a second look, as if he couldn't believe it, and I thought he wasn't going to part with the ball. I thought he was going to shoot and he feinted to drive it to the near post. The centre-back left me and George cut the ball back beautifully. I couldn't have missed. I just swept it into the other corner. The fact that I shouldn't have been playing in the first place made it all the more incredible.

No more, his team-mates might say, than his assertion he couldn't have missed. Depending on how you read that, he is either extremely modest or revealing delusions of goalscoring grandeur. Since the latter option is totally out of character, we should accept the former. Either way, Busby was now intent on patching him up for Wembley.

After that game he just told me to get myself ready for the final. I don't think it was an emotional thing. I think he thought I could do the job and had the experience for the occasion. I don't think he would have taken that sort of risk. Munich and everything else didn't come into it because this was his ambition, to win the European Cup. He wouldn't take any chances. He thought he had a better chance by playing me. I was at the training ground on my own, then having treatment afterwards, building up muscle strength. I couldn't stop, I couldn't turn, but I worked at it to get myself fit enough and played in the final. In fact, I played on two years afterwards with it.

But come the final we're talking Torres, and, of course, when you've got a cruciate ligament injury you can't leap, and here's a guy of six foot four, brilliant in the air. But I managed. Just inspired, I think. In the build-up I was a little nervous I would let the team down, but not as nervous as I had been in the semi-final. I didn't really want to play in the semi-final, but once we got to Wembley I was hoping he'd pick me.

On the day of the final I just whiled away the hours at that big, rambling hotel in the country, and relaxed. I just went for a stroll through the gardens, beautiful gardens, and went down to the bottom of the field and back. I went into the match in a really relaxed manner. I couldn't get to the ground fast enough, even though I was limping. As soon as we went out on to the field I knew we were going to win. In Madrid, when everybody was kissing each other, I said that was it, we were going to win the final. And now I knew it. We *had* to. It was our last chance and it was Matt's last chance.

Even when Eusebio broke away I wasn't worried. It's incredible and it's happened to me very rarely in my life, perhaps a couple of times, but I knew we would be all right. Normally you would think, 'Oh no, Eusebio!' But as he shot I just knew it would go straight into Alex. I just felt it. We *had* to win that match. And then George scored and we all started flying.

The team wasn't as effective as it had been in the past, although in saying that I'm thinking of myself, really. George was great, Nobby was still there, and people like Tony Dunne. Johnny Aston came in and played out of his skin. Brian Kidd was just 19 years of age. Paddy took a lot on his shoulders as well. But, to be honest, it was nothing like the side we knew, nothing.

Stiles's role, as Eusebio's jailkeeper, was crucial to United's game plan and Foulkes's faith in his little partner was unflinching. He concedes, however, his methods would probably not be tolerated by modern referees.

Nobby wouldn't have got away with it these days. I think he would have been off. He took him once from behind and, well . . . But to be fair they were the same. They were a bit naughty as well. And Real Madrid. Kicked us all over the bloody place. This may sound ridiculous, but Nobby was not a dirty player. Nobby was a brilliant footballer and was never given the credit for it. He was physical, obviously, but I think a lot of his mistimed tackles were because his eyesight wasn't too good, and I think his optician was to blame for that. I'm sure he was given the wrong lenses and was out of focus most of the time. Lenses and dentures! That was Nobby.

He was small in stature but so intelligent and good on the ball. Our combination and the understanding between us was incredible. It was like telepathy. He knew exactly what I was doing; I knew exactly what he was doing. The other aspect was his enthusiasm and his spirit, but that had a drawback. He was shouting non-stop, and his language wasn't too clever, but once you got to know him you just ignored it.

It was a worry being without Denis that night because he was such a big influence, but he'd had a knee problem for a couple of years, so we were accustomed to not having him. Having won it, I thought Matt may have had enough, emotionally. I wouldn't be surprised if it wasn't the same for Bobby. I didn't feel the others were outsiders, but we had a different purpose. I think they were worried about being so overjoyed. I didn't show any elation because I just felt relieved. I wasn't jumping about or anything. I just stood there. I was so relieved we had done it, and I looked at Bobby and I could see the same thing with him – he was drained. The feeling of, 'That's it, we've done it.' Bobby was crying. I've never been as emotional as Bobby, but I felt it just the same, just as much.

I played on for a couple of seasons after the European Cup final. I wanted to retire. To be honest, I wanted to be a pro golfer, but Denis talked me round and Matt told me to go and get a coaching certificate. So I went to Lilleshall and got really interested in the coaching side. I'd never really dreamed of staying in football as a coach, but it fired my enthusiasm and I became reserve-team coach. Whether I became too enthusiastic I don't know, because I had my hard days, as I did when I was a player. Being strong-minded helped me.

The will made him persevere across the globe when his time at United was finally over. He went to Chicago Sting, Tulsa Roughnecks, returned to England as manager of non-League Witney Town, then was back on his travels, to San Jose Earthquakes and to Stenjker, Lillestrom and Viking Stavanger in Norway, before trying his luck in Hiroshima. He has retained working contacts with the Japanese but has returned to his home in Sale and the embrace of his three children and six grandchildren.

I'd been abroad for so long – 17, 18 years – but I kept my house here. I belong here. It's home. In a way, Old Trafford is my second home. I think there was a certain bond between the players we had, almost a family feeling.

I wouldn't say the game has changed all that much since then, but the finances have. Money plays a big part in the game now. I would love to have had some of the salaries being paid these days. I do envy the modern players. These guys are secure for the rest of their lives, most of them. I'm not bitter but I just feel we were exploited a wee bit. Over a five-year period we made a real impact. We reached the pinnacle. We won the European Cup. I also got to four Championships, three Cup finals and numerous semi-finals. The fact that I have had to sell my medals is sad.

Sad and, alas, not a unique course of action for one of the game's old soldiers and heroes.

I needed some cash, not for myself, and decided this was what I should do. I think there were nine medals in all. We only found out afterwards it was a record. I don't like to disclose what they raised, but it was quite substantial. It was hard to do but my wife was relieved, because with my moving around so much it was a responsibility for her. Although I was sad to see them go it's nice to know they are here, at the museum. They are sort of within the family.

The new generation at United have matched Foulkes's achievements in the Championship, and now endeavour to retrace his steps to the pinnacle of European football.

You shouldn't really compare teams from different eras but people do, and I am always asked to make comparisons. The Munich side was brilliant, full of young, world-class players. Our team in the '60s had three European Footballers of the Year. How many teams can say that? In '68 we actually won the European Cup. This team is good, but it can't be as good, can it? They've got to be in Europe for a while, and they've got to win the European Cup. Alex Ferguson has made fantastic strides here and he's going the right way, but whether they are ready I don't know. I don't think they are skilled enough yet.

There's a lot of talent, young talent, which is again the strength of the club. Beckham is a bit like the old Bobby with his shooting. He has the confidence to shoot from 25 and 30 yards, as Bobby had. He's an exciting player. Giggs still has talent to develop. It's there, no question. Keane is a very important player. He's got to curb his enthusiasm just a little bit but not lose any of his game. Like Paddy and Denis, he's very fiery. He's a Celt, just the same. Central defence has been a problem. The nature of the game is changing. Possession is important now. You've got to keep the ball in your own half as well as theirs and help create space. Pallister can do that but his fitness is suspect. You also need people in there who intimidate the opposition.

I'm pleased to see Solskjaer doing so well because I sent a fax to Japan two or three years ago recommending him. I knew him from my time in Norway. He's got loads of talent. He's cunning and an instinctive goalscorer. It's no surprise to see him coming through. But he may need a physical player, a Mark Hughes-type player, to take the weight off him. I think the experience of recent seasons will help them this time. It was our experience that pulled us through. We'd been there so many times we knew how to cope with it.

A few customers have come and gone from the café. Some threw inquisitive glances the way of the big, amiable man cradling the coffee mug. Eventually two members of staff approach him and ask for autographs. He signs them with a gracious smile and great deliberation. 'I think it's nice if people can actually read your name,' he says. 'I got Eric Cantona's autograph for some Japanese people and, to be honest, you couldn't tell what it was. Don't get me wrong, though, they were very pleased.'

It would be difficult to get Bill Foulkes wrong. 'He's like that all the time,' the man behind the counter says as the old cowboy heads back to the ranch. 'He'll talk to anyone but never in a big-headed way, you know? He's very polite, very quiet, really quite shy, you know? And when you think what he's done, what he's gone through for this club, you know?'

# 6.  NOBBY STILES

Born: Manchester, 18-5-42
Debut: v Bolton (a), 1-10-60
United career: Football League – 311 appearances, 17 goals;
FA Cup – 38, 0; Football League Cup – 7, 0; Europe – 36, 2.
Total – 392, 19.

The United side of the '60s conjures all sorts of images: players with elegant strides and explosive shots; players with quicksilver reflexes and predatory instincts; players with incomparable ball control and audacious self-belief; players with inventive compulsions and radar passing. And there is another image, equally vivid, equally enduring, equally significant: the image of a player with menacing fangs and snarling challenges. It is the image that intimidated opponents across the spectrum of the game. It inspired that busload of Benfica fans to dub him 'The Bad One'. And yet that was only half the player, half the image. He read the game like few others and infected everyone with his boundless enthusiasm, capturing the childlike joy of ultimate success with his Wembley jig after England won the World Cup in 1966. That image was revived for a new generation circa Euro '96, but for a certain generation that and the many other images of Nobby Stiles were always in the consciousness.

Stiles was a United man: born, bred, besotted. He was a Collyhurst Catholic, ripe for United's picking. Or at least that is the way folklore would have it. A small, scrawny kid, he learned how to look after himself. Courage and tenacity were essential, not least on a football pitch against much bigger lads. To flourish, rather than merely survive, required still more. It demanded skill and perception. Young Norbert had the mix, which is why he emerged from the throng of hopefuls in schoolboy football to play an integral role for club and country as they accomplished the game's greatest goals.

He was a genuine wing-half, which he effectively confirmed when that traditional position was rendered obsolete. For United he settled into the back four, supporting, covering and sweeping up for the recognised centre-half, Bill Foulkes, with whom he developed a symbiotic relationship. For England he was a 'midfielder', supporting, covering and sweeping up for the recognised creators, who included his club-mate Bobby Charlton. He operated in either job with efficiency and intelligence, breaking up the opposition's attacks and swiftly supplying Charlton and company.

Stiles left United in 1971 for Middlesbrough and began a career in coaching and management at Preston. His new life took him to Canada and West Bromwich before he returned to Old Trafford for four years as Alex Ferguson's youth-team coach. More recently he has rekindled the 'hard man' image for the benefit of insatiable dinner audiences. But with tongue, not boot, firmly in cheek.

\* \* \*

Bill Foulkes's words spring to mind the moment his little partner comes into view. 'Lenses and dentures,' the big man had said, with an affectionate giggle. Off the pitch the lenses always gave way to chunky spectacles, while the dentures filled the gaps on his gums, and here he is now, with familiar large-framed glasses and a smile revealing a full set of ivories. He has three layers of protection against a fresh spring breeze and, not surprisingly, is content to sit out in the open, drawing on a cigarette.

He lives just down the road, barely a hoofed clearance from Old Trafford. 'In fact, we're in the next road to where we lived after we got married,' he says. 'I was 21 then, so this is an area I've known a long time. A lot of the lads went to a pub called the Quadrant, near the cricket ground. If they'd been in for treatment on a Sunday they'd go on there for a game of cribbage or whatever – Maurice Setters, Shay, one or two others. That reminds me, I've got to get that sod [Shay, that is]. He's always giving us these stupid questions and the last time I saw him he asked me, "Who was the chief baddie in *High Noon*?" I went through all the names, all wrong. Anyway, I've got it now, somebody I'd never heard of. I'm telling no one till I get Shay.'

He chats easily, almost cosily. An unassuming grandad and man-next-door, a typical lad from Collyhurst, just the other side of the city centre. Can this be 'The Bad One' from Wembley? He went to St Patrick's School, another institution in United lore, and yet Stiles remembers more Blues than Reds among his pals in those distant, sepia days.

In the playground you always played United–City, and we were outnumbered two to one. It was only a few years after the war, and although United had won the Cup in '48, City had Frank Swift and all those players. They were a big team. In our area your team was passed down to you, generation to generation, father to son, and I was always a United supporter.

Kiddo went to St Pat's as well. I played football with his older brother, Jimmy, who was a year younger than me. His next brother was Bernard. I played cricket with him. I can remember Kiddo as a little kid. He was only tiny and he used to join in with the big lads. He had a lot of go about him.

In the playground the young Reds and Blues would emulate their idols. For young Norbert, that meant the United team led by Johnny Carey.

I remember going in '52 to see them in a League match against Chelsea and Johnny Carey scored one of the most fantastic goals I've ever seen, and they won 6–1. I'll never forget it. At that time there were seven or eight from the 1948 FA Cup side and they won the League in '52. Then Matt said, 'Right, the youngsters are coming in.' It's often said Stein and Shankly were the ones who won things and then changed the team, but Matt did that as well.

In doing so, Busby introduced a new set of heroes to the infatuated Collyhurst schoolboy.

That was the start of the Babes: Duncan Edwards, Eddie Colman, all of those great players. In those days you'd got no television, no videos, so you went to watch them. My idol was Eddie. Snake Hips, he was called. I tried to do some of the little things he did, but I couldn't. That's what we did, though. We went to the games and then came back and tried to copy what we'd seen. For me, as a United fan, to join United was a dream.

And the European games filled impressionable young minds with more fantasies.

One of the greatest nights I've ever known was United playing Bilbao. That night, at Maine Road, was fantastic.

The one I missed, because I was playing that night for the school and couldn't get back in time, was the 10–0 against Anderlecht. So for me, as a Manchester lad, the European Cup was very, very special.

Also as a Manchester lad, he felt the pain of Munich almost as acutely as a family bereavement. Stiles was by then at the club and he recalls the poignant moment when he was instructed to tend to a duty familiar to all groundstaff boys.

We used to clean the boots, and when the skips came back after Munich, the kit caked in mud, Bill Inglis, who was the second-team trainer at the time, said to clean the boots of the lads who had survived. I said if I cleaned them, could I keep Tommy Taylor's. So I put them in my mac, took them home and had them for years. Then I gave them to an old school pal, who became a United scout, and eventually he gave them to the club. They're now in the museum.

Obviously Matt didn't have the base to build on, as he had in '52, so he had to bring in the likes of Noel Cantwell and Maurice Setters, and bring on the younger lads as well. And that's where Jimmy Murphy was so good, not just in that period immediately after Munich. He taught me the game was simple. It took a while to drum it in, but he did. It was so simple you couldn't see it. You were looking to do difficult things which weren't necessary. All the great players knew when to keep it simple. Jimmy was brilliant for me.

Johnny Giles reminded me of what Jimmy taught us some time later when he said Pele would do the simple thing when it was on to do the simple thing, but when he had to perform a miracle he could do that. The point he was making is that it's not all about miracles. The great players can perform them and I don't class myself as one, but Jimmy Murphy didn't tell me what I *couldn't* do, he told me what I *could* do. He told me to play to my strengths, which were winning the ball and giving it early. Five- and ten-yard passes. Bobby couldn't win the ball. I won the ball. But I couldn't do what Bobby did with it. So that's where you get the compromise.

We had great players in the '60s side, Bobby, Denis and George, and when you think about them you think of the great games they had. But they didn't always have great games. They couldn't, because week in, week out, they were being man-marked. That's why we, as a side, would complement each other. You'd have somebody else turning it on, like Paddy. At Wembley Johnny Aston was the best player on the park.

Man-marking was another of Stiles's strengths, a resource harnessed by club and country with crucial effect. That, however, is not the only role for which he would like to be remembered.

Everybody says that's what I did, especially on Eusebio, and of course it's nice that they remember that. But I did that job only five or six times in my career. The first time I had a man-marking role as such was in '62, in a Cup semi-final against Spurs. I marked John White and got the biggest chasing of my life. They beat us 3–1.

When you are an attacking side you want to join in, and if you do that it only takes a second for them to destroy you. So what you've got to do is sacrifice your urge to join in and attack and have the discipline to say, 'I'm staying with you wherever you go.' I next did it in '66, against Benfica in the European Cup, when I marked Eusebio. I did it for England in the World Cup that summer, against Argentina and Portugal – again marking Eusebio – and then for United in '68 against Madrid, on Amancio, and, obviously, in the final. But these were the only times I played in that role.

With England I played in the middle. At the back, of course, we had Bobby Moore, the best reader of the game I ever saw. Mooro was absolutely brilliant. At Old Trafford I played at the back, alongside Bill Foulkes, who would attack everything. We had two quick full-backs in Shay and Tony, and we had a good understanding between us. I was the reader, slotting people in, talking and whatever. That was the strength of my game, but people seem to think I was always a man-marker.

The fact is that I came to Manchester United in 1957, when all those great young players were there, and you don't get invited to a place like that if you can't play. So no matter what people remember, I never underestimated myself. To me it was a great honour anyway, but to be coming to a club with the likes of Eddie and Duncan, it has to be because they think you can play a bit.

Stiles's colleagues, to a man, will testify there was more to his game than the terrier-like attention he lavished on Eusebio and the others. They will also concur with his observation that he was a 'talker', although they might argue that is a euphemism for a communicator of a less agreeable nature. Hence the bestowal of the sardonic nickname 'Happy'.

He confesses, 'It was certainly not because I had a nice nature or anything like that. Quite the opposite. I got christened that because they said I was a narky so and so on the pitch, always moaning at my own players. But off the pitch I'm a completely different character, not like that at all. In fact, people say I'm easy-going.'

Eusebio and the other chosen few would doubtless receive that message with a wry smile. Or is that a grimace? The contention that he would not get away with his interpretation of man-marking in today's game provokes a characteristically spirited defence.

> I don't agree with that. People complain now that they've taken tackling out of the game, so what do you want? Bill Foulkes and I were always told, 'Don't let your front man come off you.' If you were playing against Jimmy Greaves or Denis Law and you went diving into them, they'd be off, they'd be round the back of you. You watch Italian football – they don't let forwards come off them. So you had to learn to stand up and know when to tackle. That's the way I played Eusebio, not whack, whack, whack, because he'd see that coming. But tackling at the right moment.
>
> My father used to talk to me about this. When I was young and we watched Johnny Carey playing at right-back, even on the heaviest of pitches, my father would say, 'Watch him go in at the end of the game, never a mark on his shorts.' As he told me, that was because he didn't go down on the ground; he stood up, and that's what tackling is about. I took that in as a small boy. Jack Crompton later told me the same thing about Johnny Carey. He didn't sell himself and go down; it was all about timing the tackle.
>
> When I'm told these days I wouldn't last five minutes it makes me laugh. You would change and adapt to the times anyway, but I think a lot of defenders these days, faced with a one-to-one situation, don't know what to do. They don't

know whether to tackle, whether to hold or what. That's because they're used to playing this tight thing where they're looking for offsides, and so the tackling starts to go. Mind you, I've got to admit, when we look back now at some of the things which they sometimes show on television, my wife says, 'Oof, did you do that? They don't do that now . . .'

The words trail off in a giggle. But can he share the laugh with Eusebio?

Oh, yeah. He was a great player, and he's a lovely, lovely man. A gentleman. He came over for a function Bobby was involved with a few years ago and he was great.

I remember in the final he hit one which whistled just past the post. The thing you couldn't do with Eusebio was let him get set. You had to keep pushing him, pushing him on. He had only a short back lift and he could whack 'em, so you had to keep him going, keep him going; pushing him, pushing him. But obviously he got through that time when Alex made the save.

We'd been attacking – that's Manchester United and Matt, still attacking so close to the end – and Shay had gone forward and was out of position. They broke, with Simoes, to the halfway line. There was me, Eusebio, Torres and Bill. Tony was out wide, with Augusto, I think, and I thought, 'We're in trouble here.' Simoes was very fast and I thought, if he pushes in too far I've got him. As I went for him, Torres made the run out and Bill went with him, as he had to, but I didn't know that at the time. Simoes toe-poked it and I thought Bill was still behind me, but by then he'd gone and Eusebio was right through. Alex made a terrific save.

People talk about how well I marked Eusebio in '66 and '68, but I don't think they would say that if it hadn't been for Alex. He was a great keeper. He never bragged about things; he was never flashy. He was a great keeper to play with because he always knew what he was doing. He told you when he was coming and that was it. To Alex it was just a save.

What Matt said to us before extra-time was more or less what Alf said before extra-time in the World Cup final. He said we'd been playing not to lose the game instead of playing to win it. They both said, 'You've won it once, go out and win it again.' And that meant, 'Keep the ball, don't be trying to hook it into the stands.' Mind you, when Mooro pulled the ball down on his chest Big Jack [Charlton] and I were screaming at him to knock it out. But, of course, he played that great pass and England had won the World Cup. We'd not had that composure in the last ten minutes of either game and I thought it was great for both Alf and Matt to have that coolness in such a situation. I know I couldn't have done it if I was the manager. Matt got us to do it, as Alf had, and I think we did it more for the boss than anything in '68.

At the end of that final against Benfica it was just fantastic. Manchester lad, United fan – and now I'm in the European Cup-winning team. That made it special to me. Very special. The only sad part was the following day. All my life I'd wanted to come back with the Cup in an open coach, through Manchester to the Town Hall. I didn't in '63 when we won the FA Cup because I didn't play in the final. And I couldn't in '68 because I'd gone off with England the next day. That was a big disappointment, missing that. I'd have loved it.

In '69 we should have won it again, and perhaps I would have got my coach ride then. We were unlucky. But I think in a lot of our minds it was a case of, 'Yeah, we've done it.' It was ten years after Munich and we'd done it – the lads who grew up in the club, like Shay, Bill, Bobby and myself – and I think we did, in a way, subconsciously, let down George and the younger lads. I remember George saying in a television interview that should have been just the start for him, and I think he felt let down. At the time I didn't agree with him, but when I look back now I have to say I think he was right.

It was difficult for Wilf to come in but he was very unlucky. To take over from Matt was hard, and yet he got us to several semi-finals in the cup competitions and there's a fine line between that and success. For me it was also a difficult period. I had two cartilage operations, so I was basically looking on at that time.

Stiles left his beloved United in 1971 and joined Middlesbrough, where he would link up with Jack Charlton. Later he was reunited with Bobby Charlton at Preston, and then he became manager at Deepdale. He worked with his brother-in-law, Giles, at Vancouver Whitecaps and West Bromwich Albion, and had been assistant manager, manager and coach at The Hawthorns when, in 1989, Alex Ferguson brought him back to Old Trafford as youth-team coach. In 1993 he left his beloved United a second time.

Inevitably, there were tales of discontent and we were reminded Stiles had not had a testimonial. Whatever his inner thoughts may be, he has no inclination for recrimination now. Life has dealt him a hand he could never have hoped for, making him an unlikely star of the after-dinner circuit. Above all, he has his family and he has his memories.

I don't want to talk about the times I left United, and, in any case, there was no problem the second time. It was good of Alex Ferguson to invite me back in the club and I enjoyed it, working with the kids. I'd been travelling to West Brom all those years so it was nice to be back in Manchester. That period was great. It got me back in touch with people. Now I'm settled again and, touch wood, I've never been happier.

I enjoy doing the after-dinner stuff. I meet so many personalities from other sports. I work with Tommy Smith and Norman Hunter. Tommy's a good pal. We do the 'hard men' thing. Those who know me will tell you I'm not like that, but we have some fun and people seem to get a laugh out of it. I never dreamed I could do anything like this but it just goes to show. I dreamed I would play for United when I was a kid. When I went to the games with my brother and uncle I dreamed that the man announcing the teams over the Tannoy would say, 'And at No. 4, Norbert Stiles.' It's true. In doing that, and winning the European Cup on top of it all, I lived the dream.

But this is something I never imagined doing. People around the country are lovely. They remember me with no teeth, the dance with the World Cup, and say they remember where they were on that day. And all that seems to have passed on to kids and grandkids. When the old clips were shown at the time of Euro '96, kids were asking 'who's he?' and wanting to know all about it. I've got four grandkids and the eldest has begun to pick up on that sort of stuff. He's a United fan, of course. Absolute Red. It was lovely going to Old Trafford for a match with him and my son, three generations of us there. I don't go very often because I'm usually working on a Friday night and don't get back till three or four o'clock in the morning.

I think this team have learned an awful lot from their experiences in Europe, and it is a learning process. We saw how Dortmund were happy with a one-goal lead at home [in the 1996–97 European Cup competition]. Over the years United supporters have come to expect their team to play a certain way; there's a tradition of attacking football. United would rather play for a 5–4 than a 1–0. If United had been 1–0 up at home they'd have been going for another.

But I think United will do it soon. It's a similar situation to the one we had. Matt took United to the semi-finals in '57 and '58 and I believe they would have won it but for Munich because they had learned. But over the next few years Matt made sure we played Real Madrid every year in friendlies because they were the best side in the world. The first year they beat United 5–1 at Old Trafford, the next year in Madrid United lost about 6–3. Next year Madrid came over here and I played. We drew 2–2 after leading 2–0 at half-time. And the next year we went over to Madrid and beat them 2–0. Now we knew we were starting to come of age. And that was because Matt had kept us playing the best.

After five years out of Europe because of Heysel all English clubs have had to catch up, but gradually you get there. We should have won it in '66 – everybody says so – but we missed George. We got there in the end, though, and this team is getting there. There's quality and blend. But you've got to be strong at the back as well. People like Gary Pallister, young Gary Neville and Denis Irwin are very important. Irwin is one of the unsung heroes. Like Tony and Shay. When people talk about the '68 side they don't mention Tony or Shay, but the other players know how important they were.

We won the League in '65 and then again in '67, scoring 100-odd goals, but we conceded only 35. We won a lot of games 1–0. People don't realise that. Tony and Shay were very quick, and gave the ball early and simple to George and the others. To win leagues and trophies you've got to have that strength at the back. We had that – and the rest.

So how does he respond to Peter Schmeichel's proclamation that the '68 side would not live with the present team? With a quip worthy of an accomplished public wit and raconteur: 'He's quite right – but then most of us are well into our fifties!'

Stiles wonders, by way of doubled-edged riposte, whether Schmeichel and his chums have as much fun on their European jaunts as the '60s boys had.

> It seems to me to be a very different scene now. But then we were able to relax and have a drink without having to watch out for the press. In fact, the press lads were often with us. There was that trust. I don't think that's there now. One of the great football writers and characters of the time was Frank McGhee, and he could be a cantankerous so and so when he'd had a drink. He used to rev up Paddy and, well, we all know what Paddy's like. Paddy got up one night and said, 'Right, that's it,' but just as he walked over to Frank to chin him, Frank's head tilted over as if he was fast asleep. Ah, good days.

So are these. The old nickname has become appropriate in a more literal sense. And now he has to go, to pick up one of his grandchildren. He leaves not by car but on foot, heading for the tram. 'Yeah, it's only a couple of stops.' So off he goes, just another grandfather in three layers and large glasses. Somehow you cannot imagine the current players taking the tram. Or some of the other '68 players, come to that.

# 7. GEORGE BEST

Born: Belfast, 22-5-46
Debut: v West Bromwich Albion (h), 14-9-63
United career: Football League – 361 appearances, 137 goals;
FA Cup – 46, 21; Football League Cup – 25, 9; Europe – 34, 11.
Total – 466, 178.

That 14th day of September, 1963, roused like any other match day in Manchester. The bustle of shoppers and people going about their business fused with the familiar swell of anticipation among those merely marking time before heading for Old Trafford. Those converging on the city's Central Station – since deemed obsolete and then regenerated as the G-Mex exhibition centre – for the short train journey that deposited passengers on the very doorstep of United's ground eagerly checked the early edition of the *Manchester Evening News* for any word on the team to line up against West Bromwich Albion. There was. A 17-year-old from Belfast would be making his debut at outside-right, in place of the injured Ian Moir.

The instant, gut reaction was one of mild dismay. This was the season when United were supposed to be re-establishing themselves as the best in the land. They had just won the FA Cup and now they were back on the trail of the League Championship. That meant fielding a settled, proven side that would instil fear in the opposition. This selection smacked of problems, even panic. Of those dark, confused, indecisive days that were supposed to be consigned to the past. And when he trotted out on to the pitch we were convinced problems, even panic, had set in. The kid was little, skinny and might have been aged 12.

What happened in the following 90 minutes of football depends on your memory, imagination, romanticism or source of information. One of the most distinguished writers of that or any other time, Arthur Hopcroft, considered it one of the two most memorable first appearances he had seen in League football. Others were more sceptical. To many of us standing in the Stretford End Paddock, this was another kid brought in for the ritual try-out. A kid with a few nice tricks but who was not ready yet, and who, like so many before him, might never be ready. He was marked by Graham Williams, the Wales left-back, and given an inevitably uncompromising reception to the grown-up game. In the second half the youngster was mercifully switched to the other wing and played better, though not well enough to figure in the first team for another three months.

The legend, like the boy from Belfast, needed a lot of developing yet. He had arrived in Manchester, the son of a useful amateur footballer and outstanding hockey player, in 1961, only to return immediately to Belfast along with his travelling companion, Eric McMordie, homesick and terrified. Fifteen-year-old Best was persuaded to come back to Old Trafford and give it a go, while McMordie would try his luck at Middlesbrough. Glowing communiqués about Best's talent had preceded him, but here he was, five foot three inches tall, weighing seven stone ten pounds and apparently as timid as a dormouse.

He was entrusted into the care of Mrs Mary Fullaway, a landlady whose name would also pass into Manchester football lore. She and the club fed him and built him up sufficiently to enable his gifts to take their natural course. Busby was one of those who evidently felt his protégé required more time after that baptism against Williams and West Bromwich, and probably had no intention of exposing him to the rigours of a second League game until well into 1964. Then problems, even panic, brought a change of plan.

United were thumped 4–0 at Everton and 6–1 at Burnley over the Christmas period. Best, so far out of contention for a first-team place he had been allowed home for the holiday, was summoned for the return fixture with Burnley on 28 December. Making his debut on the other wing was a 16-year-old called Willie Anderson. The younger winger was terrific, spearing the heart of Burnley's defence with his crosses and corner kicks. The 'senior' partner was a revelation. He destroyed Burnley's defence and scored his first League goal in the 5–1 victory. This was the day we knew something special was happening at Manchester United.

Anderson was one of those who never quite made it in the major league, but Best had arrived and over the following decade would subject United's management, players and supporters to the gamut of emotions. They would be beguiled, inspired, sometimes exasperated and occasionally feel betrayed. But they would never be bored. Best on the ball was an art form, a thing of beauty. His mastery of it was something they had never seen, even at Old

Trafford. Duncan Edwards is immortalised as the greatest, the complete player, his stature sacrosanct. But Best flaunted something else on the senses: the images of a wizard, his willowy frame bending round defenders and over flailing challenges, always balanced, and always with the ball at his command. He was impish, inventive and utterly self-assured. He played to the gallery and he played for the team, scoring goals – 32 in the 1967–68 season – and creating goals and tackling back. He could shoot with either foot and was excellent in the air for a player of his height.

He won Championship medals in 1965 and 1967 and scored the pivotal second goal in the European Cup final, which effectively sealed his European Footballer of the Year award. But perhaps even more memorable and certainly just as defining in his own career was his mesmeric display at Benfica's Stadium of Light in 1966. His two early goals propelled United to an astounding 5–1 victory and had all Europe talking about the 19-year-old 'Beatle'. Best, with floppy dark hair, irresistible smile and a taste for trendy clothes, was a young man of the '60s, projecting a public way of life more familiar among pop stars than footballers. He moved into a futuristic house and dated actresses and beauty queens.

There were, however, voids in his career. He never had the chance to strut on the World Cup stage because the rest of Northern Ireland's team were not up to it, and he never experienced an FA Cup final. Even so, he left his impression on the grand old lady of football competitions by scoring six goals in United's 8–2 victory away to Northampton Town in a fifth-round tie in 1970. During one of his 37 international appearances, against England, he deployed his speed of thought and movement to steal the ball from the great Gordon Banks as it left his hands bound for his boot, and nodded it in the net. The goal did not stand, but the magic did.

Alas, he also left marks of a different kind. He began to make headlines for his drinking, gambling and womanising. And then a new idiom came into the game: 'Best goes missing.' United were falling apart and his disenchantment pushed him over the edge when, at the age of 26, he announced he had quit football. He returned but his halcyon days could not, and he walked out on United for the last time early in 1974. The legend remained a draw for many years thereafter, and he took his one-man show on the road, around Britain – enjoying a particularly acclaimed run with Fulham – Ireland and the United States, where he scored what he considers his greatest goal, and, finally, Australia, in 1983.

His playing days had ended but his penchant for attracting headlines had not. His marriage broke up, he made several visits to clinics and Alcoholics Anonymous in an attempt to beat the booze, he was declared a bankrupt and he served two months in jail after a drink-driving charge accelerated out of control. He failed to turn up for the court hearing, then resisted arrest and was accused of assaulting a police officer.

From that nadir he has made a seemingly remarkable recovery, even if his friends still worry and the sceptics still sneer that he remains susceptible to drink. He has developed an after-dinner and theatre club act, has regular employment with Sky television, promotes a number of business ventures – including his own wine label – and is involved in plans for a film about his life. He is married for the second time and lives in apparent new order and bliss in Chelsea.

* * *

You would expect him to live in Chelsea. Near the King's Road. And you would expect his watering hole to be hip and decorated with long-legged creatures. This part of Chelsea, however, even so close to the King's Road, is not what you would expect. Nor is the watering hole. It is discreet, reserved, unpretentious, unsophisticated. Almost village-like.

He is just another regular, popping into his local. A couple of other regulars nod; a more presumptuous patron greets him with an enthusiastic 'Hi, Georgie boy'. Their salutations are acknowledged politely, though not ostentatiously, and he perches himself on a bar stool. He is wearing black tracksuit bottoms, a black sports shirt and trainers. The long-established beard is greying and he pulls out a pair of glasses to tackle the newspaper. A couple across the bar try to make out what he is drinking. 'Looks like a spritzer,' one says to the other.

The legend is alive and looking well at 51, even if the eyes are not as sharp as they were. He is carrying more weight than he did that night in blue, but not as much as people have made out. And you are soon reminded of what his team-mates and confidants say of him: that he is demure, respectful, friendly. Even vulnerable. He is also a doting husband and father. His wife, Alex, is half his age and by all accounts has taken years off him. Calum, his 16-year-old son by his first marriage, is over from America and dad is as proud as dads should be.

When George Best was 16 he could belittle grown men with a ball at his feet. Clever ball-players landed on the doormat at Old Trafford as regularly as the post, mostly to be discarded like junk mail. This kid was different, and on the training ground and back at Old Trafford, on the tarmac between the stadium and the railway line, where private scores were settled and cocky recruits were cut down to size, his talent ranged beyond their constraint and comprehension.

As Best recalls those days, a flicker of mischief returns in the smile.

I was the new kid on the block and all these other players were big names, internationals. We played at the Cliff or in the car park at the side of Old Trafford, amongst broken glass and bricks and all sorts, and it got a bit tasty. They didn't like it when I nutmegged them, especially Harry Gregg. Harry was crazy, but usually in a nice way. He was such a pro. He'd come through the disaster and then went through a terrible spell with injuries. But even in practice matches Harry was so serious about his game. You didn't score against Harry. You were risking your life if you did.

When it came to the real thing there were obviously doubts about me, but the club realised that with proper training and proper food, living in digs and getting looked after, I was going to get bigger. I never got massive but my legs strengthened. The upper body didn't matter that much. In those days we didn't do weights. It was a worry for me, wondering whether I could make it at this great club with all these other lads.

Busby, wrestling with a few injury problems early in that 1963–64 season, decided to gauge the development of the skinny kid from Belfast in the home match against West Bromwich Albion, coincidentally also the opposition when Denis Law had made his debut for United a year earlier.

It was a test all right. I was up against Graham Williams, the Welsh international full-back. Off the pitch he's the nicest bloke you'd ever want to meet. I've bumped into him many times over the years and he's a lovely man. But when you were out on the pitch playing against him you knew you'd better realise there were no prisoners taken. That was my introduction to the First Division. He gave me a couple of smacks and dear old Sir Matt moved me over to the other wing in the second half to get away from him. Funnily enough, I made my international debut against Graham, as well.

To be honest, I didn't find it any more difficult playing in the first team than in the reserves, but then I didn't play that many reserve-team games. I played mainly in the A and B teams. After that first-team game in the September I was back in the junior teams. I was actually at home in Belfast that Christmas when they called me. They'd just been to

> Burnley and got stuffed well and truly, and they sent a
> telegram asking me to come back. I told them I wanted to be
> back home in Belfast after the game, and they booked me the
> flight. So I played the game, we beat them 5–1, I got my first
> goal and that was it. I was in the side for ten years.

It sounds so simple. To Best it was, at that stage of his life. He had made a natural progression from the streets of Belfast to the glass- and brick-strewn initiation ceremonies at Old Trafford to the grand stage of English football. He represented a fresh, invigorating and successful period at United.

> Other kids were coming along as well. People like Willie
> Anderson, who was younger than me. He was 16 when he
> first played. He was on one wing, I was on the other, and
> there was a lot of controversy about playing two young kids.
> I remember a Cup tie at Southampton, who had a good side.
> We both played in that game and we won 3–2. We were a
> bonus for the boss because he had so many top players and
> it was developing into a terrific side again. He had Bobby,
> Denis, Paddy and Bill. Noel Cantwell was the captain, and
> he had Shay and Tony, Maurice Setters and Nobby. Then
> later came Alex Stepney.

To achieve fame and distinction at home is one thing; to bewitch Europe is quite another. Best accomplished that second feat in 90 of the most memorable minutes in football. United arrived at the Stadium of Light in March 1966 with a fragile 3–2 lead over Benfica in the quarter-final of the European Cup. Busby, for all his reputation as the unsullied purist, was pragmatic enough to demand containment in the early stages, to frustrate their opponents and turn down the volume of the towering stands. As Nobby Stiles would say, 'Nobody told George what the plan was.' Best scored twice in an extraordinary opening burst and the strategy of containment was rendered redundant. United were on an irresistible course to a 5–1 victory. Best recalls,

> Domestically I was starting to do it, but the big thing,
> especially for this club, was always Europe. Benfica had never
> lost at home in Europe. They had almost a full team of
> international players. But we went there and produced an
> unbelievable performance. I've always thought the two club

teams closest to perfection were the great Real Madrid of the late '50s and 1960, and the Tottenham side of 1960–61. But I think that night we got as close to perfection as you can get. We played a terrific side and absolutely demolished them. It could have been more. I think we had a goal disallowed in the first half, when John Connelly scored.

United had a place in the semi-finals of the European Cup, and George Best had a place in the consciousness of a world beyond the white markings of a football pitch. Overnight, this lean young man with the dark, floppy hair, pictured returning to Manchester wearing a sombrero, was 'El Beatle'. Iberian tongues may have been crossed, but no matter. It was a great headline and Georgie, the Belfast boy, was no longer merely a footballer.

The El Beatle thing actually makes me smile, because when you look back, my hair wasn't that long. But for those days it was, of course, and it was the time of the Beatles, so that was it. I was just a kid, enjoying myself. I was 19 and I was getting paid for doing something I loved doing. I'd have played for nothing. But I was able to buy nice clothes and I could afford nice cars when most of my pals couldn't. I was into music because that was just massive in the North. Fashion was changing. Hippies were coming in. Everything in that period was just special.

Football was the thing for me above all else, but I realised something different was going on when I came back from Lisbon. I bought a sombrero for a friend and wore it as we came off the plane, for a bit of a laugh. Pictures of me wearing the sombrero actually appeared on the front page as well as the back page of a national newspaper. Footballers just didn't appear on the front page. Not in those days. It just snowballed after that and the next few years were terrific.

For a few years, too, he seemed able to balance his football with his celebrity status, the boutiques, the personal appearances and the glamorous girlfriends. He had an agent to handle his business affairs and secretaries to deal with the daily mountain of fan mail. On the field, he could take care of himself.

Best's performance in the Stadium of Light was perhaps too dazzling for his and the team's good. Busby risked him in the first leg of the semi-final, away to Partizan Belgrade, despite a knee problem. Their relatively unknown and generally unfancied opponents won 2–0. Best missed the second leg – and the rest of the season – and Stiles's late goal was not enough. Another Championship, however, gave them another chance in 1967–68.

> Although I got a goal in the home leg against Real Madrid it was going to be hard over there, and sure enough we were 3–1 down at half-time and it might have been all over. I'd been marked closely and hadn't really done much. But a fortunate goal got us back in it and then, after one of the few times I got past the full-back, I knocked it back to this red shirt. When I realised it was Foulksey I thought, 'Oh, no.' But he didn't half stick it away. It was unbelievable.

But Bill says he couldn't have missed. Best stifles his guffaw to respond.

> He had a lot of choices. He could have stopped it, he could have walloped it. Instead he side-footed it in. It was brilliant. At 3–3 we knew it was ours.
>
> I think we might have relaxed a little too much after Madrid, because that was some result. There was a danger of thinking we'd already won the final. We'd beaten Benfica twice two years previously and the final was virtually a home match for us. Nobody said publicly that we thought it was all over, but we did think we couldn't really lose this one. In the end, the script couldn't have been written better.
>
> I don't remember anything about where we stayed before the final or what happened afterwards [it can be safely assumed he had a good night], but the two hours of the match I can see almost perfectly. I do remember I just couldn't wait to get out there. I've never been superstitious about anything, so playing all in blue didn't worry me. I was never physically sick before, during or after a game. I loved it so much, I suppose I was able to take it in my stride. It didn't matter if it was a five-a-side, an international in front of 120,000 or a European Cup final.
>
> Shay Brennan insists he made my goal. He passed it back to Alex, who cleared it. Brian Kidd flicked it on and then I stuck it through the legs of the centre-half, who was the last defender. I get a bit annoyed when I see the goal now because they only show the end of it, never the whole of it. There was

a bit of work to do, especially sticking it through his legs. Then the keeper came out. I always dreamt that if I was in a position to do it, I was going to stop the ball on the line and head it in. But the keeper was a bit too sharp, so I thought I'd better not risk it. Kiddo and Bobby finished it off in style.

Sir Matt realised his dream that night but, remember, we had a pretty special side over a number of years, and the more successful you are the tougher it becomes. Every week was a battle for us because we were Manchester United and everybody wanted to beat us. That made the job even harder for Matt.

You just had to see the respect people had for him to realise how special he was. He knew how to get the best out of his players. He was always paying us compliments. He'd tell me I was the best tackler in the club. Coming from him that was brilliant. He gave you such a lift. But he knew how to bring you down to earth as well. He didn't call you in to his office and tell you that you were dropped, he'd call you in and ask you, 'How do you think you're playing?' You would have to say, 'Not very well, boss.' After that you had to be dropped. And that was the way he did it.

He was like a father to me. Remember, I left home at 15 and this great man treated me as if I was a son. When I was going through hard times he never lectured me. He talked to me. I came back from Spain in 1972, after announcing I was retiring, with a thrombosis, and he was the first person to come and see me in hospital. He stayed for about 20 minutes, we talked about old times, and as he walked out of the door he popped his head back in and just said, 'Don't you think it's about time you were back playing?' And that was it. He was no longer the manager, but he was still the Great Man.

The trouble was, it was never going to be the same. Those ten years were just magic, but the King was no longer on the throne. The fact that the club went into the Second Division just six years after being the best in Europe was a disgrace. It doesn't matter that they came straight back up.

We all know what should have happened. The team should have been strengthened before it was too late. But the club signed a lot of players who weren't good enough. It was as simple as that. I was still quite young. If I was lucky I had another seven or eight years. At first I didn't think there was extra pressure on me after Wembley, but there was. I was coming back to the dressing room after getting stuffed by teams who a couple of years earlier couldn't have lived with us.

It was like revolving doors with the different managers. Some would come in and hardly say two words to anyone and they were gone [an obvious allusion to Frank O'Farrell]. And some of the team-sheets! Some of the players who were putting on the red shirt . . . well, it was an insult to the great players who'd worn it in the past. When you think of Bobby and Denis, Paddy and Nobby, and, yes, me, there's no comparison. Good players could and would have signed for the club. Mike England and Alan Ball were two who should have joined us. There weren't too many players who didn't want to sign for Manchester United. In that respect the fans were let down.

I'll probably never know whether that pressure on me led to my problems. Nobody will ever know. But I knew one thing: that something I loved more than anything apart from my family had been taken away from me. It was something I'd been doing since I was a year old and the only thing I'd ever wanted to do. And all of a sudden it had been taken away from me.

As we shall hear from Bobby Charlton, he felt Best let down the fans and his colleagues when he went missing in those later years. Some observers maintained the differences between the two men extended to disdain and even jealousy. Best sees it differently.

I never let anyone down on the field. That's one thing no one can say against me. I suppose I can understand the accusation that I let down my team-mates in terms of training, but I would go back and train in the afternoon with Bill Foulkes and Paddy Crerand. I was top scorer in the League for five years in a row, playing on the wing. That's hardly letting them down.

I've never felt people were jealous of me. Not then, not today. I see Bobby now regularly and we get on great. We were just different characters. He was a real family man. After training he'd be off to his family, whereas I went with the lads for a game of snooker, and at night maybe had a few drinks. Sometimes we'd lay a few bets. Bobby was different, that's all. But on the field, we were part of the same team and we wanted the same thing, which was success for the club we both loved. And still do.

Denis has the same feeling, but is a different character from Bobby as well. I'm a different character from Denis, though probably closer than Bobby is. If you've got a squad of 15 or 16 players, you are going to get differences of character, differences of opinion and fall-outs. We had some punch-ups in training and rucks and arguments. But it's forgotten as soon as training's finished and you get on with things. And come the Saturday, we all did the business.

David Sadler was my room-mate, a really quiet lad who kept himself to himself, and we got on well together. I was also shy and quiet – but I came out of it a bit later! David's never changed. He's the same today. Different class. He's always sending me messages about old boys' get-togethers. I try to get up when I can. Denis and Shay became two of my best friends later. Our relationships developed after we finished playing, really after I came back from the States, in '81. Since then the three of us have become very close, regularly seeing each other in twos or threes.

We had a team get-together for the 25th anniversary of the final and it was very special, because they can't take away from any of us what we achieved in '68. Some players have maybe fallen out with the club, for whatever reason, and some maybe aren't seen as regularly as others, but there is still that feeling within the team. And when we sat down together to watch a rerun of the final, I think some of us realised we'd forgotten how good we were. Some of the football was fabulous, and you could see the confidence running through the whole team.

We never went out believing we were going to lose, home or away. When we won the Championship in '67 we went to West Ham and knew we could finish it there. But they were a terrific side. It didn't matter. We went to Upton Park and stuffed them 6–1. That's some way to do it. Other teams would have gone there and had their backs to the wall. We just thrashed them.

By 1972 the days of virtuoso football had gone. United were the team on the wrong end of thrashings. Best quit, then returned; then the club announced there was no future for him at Old Trafford and Tommy Docherty succeeded Frank O'Farrell as manager. Desperate for a spark of inspiration to ignite his fading team, Docherty sanctioned another comeback by the Ulsterman and Crerand brokered the deal. Even 75 per cent of Best, even in a more withdrawn role, had to be better than most of the rest had to offer. He played a dozen games, the last on New Year's Day 1974, a 3–0 defeat at Queen's Park Rangers. Four days later Docherty dropped him for the third-round FA Cup tie against Plymouth Argyle at Old Trafford and Best walked out on United for the final time.

Best gives his version of the closing scene.

There were stories that I had hit the booze again that weekend, but I had not. Those stories are always going to come along. The Doc had said to me that if I ever missed training, for whatever reason, it would be kept quiet. I'd take my punishment and do extra training. And I'd been training really hard, doing extra work with Paddy and Bill. I think we'd played Spurs the week before and I'd scored, and it was the first time I felt I was getting there. I was starting to get past players and away from them.

On the Wednesday I went out with some friends and had a late night, and I missed training on Thursday morning. So I came in Thursday afternoon. I came in on the Friday morning and trained, and nobody said anything to me. I turned up on Saturday with the rest of the boys and the Doc took me in the referee's room with Paddy. He said, 'I'm leaving you out today because you missed training Thursday morning.' That was it, I said to myself, 'If I can't play today, it's over.'

What might have happened after that we'll never know. But I don't regret walking out because I realised it wasn't going to work. I'd worked my socks off to get back into it, and I still wasn't happy about the team and the sort of players that were playing. So I think it was just a matter of time anyway. I just figured it would be best for all concerned to do it there and then.

Even to this day I sit and wonder whether it really was the best thing to do. It was like being with a woman you loved, knowing it was going to end sooner or later. It was probably braver to make that decision sooner rather than let things carry on. I couldn't have achieved any more at Manchester United, the team being as it was. And after those fabulous years, when we won everything, I didn't want this. And anything after United would have been second best. I didn't want second best.

I could have gone to another club and started anew. I had a lot of offers. I could have gone abroad. There was talk about Chelsea, which might have been a good move for me. In London. Then again, that might have been the worst move I could have made! But the bottom line was I didn't want to play for anybody else. So the next few years I was a maverick, and I played everywhere in the world.

His wanderings took him to some unlikely watering holes: Dunstable, Stockport and Bournemouth, to name but three. He revived the soul with a cameo spell at Fulham, teaming up with fellow showman Rodney Marsh and Bobby Moore. He maintains he performed his real show-stopper, however, playing for San Jose Earthquakes in 1980. 'Yeah, I enjoyed that, going round five players and sticking it in. When you score a goal like that it's a bit special, no matter where you're playing.'

Best always had a yearning for that special something and he weaned his public on to the drug. He remembers how, as a youngster, he was mesmerised, along with Sheffield Wednesday's exceptional goalkeeper Ron Springett, by Pele's penalty for Santos in a friendly at Hillsborough.

He dummied three or four times and the poor keeper was just bewildered, rooted to his line, as Pele eventually smacked it in. Pele made ten the magic number, and since then it's been a symbol for some of the great players – Platini, Zico, Maradona – and, I must say, I enjoyed the game I played with it on my back. Yeah, that has to be the number to have. I've been eight, but, of course, more often seven, which I had in the final, and 11. I suppose really I think of myself as 11 and my son wants 11 on his shirt.

Unlike Pele and the rest, as well as several club colleagues, Best never had the opportunity to demonstrate his talent on the World Cup stage, but he maintains,

I don't really regret that, because dear old Northern Ireland were never going to make an impact at that level. Sure, I'd love to have played with a great team, with ten Brazilians, but we were never going to have a great team.

As his football prowess ebbed, the booze flowed evermore freely. Best was in a twilight zone and in danger of being sucked into eternal darkness. That he has emerged in daylight seems a minor miracle. He has learned his lessons the hard way, yet appears none the harder for the experience. Cynicism has mercifully passed him by. He is simply grateful to be able to tell the tale.

I have to be thankful for the way I've ended up. When you consider what I've been through, I've got to consider myself lucky. I've been in prison, I've been in clinics, I've been treated three or four times for alcoholism, I've been bankrupt and I've had car crashes, fights and all sorts of dramas with women. And yet I couldn't be happier than I am today. I go to bed at night and I sleep. For years I couldn't. I'd got that many things going round in my head.

My life is under control now. Brilliant. Totally different from when I came back here from the States in '81. Calum was a year old, I was getting divorced and I'd had to leave him over there while I came here to get things sorted out. Today it's a nice family and Calum is over here with us for a while. I say to my wife, Alex, 'Isn't it nice we don't have a nine-to-five working life?' We don't know from one day to the next what we're going to be doing, but there's always plenty for us to do.

For the past three or four years I've been working with Sky. I'm on the after-dinner circuit, although I cut down on that a bit because I was doing too much. I do some with Rodney, some with Denis and quite a few on my own. I'm involved with a few companies and businesses, basically to make personal appearances, and there's a movie in the pipeline. It's really my life story and it looks like it could be a biggie.

One of the places I got involved in was Bobby Keetch's 'Football, Football' restaurant, in London. Poor Bobby died not long after it opened and I was supposed to speak at a memorial dinner organised as a tribute to him. I was actually going to read a letter he wrote me just before he died but I freaked out. I couldn't do it. I had to get Marshy to read it.

Keetchie's death, and Bobby Moore's, not so long ago, have made me think a lot about myself. I was the one who had all the problems, I was the one who wasn't supposed to be around much longer, and yet I'm still here, feeling as fit as a fiddle. A lovely old doctor did some tests on me and said he must have got them mixed up with somebody else's because as far as he could see there was nothing wrong with me. I don't do any sport now because one of my knees is really bad, and I have my circulation checked following the thrombosis. I go to a health farm about four times a year, just to relax, and I feel great.

I'm thankful because I think I'm lucky. I'm travelling the world first-class, I stay in the best hotels, all paid for. I'm married to a beautiful lady and I'm madly in love. And I've got a terrific son. And you know what's really nice? That despite all the trouble I've been in and the scrapes I've had and all the bad publicity, people remember me above all as George Best the footballer. That's lovely.

I took Calum to 'Football, Football' for lunch and there must have been 50 or 60 kids who came up and asked for my autograph. I've spent three hours signing autographs in New Zealand and even then had to be dragged away. Sometimes on the theatre tours I'm amazed how many youngsters are in the audience. I haven't kicked a ball at top level for 25 years, but they know about George Best the footballer.

There was a time when being George Best meant a lot of hassle. About 50 per cent of the time, in fact. Now it's maybe 10 per cent. I tend to have regular haunts, where I know I'm going to be looked after. You still get the odd idiot and that's never going to change. I don't know whether I'm getting smarter or just too old to fight, but I tend to walk away from it now, whereas a few years ago I wouldn't have done. I was up at the local pub for some charity do and this guy wanted to be Jack the Lad. He's with half a dozen of his mates, all having a few drinks, and he starts effing and blinding. I'm there with my wife and in-laws and I'm tempted to walk over and smack him in the mouth. But that's probably what they want, and then, of course, they're the first to complain and it's 'George Best in brawl again'. Unfortunately that's how certain people look on you, but the kids don't.

You can imagine what Alex's mum and dad said when she

told them about me. She's half my age and they've heard all these stories about me. But I went to meet them and we've become good friends. When her mum said to me, 'I've never seen my daughter happier,' it made me feel pretty good about life. My relationship with Calum is great. He's football-daft. A United fan, of course. The team he plays for have just won their championship. He fancies a career in the game, but he'd need to live here. He's got an American accent but hates to be called an American. He says he's half Irish and half Scottish, because his mum's got a Scottish background.

The doting father has arranged time off from his Sky commitments to take his son to a match at Old Trafford, the first of two trips to his old club in three days. He explains,

> We've got a box organised at the game against Coventry and we're getting there nice and early so Calum can go to the megastore. I've also got to go up there to interview Alex Ferguson for Sky. This is a bit of a first for me and I'm looking forward to it. Fergie's done a terrific job, no question about that.
>
> You've got to say this team does compare with ours, except in one important respect. They haven't won the biggie, and until they do the comparisons are only words. Cantona was the one who brought back the style and flair, and I think every team at this level needs a genius, with ten good players around him. What he's left behind is the confidence, and you can see that in the kids. We had that with kids like Kiddo and Johnny Aston coming in. They have that same feeling that they're not going to lose. Domestically they are the side to beat, and they should have got to the European Cup final last season. But that's where they've got to do it.
>
> Having said that, the European Cup's not really the European Cup any more. It's not the Champions' Cup it used to be. I think it has been devalued by allowing runner-up teams into it, but at least United did qualify as champions.

Best would be similarly resistant to change in his own life. He is adamant, in fact.

I wouldn't change anything, because although I have had bad times, the good times outweighed them. I had those fabulous years in the game, which the older fans remember and the younger ones can see on video, and I've certainly no complaints about my life now. I have to smile when people talk about 'poor old George'. I wouldn't swap places with anyone.

The respect people show me means everything. When I go to Old Trafford I always get respect, even from the present players. I went to Coventry to kick off the celebrity game at David Busst's benefit and Peter Schmeichel, who was warming up for the main match, came sprinting over to me. He shook hands and said he wanted me to know that business about the present team walloping our team 10–0 or something was all a load of rubbish. The thing is we did it – and you have to respect that.

# 8. BRIAN KIDD

Born: Manchester, 29-5-49
Debut: v Everton (a), 19-8-67
United career: Football League – 195 (8) appearances, 52 goals;
FA Cup – 24 (1), 8; Football League Cup – 20, 7;  Europe – 16, 3.
Total – 255 (9), 70.

If Busby's story was the main theme of the fairytale, there was also a sub-plot to intrigue the romantic: local boy, United fan, called up to the first team at the start of the 1967–68 season and, on his 19th birthday, scores in the European Cup final victory. And, by way of a further sentimental twist, he is back at Old Trafford today, assisting Alex Ferguson's endeavours to reclaim the club's position as the continent's No. 1. Brian Kidd, like his original manager, has his heaven right here.

As a youngster raised in a Catholic family in Collyhurst, Kidd followed Stiles to St Patrick's School and developed the same devotion to United. At the time of the crash, however, he was only eight and his heroes would be those of the next generation. Of Stiles's early teams. His idol was Denis Law, so imagine the pride stirring inside Kidd when a fan ran on to the pitch and 'crowned' him the new King in succession to the Scot.

Kiddo had been in dreamland since joining the United fold as a schoolboy. Two years on he was an apprentice and beginning his rapid progress through the junior ranks. When the 1967 Championship-winning side went on tour to Australia, Busby added Kidd to the squad. He needed a replacement for David Herd, who was recovering from a broken leg, and had been impressed with the youngster's performances for the reserves. Like Herd, Kidd possessed a venomous shot. He was particularly strong on his left side but the right foot was no mere 'swinger'. He was big enough to be a physical handful yet mobile enough to exploit exceptional close control.

Kidd returned from the trip with his graduation certificate. He played in the Charity Shield game against Tottenham Hotspur and made his League debut the following week. He appeared in 38 of United's First Division matches that season, scoring 15 goals. He also played in all nine European Cup games, culminating with the Wembley final and that birthday goal.

He was unfortunate his arrival coincided with the erosion of the great '60s team. Like Best, he was blossoming as others were wilting. The years of turmoil can scarcely have eased his development, and yet his powerful displays devastated opponents and captivated subjects yearning for their next King. It was a short reign. There was no future for the old monarchy in Tommy Docherty's republic and Kidd left relegated United for Arsenal in the summer of 1974 in a £110,000 transfer.

The move resuscitated Kidd's career but he seized the opportunity, two years later, to come home. Home to Manchester, anyway. He had to withstand some ribbing from his old pals when he signed for City, as well as a few scrapes with the authorities. The seemingly shy, humble demeanour hid a wicked inclination to mischief and a sharp temper. He joined another major club, Everton, before completing his regular playing career in England with Bolton Wanderers. Considering the stature of his employers it is perhaps surprising his only club honour was that European Cup winner's medal. He won his two full England caps – after international Youth and Under-23 appearances – as a United player.

Kidd followed the trail of the prospectors to America, panning for gold in Atlanta, Fort Lauderdale and Minnesota, before trying his hand at management with Barrow, Swindon and Preston as first or second in command. But he remained a Manchester boy at heart – a United boy, in fact – and he revelled in the opportunity to forge links between the club and the community and to activate Ferguson's desire to bring the best of the local talent to Old Trafford. Kidd's work with the School of Excellence and as youth development officer convinced the manager he had the ideal No. 2 on his doorstep.

\* \* \*

Less than 45 minutes to kick-off and the bars and kiosks inside the stadium are humming to the familiar tune of brisk business. The moment the customer is released from the turnstile into the concrete cavern beneath the stands, he or she is assailed by earnest invitations to buy half-time draw tickets. Programmes are sold by the bunch. 'Must take one home for little Jimmy. Oh, and I bet your Fred would like one.' Groups gather to sip from plastic cups, master the art of excavating a pie from its container one-handed and listen out for team news. Few have yet taken their seats. Early arrivals in the top tier of the new stand (what time did they set off?) are distant specks.

Down on the pitch, however, there is activity already. Peter Schmeichel, the United goalkeeper, has begun his warm-up routine in front of the old Stretford End, fielding short-range shots from a man once hailed in these quarters as 'King Brian'. Today Kidd is slightly chunkier, but he still has a good head of hair and those boyish features, and that trusty left foot looks as lethal as ever. The right one is still no mere swinger, either. Schmeichel asks for crosses and the assistant manager obliges. From left and right, they stretch the magnificent Dane, who has been given the captaincy in the absence of the injured Roy Keane.

We have a delicious irony here. It was Schmeichel who told the press his team would have demolished Kidd's European Cup-winning team. It was later dismissed as a tongue-in-cheek, throwaway, not-to-be-taken-seriously wind-up. But rivalries cross the generation time zones, and here are two fiercely proud and competitive characters. Should we discern a little extra venom in Kidd's shots now? And a steely determination by the goalkeeper to defy him? After 20 minutes of entertaining sparring Schmeichel is satisfied, and they conclude the session with a ritual handshake. Schmeichel, whose stature here has grown in every sense, leans over the perimeter fencing and gives his gloves to a thrilled youngster, then walks back towards the dressing room accompanied by warm applause.

Kidd now turns his attention to the other players, who are into their final preparations: stretching, sprinting, juggling, passing. Kidd is joined in the arc of the penalty area by an apparently self-appointed lieutenant, Brian McClair, and together they supervise the mosaic of moving patterns. There is an air of confidence and control, as you might expect from players who have just won a third consecutive match in the Champions League. The flicks, tricks and smiles are those of young men utterly sure of their course. Giggs and Beckham, the crown princes, trot out together, sprint together, laugh together. Kidd, an earlier product of the United nursery and symbol of the club's faith in youth, maintains a paternal watch, occasionally reaching out a guiding hand.

For all it is an easy, happy atmosphere, but this is another day at the office and Kidd ensures they go about their business. At 2.45 he winds up this part of the proceedings and herds the players back up the canvas-covered tunnel, conveniently positioned at this end of the ground. He, too, looks content and relaxed, proffering a thumbs-up sign and wave aimed in the direction of the players' and staff guests' enclosure. In a few minutes Kidd will re-emerge and take his place alongside Ferguson on their pitchside platform, and hope he is still content and relaxed after the game against Barnsley.

Kidd has not always been able to hold station on the sidelines. One of the abiding images of him is his delirious celebration when Steve Bruce plundered a crucial and improbable victory against Sheffield Wednesday in 1993 with a goal some six minutes into stoppage time. Kidd leapt into the air, then sank to his knees, fists clenched, paying homage to the One responsible for divine deliverance. Manchester United were never merely a football club to Kidd, and in moments of extreme emotion he was never afraid to show it.

As a player his passionate reactions sometimes brought him into conflict with the game's officials and authorities, but it was usually the tantrums of childlike innocence rather than premeditated cynicism. Kidd by name . . . And yet, when he was entrusted, at the age of 18, with a man's job, he responded with a stoicism and maturity even Busby cannot have anticipated.

Herd's injury in 1967 appeared to have secured David Sadler a permanent place in the attack, but by the start of the new season Busby's perspective had changed. Sadler's versatility had provided new options. If anything he was a better player in midfield or at the heart of the defence. And, in any case, the young boy Kidd was looking the part. He would be given his chance in a forward line that also comprised Best, Law, Charlton and Aston. It is a measure of how well he took the chance that he woke up on the morning of his 19th birthday contemplating the European Cup final.

By then his more experienced and renowned colleagues had come to admire his talent and muse at his taste for mischief. As David Coleman recalls, he found ready-made material in the Stiles family trade. It was Collyhurst Jack the Lad humour, a chattering Mancunian parody. He would always play the humble, self-deprecating boy-next-door role for public consumption, but here was a young man not out of place with Manchester United and not out of place at club football's showpiece event. He tells the story in an accent as authentically Manc as it ever was.

> It was my first season in the first team, and to be involved in the European Cup final, I don't think anything could have topped that. You had every type in that team. Bobby, so graceful. Bestie had everything, so explosive. Paddy, what a passer of the ball. You go to Tony Dunne, who for me was the best full-back in Europe that season. Bill Foulkes, who'd seen it all and what a great servant he had been to the club.

You go through to Johnny Aston and myself, the local lads. It must have been nice for John because his dad was youth-team coach here. We'd Dave Sadler coming in as well; he was a young lad. Nobby, again, we went to the same school, St Patrick's, Collyhurst, so it was another double, two lads from the same school playing in the European Cup final. And then Shay and Alex. It was a really nice mixture of talents.

With the great players in the team we had, nobody from Benfica was worried about me. My marker wasn't. He didn't kick me as hard as I expected! I remember reading in the *Daily Express* about Eusebio saying, 'Who's Kidd?' So obviously nobody knew me. I was only an 18-year-old that season and nobody was really worried about me.

Equally obvious was his relishing the opportunity to introduce himself. He had no doubts about his value to the team. He had held his place on merit and, for all the politically correct tributes to the 'great players' around him, he felt comfortable in their company. By the end of the long evening the Portuguese had been made aware they ought to have done their homework on the other lad from Collyhurst. Kidd not only headed his birthday goal but also played supporting roles for United's second and fourth.

Because I'd played all that season it really wasn't as much of an ordeal being the youngest member of the side as some might imagine. It probably seemed odd to see us in our blue away kit when they were in white, but as we both usually played in red we both agreed to change, which seemed fair. The 90 minutes was really a non-event. It was only the first 15 minutes of extra-time when it came to life. We possibly lost our way near to winning the game. We were 1–0 up and really, subconsciously, we tried to protect it. Obviously it didn't work out that way but we were never going to be short of legs.

Memories of my goal are vivid. It was pretty straightforward. It came from a corner and I got a double header in. A lot of people think I hit the bar with my first header but I didn't. Henrique, the keeper, made a save and it came back out. I just lobbed it over his head. It was a soft head, really; I can see it now, just going over his head into the back of the net. Then I was away and running, like the greyhounds round Wembley. No one could catch me. Because, obviously, I couldn't believe it. It was a dream come true.

At 3–1 it just gave us that bit of a buffer. And then Bobby went on to get the fourth goal, which I was involved in on the right wing. My right leg was for standing on, but I could see the defender coming in to kick me and I just managed to kick it past him and go down the right wing. I didn't hit it well but you don't have to with Bobby. Hell of a strike. Rifled it in.

We had the reception back at the Russell Hotel, with Joe Loss and his orchestra. Joe Loss presented me with a birthday cake. That was nice. My mum and dad were there. Three or four of the lads were emotionally drained. I think it had all come to a head for them. To be honest it was a bit of an anti-climax, but for a local boy it was still a wonderful experience.

Like Best and the other young players, he anticipated many more wonderful experiences with United. The scoring touch deserted him the following season – he managed only one League goal in 28 starts, and that in the 8–1 thrashing of Queens Park Rangers – but he was more productive in 1969–70. He also felt inclined to be more assertive and when, midway through 1970–71, Wilf McGuinness was sacked, the Kidd from Collyhurst angrily turned on his illustrious team-mates, accusing them of letting down their manager and precipitating his demise.

Supporters warmed to the local boy's commitment and loyalty. He was one of their own, a surrogate wearer of the red for each and every one of them. To Kidd passed Law's crown. Alas for Kidd, and United, he was not as prolific a goalscorer as the Scot. He was capable of spectacular strikes, the type Law admits he was incapable of. But not the quantity of goals the old King delivered; the scraps and six-yard stuff the great goalscorers fed off.

United were relegated to the Second Division at the end of the 1973–74 season but Kidd did not go down with them. Instead he went south, to Arsenal. He talked of the wrench leaving his club, yet accepted he did not figure in Docherty's plans. The new environment invigorated Kidd, but the chance of a return to his roots was irresistible, even if it meant wearing the sky blue of City. The Maine Road fans made him feel at home, especially when he became their top scorer. He helped them to second place in the 1976–77 First Division Championship. There were, however, bouts of frustration and brushes with opponents and referees. 'You know me,' he would plead with that wide-eyed local-boy-misunderstood-and-picked-on expression. 'I'd never kick anybody.'

He had almost three seasons with City before moving on to Everton, and from there to Bolton. After the then regulation sample of football Stateside he came back to England to mould a career in coaching and management, although he never envisaged circumstances conveying him to the No. 2 job at Old Trafford. Kidd went back to the family circle as community officer and extended his influence to luring youngsters to the club and coaching. City's scouting and coaching system had outmanoeuvred United in the area and even Oldham were having more success with the local talent. Kidd's name, enthusiasm and dedication were hugely instrumental in changing the trend. Many of his discoveries have made it all the way to the first team.

Ferguson had seen enough in Kidd's work to be assured the 'United man through and through' should become his assistant in August 1991. Kidd reluctantly accepted the promotion, but since then United have won the Championship four times and been runners-up twice. They have also twice completed the League and FA Cup double. Ferguson has no doubt about Kidd's contribution: 'He's been fantastic for this club. His heart's in the club but also he's dedicated to the job he's doing. He's loyal to me, and his commitment to the players is great. His training sessions are excellent. He takes a lot of care and consideration over his training.'

Kidd has formulated those training sessions after scrutinising methods used by leading clubs in Europe. His brief also includes monitoring possible transfer targets on the Continent and beyond, and future opponents in European competition. His assistance to Ferguson has encompassed extra-curricular duties, such as dragging the volatile Scot away from confrontations and potential trouble with referees, and keeping the boss's feet on the ground with a few well-chosen wind-ups about European Cup glory. Little wonder Ferguson has resisted overtures from other clubs – notably City – for Kidd's services as manager. Ferguson has indicated that when he stands down, the club would have to look no further for the perfect replacement.

Kidd himself is adamant he has never encouraged such approaches and that he never wants to leave Old Trafford for another club. As No. 2 at United he has the emotional attachment, the satisfaction, and none of the media attention a No. 1 must endure. He remains, for public consumption, the humble, self-deprecating boy from Collyhurst, happy and grateful for his role and his life.

At the end of the match against Barnsley he is palpably still content and relaxed, making his way back towards the tunnel. United have won 7–0.

# 9. BOBBY CHARLTON

Born: Ashington, 11-10-37
Debut: v Charlton Athletic (h), 6-10-56
United career: Football League – 604 (2) appearances, 199 goals;
FA Cup – 79, 19; Football League Cup – 24, 7; Europe – 45, 22.
Total – 752 (2), 247.

Pele apart, no greater ambassador has served football; no other former player is more instantly recognised, more loved or more revered wherever the game is played. That, even more than the century of caps and record 49 goals for England, the World Cup winner's medal, the European Cup winner's medal and a knighthood, is the measure of Bobby Charlton's impact and stature. His fame and appeal reached the remotest outposts not merely because he was one of the finest players of all time (in fact, his ability has been understated in some quarters), but also because of his manner and sportsmanship.

Those who have endeavoured to undermine his reputation by focusing on his non-existent tackling and dubious heading prowess, and suggesting he was moody and inconsistent, are, frankly, whistling in the wind. Tackling was certainly not part of his game and did not need to be with so many expert practitioners of the craft about him, and yet in an international when injuries reduced England to nine men and a state of emergency, he performed splendidly at left-back. Two of his most important goals – a winner for England and the opener in the European Cup final – were headers. If he had moods they provided confirmation he was human after all and reflected how much he cared about his club, a commitment his team-mates confirm. Inconsistent? He had the odd erratic spell, particularly when he was isolated on the left wing, but, as Stiles says, no player is great in every match.

The reality is that Charlton maintained a standard of excellence over a 15-year span probably unparalleled in the English game. His graceful, flowing style belied the awesome ferocity of his shooting with either foot. A dip of the shoulder could send a whole defence the wrong way; his sudden surge could carry him within range of a terrified goalkeeper. He could drop the ball on a colleague's little toe from 50 yards. And artist though he was, he did not consider it demeaning to lather his skills in sweat. As one eminent writer observed after a match at Derby County's notorious Baseball Ground, 'This man could play good football on a ploughed field.'

This rare talent emerged in the North-East, renowned for its productivity in coal and footballers in roughly equal proportions. He was the nephew of Jackie Milburn, a Newcastle icon before anyone knew what an icon was. He was the younger brother of Jack, the Leeds United and England centre-half who was everything Bobby was not. Bobby was a natural. The progression from East Northumberland Schools to England Schoolboys to United was natural, too.

He was a member of United's FA Youth Cup-winning team in 1954, 1955 and 1956 and made his League debut, ironically against Charlton, a few days before his 19th birthday. He scored twice in the 4–2 win. By Munich he was a recognised first-team player, alongside the tragic Babes. After the crash he shouldered the responsibility of inspiring the rebirth of United. Soon England, too, turned to him for the first of his 106 international appearances.

Charlton dutifully switched from inside-forward to left-wing for club and country before returning to more familiar territory as a deep-lying No. 9 or central midfield player. His goals against Mexico and Portugal were beacons that lit England's path to World Cup triumph in '66, his goals against Benfica a fitting contribution to United's finest hour.

He retired at the end of the 1972–73 season to begin a career in management with Preston North End, but he resumed active duty in an attempt to rescue the cause and had a brief spell with Waterford. He became a director of Wigan Athletic and stepped into the breach when the club had a managerial crisis. In 1984, however, he was back at Old Trafford as a director and he has since combined an obvious ambassadorial role for club and a range of worthy causes with his business and television enterprises.

\* \* \*

A group of Porto supporters are gathered, as arranged, at reception, awaiting their conducted tour of Old Trafford. Later they will doubtless plunder the megastore and later still sit on the edge of their seats for the first leg of the European Cup quarter-final tie against United. Suddenly, their meticulously planned agenda is interrupted. Their guide is abandoned as they spot the bald, bespectacled gentleman, wearing a suit and raincoat and carrying a briefcase, stepping from his car. Legends are unmistakable.

Sir Bobby Charlton CBE is swallowed up by the adoring visitors and smilingly poses so that every member of the group may take a photograph of him with the rest of them. He is polite and modest. He has no need to flaunt his greatness. He radiates it. Autographs collected, hands shaken, the beaming Portuguese respectfully form a phalanx as he turns towards the door of the building. He makes his way up the stairs and through a labyrinth of corridors connecting offices, restaurants, bars and suites. Finally he unlocks a door and announces our arrival in the 'inner sanctum'.

It is the directors' private lounge, sculptured within the structure of the old main stand. It is impeccably appointed and decorated. A huge table dominates the central area, settee and armchairs offer comfort in a corner. Pictures of matchstick footballers hang on the walls. The eye, however, is inexorably drawn above the fireplace to the imposing roll of honour. It lists only United's wins. Runner-up places do not belong here. The most treasured entry is in the top left-hand corner – 1968 European Cup.

So much of Charlton's life had been dedicated to the pursuit of that simple inscription, and after so many lives had been lost it was almost as much his crusade as Busby's. He oozes pride. Not on a personal level but on behalf of his club. No hint of the moody player here. He is warm, buoyant, effusive.

> I've been here since the start of it all. Sir Matt had been to see a few matches in Europe and came back saying it was the only place for the best players, a different world. We had to go there. The Football League were against it, complaining there were already enough matches, but I think their concerns were more financial. They got more of a cut from fixtures here. It was a bit of sour grapes. But the Old Man was always progressive. He'd come back from the Giants Stadium in America talking about the corporate thing, people enjoying much more than the match. His plans were in place. So we went into Europe.

United had always held an exotic attraction for the quiet miner's son from Ashington.

I was first drawn to United when I listened to the 1948 Cup

final on the wireless. I remember wanting them to win when everyone else wanted Stanley Matthews and Blackpool to win. I think I must have been reading about them and made my mind up I wanted United to win.

Charlton's native instincts took him to matches at Newcastle, and the Milburn genes, augmented by the encouragement of his mother, Cissie, created another future star in the fair-haired boy. He sharpened his appetite for the game and prepared himself for its earthier characteristics on visits to another of his footballing uncles at Chesterfield. 'I learned all about swearing when I went to see Uncle George,' he chuckles.

Newcastle must have cursed when they watched Charlton's development in Manchester. The young player, however, grew restless for his chance to graduate in the Babes academy and defied an injured right ankle to make his debut. Fortunately for him and United, he had already worked on improving his weaker left foot, so much so that many became convinced that was his favoured side. The club, meanwhile, had embarked on its maiden European voyage. Charlton recalls,

> I missed the first European matches. I wasn't in the first team regularly and I was doing my National Service, stationed in Shropshire. When any little aeroplane flew over I used to think it would be the lads going off, to Dortmund or Bilbao or wherever. It was just a great adventure, so exciting for the fans and the players, something totally different. You were seeing players you'd only read about. The atmosphere at the matches was sensational. It made what you'd call exciting cup-ties pale into insignificance. They were all midweek games, at night, and people were having to rush from work to get there. And we had the advent of floodlights. We didn't have lights here at the time so we had to play at Maine Road.
>
> And you were going to all these places, playing all the really great teams. We knew we had really great players and we weren't afraid to play anybody. The best way to show how good you are is to play against them. I wouldn't have liked to have played against our team at the time. It was the best we've had – Duncan and all those others. There were times, when George and Denis performed at their peak, that the '60s team was sensational. But regularly the team prior to Munich was great.
>
> When you think that now we're restricted to crowds of

55,000 and at that time I think we could have got 200,000 in, it is amazing. It wasn't like now, when you see the stars all the time on television. Then your only chance was to go to the games, and here were Puskas and Di Stefano and Rivera.

The excitement was extinguished on 6 February 1958, and no one did more to rekindle it than the young man suddenly elevated to leading player. Recovered from his injuries, he returned to steer a patchwork team to Wembley, only to collect his second successive FA Cup runners-up medal. The European adventure almost inevitably ended that year in Milan. Charlton offered his soul to the crusade and insists he was willing to make the switch to outside-left.

> I didn't have any difficulty with that. All I wanted to do was play, so if it meant I played every week on the wing, that was okay. The Old Man explained he didn't have any wide players. Albert Scanlon, an orthodox left-winger, had gone. United teams were always expected to play with wingers. We had plenty of midfield players but nobody left-sided, so he asked me if I'd play there and I said yes. I preferred the freedom of the middle of the field, but I did quite well on the wing and played a lot of times for England there. Because I'd done quite well he kept me out there. But I was frustrated at times because I had to depend on other people to get the ball to me, whereas in midfield you can go and impress yourself on the game. Once I came back inside it was better.

By the time Charlton had his FA Cup winner's medal in 1963, he was having to share top billing with Denis Law. Come the first of their two Championship successes, in 1965, George Best was up there too. Charlton was very different from the other two, in character as well as playing style. He was more of an introvert, more sensitive. It was his club, and he had gone to hell and back with them. United watchers sensed friction, even envy, between them. Charlton now proffers his version of their relationship.

> The only criticism I would ever have of George is that he didn't give the people what they wanted in his later years at the club. He was a young lad and he could do whatever he wanted in private as far as I was concerned. All we were interested in was winning the games. He was a really sensational player and all he had to do was come and train

and play. When that stopped I think he was on a downward spiral.

He denied the public seeing him at his best. To stop at 26 was nonsense, really. He knows that. But at that particular time I don't think George listened to the right people. It was very frustrating for me and the other players. All the other players were coming down training when sometimes he wasn't. When you're doing six-mile runs and you don't know where he is, it isn't right. We were all pros and we expected everyone to behave as pros. The lads were complaining about it and as I was captain I had to go and see the boss about it. He took it in but, at the end of the day, nothing really changed.

There was, though, no friction between me and George, or between me and Denis. George was in a different age group to me, that's all. I didn't go out to night clubs. By the time George came on the scene I was married and we'd started a family. I was settled. My night-clubbing was over. I used to hear about some of the things he'd got up to and I couldn't believe it [his laughter emphasises the incredulity]. But, as I say, if he played, that was okay by me. I think one thing which perhaps didn't help George was the fact he played for Northern Ireland rather than England, and he never got on to the world stage. That always frustrated him.

I had no problem with Denis, other than when he didn't get the service he wanted. Denis was an out-and-out goalscorer, and if you didn't give him the ball in the 18-yard box he would argue with you. And if you tried to score . . .! If I got in a good position and didn't give it to him, he would have a right go at me. But that's the striker's way. Denis and I are fine. In fact, we play golf together.

It's the same with George. No problem. Honestly, I'm really proud when people talk about 'the three' of us, about the 'Best, Law and Charlton era'. Somebody came up to me at a function and said he'd got a great picture of us in some match. I've never really seen an action picture with the three of us together, and I asked him if he'd let me have it. Because that's how I feel about us. They were great players.

Nobby Stiles was a great player as well. I don't have any hesitation in saying that. In people's minds he's probably that dirty, argumentative, irritating little sod. In reality, his defensive qualities were just sensational. He was an unbelievable reader of the game. He could sense where danger was coming from. If it was coming from the side, he'd be over and nip it in the bud there. His timing was amazing. Technically, he was brilliant. If you turned round and saw him there you'd feel at ease. He'd tidy up for Shay, for Bill and for Tony if necessary. He was an instinctive, natural defender, and when he went into coaching I think that took something from him. But when people ask me who were the great players I played with I always include Nobby Stiles. No question.

Charlton toes the party line that it was the club's destiny to win the European Cup after the great escape at the Bernabeu.

We were fated to do it that year. Having been 3–1 down and overrun for 45 minutes by Real Madrid there was no way we should have got back, but we did. Half-time was the turning point. Jimmy Murphy, the Old Man and all the staff were stunned. The players were. Gento had gone on a couple of runs and they were just alive. The goal we got in the first half was an own goal, scored by Zoco. You'll see him now, standing next to Real Madrid's manager on the touchline at matches. It turned out to be vital.

The Old Man said, 'Come on, keep going,' but there was no great conviction. Then we realised another goal would give us a replay in Lisbon, and I remember going down the tunnel behind the Spanish players and they were strutting as if to say, 'Only another 45 minutes and we're in the final.' But they obviously didn't train like we did and they played in bursts – and they'd had their burst. We just kept plugging away and you could sense after five or ten minutes that the spark had gone out of them and that there was something for us.

Nobby started shaking up a few people. We didn't feel our goal was under any threat and started pushing forward a little. David Sadler somehow got one in and there was silence from the home fans. We had about 10,000 there but, obviously, they were greatly outnumbered. You could tell then that they'd gone. They started arguing among themselves and little fights were breaking out between them.

That's when there was a little incident I'll never forget. The ball went out of play and I wanted it quickly because time was running out and we felt we could win the tie. This chap in the front row picked it up and went as if to throw it down the line. I thought, 'Keep calm, don't panic,' and just walked over to him and put my hand out. He put the ball into my hand. I couldn't believe it.

Anyway, not long before the end George went past his man, which you always expected him to do, and got to the dead-ball line, and I was thinking, 'What's he going to do?' Well, instead of trying to beat somebody else he pulled it back, as you would hope, and I could see a red shirt coming on to it. Then I thought, 'Oh . . .' I was really depressed, you know? It was Bill Foulkes, and he never crossed the halfway line unless it was for a corner. Ever. But he was obviously caught up in the thrill of it all and just slotted it, side-foot, like any professional would, into the bottom corner. We'd come back from the dead. I'd never been in a match where we'd gone from such absolute depression to perfect happiness.

I broke down because it was such a hard slog, and it meant so much to win the European Cup for all sorts of reasons, all that had happened before. We'd had a couple of attempts at it and failed, and most people thought this was possibly going to be the last chance. I probably thought so, too. We had a lot of players at their peak and I felt if it wasn't going to be this year it was never going to be.

So when the whistle went it was really emotional, and I remember the United fans coming on and all the excitement. What made it so much better was that we'd done it in Real Madrid's stadium, a great stadium, maybe my favourite. I loved playing there. And now we'd won the semi-final there was no way we were going to lose the final. There was no danger of complacency. I knew we would be stronger and that the longer the game went on the better we would be. Playing all in blue wasn't a problem either. We had no superstitions about that. We were all focused.

What we didn't expect was that it would be so hot. It was so humid. It was pumping out of us. And they didn't throw water bottles on in those days. Players suffered. It was a cracking game, though. They had shots at goal, Eusebio hit the bar with about the only shot he had apart from the one at the end, and Torres was a real problem because he was so big. If you allowed crosses to him and allowed him to have a run he could do damage. But Bill Foulkes was great against him and we nullified most of the things they had, all the other dangerous players they had. And we were at Wembley. We knew it well and you could feel the will of the crowd helping us.

The fact that Charlton's opening goal was so uncharacteristic – it was stamped with the Geoff Hurst trademark – reinforced the belief that fate had decreed this would be United's year.

I didn't score many headers, and, to be honest, I went to the near post as a decoy as much as anything else. You go to the near post, as you are taught, to take a player away. I went, but David Sadler didn't knock it to the far post, he knocked it in to me, and I literally just helped it on its way. It didn't need much of a touch, but it was quite wide out and if the goalkeeper was positioned properly it was going to be difficult to beat him. It went just inside the post, into the bottom corner, almost impossible to stop.

We'd had some chances in the first half – David Sadler missed a couple – and I think their defence panicked. They weren't very big and the Latins were used to getting plenty of notice when people went at them. They didn't like people coming at them too quickly – and coming again. We pressurised them, they left a few spaces at the back, but we didn't take advantage. Having got the one we were on our way, but physically it was still a slog because we were drained and we had to keep forcing ourselves. Then they scored and it was the big man there, knocking it down, and Graca popped it in, good right foot.

When Eusebio was going through I thought that was it. We hadn't done anything wrong but it was a good pass, good run, and there's not much you can do about it. It was unlike him to miss that. If he'd placed it or taken it a bit further he would have scored, but I don't think he knew who was behind him, so he hit it a great blow and Alex Stepney, well, it just stuck. Unbelievable, really, but the thing about Alex was he had good hands.

Fate was showing its hand again, too.

We thought then that if we got to extra-time we would be okay. You are trained and prepared in the English game to push yourself through the pain barrier. Our record in extra-time had always been good and our record against Portuguese teams had always been good. They didn't like extra-time. Latins generally didn't like playing one game soon after another. I remember Chelsea drawing against Real Madrid in, I think, the Cup-Winners' Cup, and the Spaniards didn't want to play again in three days, as they were told to. They wanted a week. The Latins are much more professional now, but at that time they didn't like playing too often and they didn't like extra-time. Really, Benfica never had any sort of chance in extra-time.

We overran them and when George went through and popped in the second that was it. There was no way they were going to score again, and they collapsed psychologically. There were loads of goals to be scored. If we'd gone at them in the second period of extra-time we'd have got more, but it was over anyway. Brian knocked in the third and then rolled the ball in for me to score the last one. Again, I went to the near post as a decoy and it wasn't really a shot, but he wasn't a very big goalkeeper and it just looped over him.

When I picked up the Cup the first thing I thought was how heavy it was, because at the end I was physically drained rather than emotionally drained. I've never known humidity like it in this country before or since. I couldn't go to the reception. I lay down in our hotel room and every time I tried to get up I started to pass out before I reached the door. I suppose had I drunk water, as they do now, I would have been all right. But I was completely dehydrated. Pat Crerand was the same, sick as a dog even before we left Wembley.

And there were so many people I wanted to see. Some of the old players were there – Harry Gregg, Kenny Morgans, Johnny Berry, Jackie Blanchflower – and parents of lads who died in the crash. And I never saw them. My wife, Norma, had to go to the function on her own. She came back and said it was a pity I didn't make it because the Old Man had stood up and sung 'What a Wonderful World'. He'd lost his team at Munich and he always said it would take a long time to get anything like that sort of team together again. He used to say that in memory of the lads who had died it was right and proper that one day we should win the European Cup.

The lads in the '60s team never asked me about Munich. Even now there isn't a day goes by when I don't think about it, and, of course, I've since flown there many times. But it was always a private thing, and they respected that. They were obviously aware of the history and the significance of the European Cup. They were aware of their responsibilities, as well. But they were good players in their own right, so why shouldn't they win the European Cup? We were never really going to be a *proper* football club until we won it.

Winning the World Cup was very different, and didn't mean any less to me. But that was a six-match competition. We didn't have to qualify, and that's a lot easier than having to play over two years, win the Championship and then go and beat the rest of Europe's champions. That's hard. The quality at international level was obviously higher, but it's not a slog. I wouldn't have liked to have played out my career and not had the World Cup and not had the European Cup. I'd lived through the gamut of emotions for the European Cup, right from when we first played in Europe. It had been a long and painful journey. But we made it.

Above all, Busby had made it. That is how much of the world saw it, and some within the camp would have you believe that is how he saw it. Charlton, his ever-loyal lieutenant, maintains Busby was never so egotistical.

He never talked about himself as the manager, it was always him and Jimmy. We've seen it elsewhere in the game. The great Liverpool sides were led by Shankly and Paisley, then Paisley and Fagan. Derby and Forest had Brian Clough and Peter Taylor. There were always two. You need two. You bounce ideas off each other. We had Sir Matt and Jimmy. Jimmy was the coach. Sir Matt was never the coach. He was a motivator, but he wasn't a technical coach. He didn't work on you day to day on how to do things. Jimmy Murphy was the one who did that and the one who got me from being a schoolboy amateur to a professional player. For about two years he worked on me as an individual, getting all the bad things out of my system and teaching me the professional things.

But Jimmy didn't like it when he had to do things Matt did, because he wasn't good at it. Jimmy was good at working with the lads. After Munich we seemed to be at Blackpool all the time, because Jimmy wanted to get away from all the pressures in Manchester. He's always held in high esteem here. His family, I think, are still looked after and they are always welcome when they come.

The end of the Busby–Murphy era left United in apparent free-fall to mediocrity and worse. Even recalling that period appears to pain a man who symbolised the club's triumphal parade.

I have been presenting a series of programmes on Sky featuring some of our matches from the early '70s, and it reminds me how awful it was. It was a period of transition, when people like me were coming to the end of their careers, and to try to maintain the quality players were drafted in, but they weren't really good enough. It was a bad time for us. But it was obvious after 1968 that everyone would want to beat us, and there was a lot of good competition. The Bill Shankly era had started at Liverpool. It became much more difficult and we weren't able to go along with it. It was obvious it just couldn't continue. These days you would make it continue because you would have the money to go into Europe and buy the best players.

Charlton, having drawn an astonishing 60,000 to his testimonial match against Celtic, played his final game for United at Chelsea in April 1973. He was 35, had made 754 appearances and had scored 247 goals. A month later he became manager of Preston and discovered, as many of the greatest players do, that natural talent does not easily rub off on others. One of his charges at the time confided, 'He was trying to get us to do things that were nothing to him but beyond us. The fact is that even at that age he was twice as good as the rest of us.'

The old skills were dusted off in a forlorn attempt to revive Deepdale's glories. This, alas, was one crusade too many. Charlton parted company with Preston in a dispute over transfer policy and would return, via Wigan Athletic, to his spiritual home in 1984 to join the board of United. A decade on he was knighted for his services to the game, a game he again enjoys thanks largely to the success of the Ferguson–Kidd regime and the sight of a new generation experiencing the incomparable thrills of the European adventure.

It's really great being around the club now because you sense the same feeling and hunger that we had. I listen to some of the younger lads, like Gary Neville, and they've got so much enthusiasm for European matches, just like we had. Gary was saying how he heard the old, great players talking about Europe and never realised how much of an achievement theirs was until he actually sampled it. He now realises how hard it is, what a great challenge and adventure it is, how it demands total concentration and performances of the highest calibre. Anything short of that will not be good enough.

Gary's a really intelligent and sensible lad, as well as a terrific player. He reads the game so well. He is a leader and I think he will be captain of England one day. David Beckham is another tremendous player for this club and the country. He's a bit like me. He likes experimenting. He likes short passes, he likes long passes. He likes shooting, he likes all the glamorous parts of the game. That makes him exciting to watch. He's not afraid to have a go. He's not afraid to miss. Too many players are. And he can hit a ball. He concentrates on his technique. We've also got Phil Neville, Nicky Butt and Paul Scholes in the England set-up. They all want to be the best.

The young lads talk to you about Europe all the time, and they're very keen to show they are up to it. They put a lot of work into it and it's a great spur to them to think that one day they might be able to achieve greatness. We've had one or two stutters in trying to get there again, but then not being able to play the full team was a bugbear for us. The team is better equipped and prepared for it now. It's not just the young ones who are hungry for it, of course – although they're all young compared with me! The likes of Peter Schmeichel, Gary Pallister and Denis Irwin want to be the best in Europe as well.

I think winning the European Cup would have been the icing on the cake for Eric Cantona. He was a great player for this club, but I don't think from a satisfaction point of view you can call yourself one of the really great players unless you win the European Cup or the World Cup. You have to be seen to do it on the big stage, in the big pressure situations.

If Busby was the Father of Manchester United then Charlton appears to have accepted the responsibility of fostering the flock. His daughters, Suzanne, who is making a name for herself as a BBC weather expert, and Andrea, will feel they have a whole dressing room of brothers in red.

For me it's great to be involved with the club again in these exciting times. This was the only place to play and it's still the only place to be as far as I'm concerned. I've no ambitions to be chairman or anything like that. My ambitions are for the club to keep going forward. I want to see us win the big one again, and knowing Alex he'd want to keep winning it. But there is something else beyond that – the World Club Championship. We didn't manage to beat the South Americans and that would be the target for us. I'm sure that's in Alex's mind as well. There's no end to his ambition. You need good management, good coaching and it is, to use the old cliché, a team game. We are all part of it here and can't win without each other.

I've never felt as sick as I did when Fenerbahce won here in the last five minutes. Losing the unbeaten record to them was bad enough, but I just felt there was no justice because they were clearly inferior to us. Having said that, you have to be good enough to break them down and not make a mistake to let them in. That's the game. Juventus was a different matter. They are a great side. But they can never have had as many shots on their goal as they had in the second half here.

This, though, is why winning the European Cup is such a fantastic achievement. It's hard – harder than winning the World Cup. That's what keeps you going at it. And I love it as much as I ever did.

# 10. DAVID SADLER

Born: Yalding, Kent, 5-2-46
Debut: v Sheffield Wednesday (a), 24-8-63
United career: Football League – 266 (6) appearances, 22 goals;
FA Cup – 22 (1), 1; Football League Cup – 22, 1; Europe – 16, 3.
Total – 326 (7), 27.

If Shay Brennan is the most-loved member of the '68 club, then David Sadler is probably the most respected. Intelligent, level-headed, conscientious and organised, he has always provided the ballast for a ship that might otherwise list beyond control. Little wonder he runs the United old boys' association. On the field and off it, he was ever 'Mr Dependable'.

Sadler's calculated course took him into a career in banking before the professional game and, at the tender age of 16, he became an England amateur international. He played for Maidstone United, in the Isthmian League, and news of a potentially sound investment reached Old Trafford. Business concluded, he joined the club in January 1963 for £750. He made his debut for United later that year, still aged 17, at centre-forward.

That remained his role through much of his early period at the club and he scored a hat-trick in the 1964 FA Youth Cup triumph. However, establishing himself as a regular forward in the senior side proved a formidable task and it was to the considerable benefit of player and club that he emerged as the versatile answer to almost every eventuality. He could operate in a range of midfield guises but found probably his most effective post as a central defender. Here his composed, discerning style contrasted with the orthodox stopper approach and earned him accolades as one of the most polished players in the land.

Sadler won a League Championship medal in 1967 and then played his full part in the European Cup success, somehow improvising the goal that revived United in Madrid and then delivering the cross from which Bobby Charlton opened the account in the final. That year he made the first of four appearances for the senior England team, thereby completing a treasured international collection. He also played for his country at Youth and Under-23 levels, and represented the Football League.

The exodus of the Docherty era carried Sadler away and he joined Charlton at Preston for a still-reasonable £25,000. Their return was more than 100 matches of elegant football. Since no obvious routes opened up for him in the game after his playing career, he retraced old steps and became branch manager of a building society. He linked up with Charlton again as a financial consultant before developing a corporate hospitality business. He chips in a few comments to the media pot and still finds time to keep his hand on the old boys' tiller.

\* \* \*

The exterior of the brick building in Chorlton is much as you would expect David Sadler's workplace to be. It is imposing rather than grandiose, dignified rather than ostentatious. Behind the door . . . things seem to be listing. Still getting things sorted, someone explains. David? His is the room at the top. Watch the boxes. Sorry. The stairs reaching ever upwards towards the attic negotiated, more evidence of disorder paves the final steps to his desk. Beneath the folders it is a simple piece of furniture, in keeping with the modest office. Organisation will doubtless ensue; flamboyance is unlikely to. A few sporting trophies give a clue to the occupant's line of interest, but nothing flaunts his involvement in Manchester United's greatest night.

Sadler's play with Maidstone had been more conspicuous and he was whisked into the fold before the big clubs of the South could convince him the 'Frozen North' was no place for such a refined boy. He settled into the 'family' with Mrs Fullaway and was in the first team three weeks before his new house-mate, George Best. A less likely pairing is unimaginable, as Sadler hears constantly.

> Yes, that's what people say all the time. But in fact we got on fine together and George was nothing like the image some have of him. It wasn't night clubs and drinking and wild goings-on, nothing like that. George was just a pleasant, quiet lad. We'd play cards or read at our digs, maybe go for a game of snooker or bowling. He was the greatest player I ever

played with, and brave with it. But he was a normal lad and we had the normal life of young footballers.

United are not readily perceived as a normal football establishment, but players come in much the same mix wherever they land and Sadler found life comfortable. The shadow of Munich was never overbearing, the ghosts never intimidating.

> As a young player coming to the club after Munich I was obviously aware of what had happened and I was with people who had gone through it: Gregg, Foulkes and Charlton. But it was something we would never raise and talk to them about, and in a sense we didn't need to. Nothing was thrust upon us in that regard. People still talked about the players, about Duncan Edwards, Tommy Taylor and Roger Byrne, but not in a depressing or morbid way, just about what great players they were. Obviously it came up in the build-up to the big European games, and especially the final, but it wasn't something that was hard to bear.
>
> Things went pretty well for me, anyway, as soon as I went to the club. I'd been playing in senior amateur football with Maidstone and there were strong leagues in the London and Home Counties region. Wimbledon, of course, came out of this environment. I scored a few goals, played for England amateurs, came to Manchester as a centre-forward and very quickly got into the team. I did reasonably well for two or three years without really establishing myself as a regular, playing my part in the first-team set-up as stand-in for the likes of Denis and David Herd.

The likes of Law and Herd, and then a youngster called Brian Kidd, represented an impregnable barrier to Sadler's long-term aspirations. There is a school of thought that suggests his versatility undermined his lasting stature, but Sadler is honest and pragmatic enough to acknowledge the switch from centre-forward effectively resuscitated his career at United.

> It all came about by accident, really. At the end of training we'd have little kick-abouts, five-a-sides, eight-a-sides or whatever, and you'd get people wanting to play in different positions, goalkeepers at centre-forward and that sort of thing. I would play in defence. I enjoyed it and found I could

play there. Anyway, at some particular point I got moved back and played for a junior side at centre-half. I also started to play a bit in midfield and I was into a period where I played centre-half or midfield according to the team's requirements, and that was around the time of the European Cup run.

We had Nobby Stiles and Bill Foulkes at the back, and in midfield we had Bobby Charlton and Paddy Crerand. There was clearly a need for somebody to do the defensive duties for players of that sort. Nobby did it and I did it. So I played all over the place, but I suppose at the end of the day I failed as a centre-forward and that's what it came down to. I didn't score enough goals. Equally, it suited me better. There's no question that by playing in more defensive positions I was able to develop my game and my career. Playing in either role enabled me to secure as permanent involvement as you are likely to get bearing in mind the sort of team we had, and I was happy with that.

The club should really have won the European Cup two years earlier than we did. I wasn't quite as regular a player in the side but I have to say it was probably a better side then. People who were near the end of their careers when we won it were two years younger in '66 and were expected to win it, but they blew it. Had it not been for that failure a lot might have changed, even to the extent of the George Best situation and how things developed with him. Because we didn't win it, the team remained much the same.

We won the Championship in '67 and it was a Championship-winning side, but it should have been fairly clear – although perhaps not to us, because it's never that clear when you are involved in it – that changes were going to have to be made. You have to think Matt must have been looking to make changes in that side. Bill was of an age when he might have been contemplating finishing and Denis was struggling with his knee, but for whatever reason the team stayed together and we won the Championship and went on to win in Europe. For me it was great. I was just happy to get in the side.

The final was actually a bit anti-climactic. We'd been to Gornik and conditions were really dreadful there. They were a very good side and we really had to battle to get through that one. We played very well against Madrid at Old Trafford and really should have taken a better lead over there. But we didn't and we got absolutely slaughtered in the first half. Of course, as everyone knows, we were only 3–2 down on aggregate, so the game was still there for us. But it didn't feel like it. We felt as if we had lost the first half 6–0. The one we got was an own goal. And then, of course, in the second half . . .!

All these years on, having rerun it a million times in the mind, this bit still seems the stuff of fantasy.

We obviously played better in the second half, and we worked much better, but I wouldn't claim enormous credit for my goal. I'd started in a defensive role again, supporting Nobby and Billy, but come the second half we had to take every opportunity to go forward, so I was starting to get more in touch with the front players and even getting beyond them. And that's really what happened. The cross came in, Bestie went for it and I sort of followed in. I don't know whether he got a touch or somebody else did, but the ball eventually found its way to me and I just stuck my foot out, in passing almost, and in it went. It was one of those situations where you take a bit of a chance, you see something, and it comes off for you.

It was quite strange then because you had this massive crowd – you read all sorts of figures as to what it was, 125,000 or whatever – and they'd been so noisy in the first half, and all of a sudden it was as if somebody had turned a radio off. For a minute I didn't really understand what had happened. It was unreal. But, of course, the ball had gone in and that was it. We were then on top of the game. I can't remember what the situation was in those days with relation to draws, but there was never any thought we would settle for that. And then we had this situation where Bill Foulkes scored the winner, which makes the story all the more incredible. When you consider everything Bill had been through with the club, for him to get that goal was amazing.

So after all that the final itself was probably a bit of an anti-climax. You have to remember there was a special relationship between Madrid and United. Matt and all the people at Madrid were very close. And Madrid, of course, had been the great European side, the team to aim at. Benfica, too, had a great record by then, but I think Madrid had a special place up there for Matt and United.

United's special place in the build-up to Wembley holds memories of walks through the grounds and bets on the Derby. Typically, Sadler's recollection focuses on something else.

Horse-racing didn't interest me very much anyway, so I don't recall too much about the Derby. But I do remember watching David Coleman as he was doing the TV programme from the grounds of the hotel and thinking how professional he was in terms of the way he handled it. Apart from that I just remember wanting to get off to Wembley.

Benfica were a side not dissimilar to us. They had one or two players, like Coluna, who were getting towards the last throes of their careers, if not actually over the hill. It was a hot day but I don't remember it as being unbearable, and I think the game was good, it flowed. I realised that when we got together for the 25th anniversary and watched the match in full.

My overall recollection, though, remains, and that is that the game had a strange look about it. I was really a centre-half-type player then, and it was hard to see how we would play with Bill, Nobby and me. Nobby was really marking Eusebio but at the same time we didn't want Eusebio pulling Nobby all over the field. After '66 it had become a bit of a battle between them and Nobby, of course, had done pretty well against him. But we knew he would try to drag Nobby all over the place, so the idea was that I would be the anchor-man in midfield, and if Eusebio pulled away from Nobby I would pick him up rather than have Nobby go chasing him. The tactics worked reasonably well, and I also had to look after people like Coluna.

Bestie had a fairly free licence, but Johnny Aston, of course, was really the star player. If Denis had been fit, Johnny almost certainly wouldn't have played – which is ironic, because he had such a magnificent game. By that time we were almost certainly going to play with Brian Kidd because he was a strong, up-front player, though still fairly inexperienced. Although I was in a fairly defensive situation I had chances in the first half and in the second, when another goal would probably have made it safe for us. If Alex hadn't made that save when we were rocking a bit, it might all have gone wrong. The fact is I had two or three good chances which I should have taken. I didn't, but we still went on to win and I felt I had contributed anyway.

That save by Alex got us through to extra-time and it was the best opportunity they were going to have. Matt and all the coaching staff came out on to the pitch to us before extra-time, just saying, 'Come on, come on, we can do it now. We've got 30 minutes.' We were tired and lay all over the place. Matt didn't change any tactics or anything like that, he just urged us on. But it just so happened that we scored fairly quickly in extra-time and then ran away with it. We just overwhelmed them.

It was a marvellous win and a marvellous night for all of us, but I think if the truth be known, some of us, the younger ones or those who had come into the club after Munich, did feel slightly like interlopers, a little bit out of it. We were all in it together, it's a team game and we were all elated with the victory at Wembley, the achievement and significance of it all. But at the same time we were aware it was about Matt, Bill and Bobby, in particular, because of all they had been through. Bobby was drained. So was Matt, and for the first time he looked old, and you wondered what was left. That's why you can look back now and use words like 'crusade' and 'destiny'.

Sadler was not among those approaching the end of their careers and his prime coincided with the period of turmoil that followed the abdication of Busby.

I was involved in the aftermath of the European Cup and probably played my best football at that time. I'd become a central defender, got England caps and was part of the England set-up in the build-up to the 1970 World Cup in Mexico, although I didn't actually make the 22. So this was very much my peak. But there were all sorts of problems at United; finding a successor to Sir Matt and all of that. Looking back, it shouldn't have been a surprise, the problems the club had. It probably needed somebody as great as Busby, and when you consider the time he was at the club and all he went through, it's inevitable it would take time to find the right man to follow him.

Liverpool maintained their level of success exceptionally well for a period of time with Shankly, Paisley and Fagan, but then they had their problems with Souness and Dalglish. I just hope there isn't a problem for United following Alex. You accept this situation as a player. Managers come in and managers go; or managers come in and players go. I experienced that at Old Trafford. When Tommy Docherty came in I was initially part of his plans, then I was no longer part of his plans, and that, as a professional footballer, is something you have to accept.

I did make mistakes, and one I made was at the end. I was under contract and should have sat it out there, but pride comes into it. You want to play first-team football and you're not getting treated as you think you ought. But then we all think we should be treated better. The fact is I'd had a great time and a great career at United. I had the best part of 11 years at Old Trafford. But having played for England two or three years before and not getting matches, I had to be interested in an opportunity to move on.

Bobby had gone to Preston and I was always quite close to him – or as close as you can be – and he asked me to join him there, so I went. It was quite a dramatic change and it would be fair to say it was something of a culture shock going to Preston. When you've played at the top and travelled and done everything first-class, you have to get used to different realities in the Second and Third Divisions and at a club like Preston, a club that was losing money and having all the associated problems.

Bobby himself wasn't used to it, and could never really come to terms with the problems. Bobby, as you would expect of him, was something of a purist and an idealist in terms of wanting to keep his best young players, bringing them on and building a team, all the things he had experienced at Old Trafford. At Preston the attitude was that if you produced a good player that was fantastic because you could sell him on and buy off six months' debt. That's the nature of the game there. Bobby didn't see it like that but then, fortunately if you like, recognised it and got off the managerial merry-go-round.

It was very difficult for me to adapt when I first went there. I got an illness – mumps, of all things – which was not very pleasant for someone of 28 or 29, so that was a bit of a setback. Then I had a good spell and enjoyed it, but by then I was having trouble with the knee and I was advised to stop playing when I was barely 31. It was the sort of knee ligament job they would do something about now, and really it didn't compare with the injuries Paul Gascoigne and others have had. I tried to play on and didn't train for the best part of a year, but you can't go on like that because you risk really bad problems later – and you've got a lot of life to live after football.

I had thought about doing something in the game, although the idea of coaching had never done anything for me. Working with players was something that never interested me. I did feel that if I had something to give it would be on the management side, perhaps running a club like Preston and having a coach who would work with me. But football never made any efforts to keep me, nobody asked me to go and manage them, and I never made any efforts to stay in football on the other side. Instead I got involved in one or two things outside football, and made myself another life. Now I've got links with sport in general through the hospitality and entertainment business.

The link with United and his old colleagues is also intact. As secretary of the Association of Former Manchester United Players, he is the axis of an organisation that reunites the Reds, rekindles the spirit and, in the process, helps replenish the coffers of worthy causes.

We've been going for about 12 years and it followed on from organising a bit of a charity team, having the odd game here and there and then a glass of beer. It was just a social thing, a nice way of seeing one another again. It's not elitist or just for first-team players; it's for any ex-Old Trafford player. A lot of my pals never got near the first team. It's broadened out and we do a fair bit of charity work, but first and foremost it was about catching up with players you hadn't seen for ages, enjoying a pint together and getting into the football chat.

We basically hold four events, including a golf day, a year. Most of our dinners are back at Old Trafford. Over the years we've probably raised more than £80,000 for charity. We support a charity Jimmy Murphy got involved with, leukaemia research, after his son-in-law died. Jimmy was such a big part of our lives, as of course was Matt.

There is really a bit of a bond with the European team, but it depends on who you speak to as to how secure that bond is. It depends also, a fair bit, on who's in power down there. By that, I really mean the manager. Certainly Alex Ferguson has been great with us. He's never been scared of the old boys, if that's the right word. Some people have been, and that's probably understandable. One who was not comfortable with it was Frank O'Farrell, though of course he came immediately after Sir Matt. The next problems will arise when Alex goes.

The question is, who's going to be big enough to take that on? They'll come in, as managers did after Sir Matt, with their own ideas about how to do it. Some of them decided the past was the past and they should leave it there, and they didn't want anything to do with it. They wanted their own men around them, their own players in and all that sort of thing. But nobody quite succeeded Sir Matt until Alex, although there were people along the way who did reasonably well. Big Ron [Atkinson] had a pretty good time there, and Tommy Docherty had a great relationship with the fans and got things moving again. Even if Fergie doesn't do anything else from here on in, he's going to be up there and he's going to take some following.

You do sense the same desire in Alex to pull off the big one. United have no divine right to win anything, and they went 20-odd years before they won the Championship again, so that became an enormous pressure for managers. Some coped with it, some didn't. When finally they pulled it off it was an enormous relief to a lot of people. To a certain extent it sort of pushed us to one side at last. There were times when it was embarrassing for some of us to be at the club, being members of the last Championship-winning side. And it got worse as the years went by. The whole thing became a bigger and bigger issue.

I never actually wanted to put the past away. If it's in the right place it should never be intimidating. It should be some sort of inspiration, something special. When they did eventually win the Championship that was great. Liverpool went on to achieve more than we did in Europe, but the fact we were the first English club to do it remained a landmark, and even Alex must have realised that winning the European Cup was unlikely to be accomplished straight after his first Championship. They'd got rid of one millstone only to find another hanging round them. But all English clubs had suffered by not being in Europe for five years. Europe is a different matter and the rest of Europe had opened an enormous gap between us. I think, though, the gap is closing, and the more experience our players get the better chance they will have.

It's difficult to make comparisons because so many things are different. The format is different for a start, and I'm not in favour of it, but then, as we know, it is money-orientated. The current side has evolved, and there have actually been two or three sides over the last six years, starting with the one that won the Cup-Winners' Cup. Older players are always moving on, younger ones coming in. The trick is to catch them all at the right time. This should be a good time for the team, providing Alex doesn't have too many injuries and can pick his strongest line-up.

I certainly never look at the current team and think, 'Oh, only two of these could get in our team,' because the game is so different. And what I admit with regard to myself is that you become a much better player than you ever were the older you get and the further away from it you get. I know I was a reasonable player, but time glorifies things to a certain extent.

What you can say is that we had some undisputed great players in our side – Charlton, Best, Crerand, Stiles and, although he didn't play on the night, Law. And then in Tony Dunne we had the best full-back around. If you could beam them to another era, they would have been part of the present-day team. Equally, you have to say that people like Schmeichel, Keane, Giggs and maybe Beckham would have been great players in our period. Cantona certainly would have been.

Sadler and his wife Christine, a Stretford girl, have long been settled in the North Cheshire belt that houses many of Manchester's footballers, past and present. Ironically, their son, Nigel, took the opposite career direction to his father, heading for London and the bright lights. Literally. He works in the theatre on lighting and special effects. Establishing a work base here in Chorlton is appropriate for his father. 'Our digs were not far from here,' he says.

He passes another reminder of a cherished past every time he climbs or descends those stairs: a concocted picture of the 11 players who won the European Cup. 'As far as I can remember that 11 never actually played together again and no photograph was taken of the complete team on the night, so I suppose that's the nearest we're going to get to a picture of the winning line-up.'

Even if they are in red, rather than blue.

# 11. JOHN ASTON

Born: Manchester, 28-6-47
Debut: v Leicester City (h), 12-4-65
United career: Football League – 139 (16) appearances, 25 goals;
FA Cup – 5 (2), 1; Football League Cup – 12 (3), 0; Europe – 8, 1.
Total – 164 (21), 27.

He was the last name on the team-sheet and somehow he always gave the impression he felt he was the last in the affections of the club and its supporters. It was evident in the body language and in the sentiments he confided to friends and colleagues. It is evident, too, in the few words he is now willing to express about his career with Manchester United. An apparent sense of family betrayal impelled him to sever all physical and emotional ties with the club and seek a new life in self-imposed exile.

The feeling of treachery is doubtless compounded by the acclaim for his performance in the European Cup final. He was the man of the match. Everyone says so. It was the night his uncomplicated wing play destroyed one of the Continent's most sophisticated and successful teams. He sucked in his marker, then left him dead for pace and invited colleagues on to his constant supply of crosses. He did not have the sublime skills or charisma of other forwards in the side, but then neither did he carry any egotistical baggage or enrage the rest with unpredictable intent. There was never any doubt where John Aston was coming from.

He had been brought up in the United household, not merely a local boy but the son of the John Aston who played for United and England in the post-war years. Aston senior was a powerful, versatile player who would answer the call to bail out a depleted forward line with gusto and goals. He was a similarly effective wing-half, assured in the tackle and on the ball. But it was as a left-back that he excelled and was renowned, partnering Bert

Whalley and then, more famously, Johnny Carey. He collected an FA Cup winner's medal in 1948 and a Championship medal in 1952. Illness curtailed his playing career and he joined the staff as junior coach. He switched to scouting duties and was chief scout from 1970 to 1972.

The young player he monitored with particular interest was John junior, who advanced through Manchester Schoolboys and Lancashire Schoolboys to an apprenticeship at Old Trafford. A boy called Best worried about his own future because Aston was ahead of him in the pecking order for the No. 11 shirt. He turned professional in 1964 and was a member of the FA Youth Cup-winning team that year. A year later he made his senior debut as the club closed in on their first Championship post-Munich. He played a more regular and influential part in the title success of 1967 and duly picked up his winner's medal.

The following season he featured in the cast not only on the domestic stage but also, and more crucially, in the grand arena of the European Cup. He was on one wing, Best on the other. Both scored in the hard-earned victory against Gornik, and Aston created the goal converted by Best in the home leg against Real Madrid. And then came Wembley. Aston, aged 20, was like a man possessed. He terrorised a defence that had expected most of its problems to come from the other flank. Best will always be remembered for his critical goal, Charlton for his double, Kidd for his birthday goal, Stepney for that save and Stiles for his shackling of Eusebio. But John Aston junior outshone them all.

And yet John Aston junior was the whipping boy of United, the player the fans turned on in less exultant circumstances. When his direct, orthodox play was neutralised he did not have the options more gifted team-mates possessed and became an easy target for the disgruntled. He was never a shirker and always tracked and tackled back, but sometimes it seemed the harder he tried the more he was ridiculed. If Best fought back it was another dimension to his genius; if Aston fought back it was a giveaway sign of his desperation and inadequacy. Some said he had an inferiority complex and a propensity to sulk which dragged his chin to the floor. Little wonder.

Aston's confidence can scarcely have been buoyed when, three months after his and United's greatest night, he was laid up with a broken leg and Busby signed another winger, Willie Morgan. McGuinness endeavoured to restore Aston's faith and brought him back into the side, but that injury had caused his career at United irreparable damage. He moved to Luton Town in the summer of 1972 for a fee of £30,000 and had five productive seasons with the club, helping them gain promotion to the First Division in 1974. He went on from there to Mansfield Town before returning to the North-West and finishing his playing days with Blackburn Rovers.

He would not, however, feel inclined to return to his original football home. His father was discarded, along with the manager, Frank O'Farrell, and the coach, Malcolm Musgrove, in December 1972, and, according to his colleagues, he could never forgive the club for that. He turned away not only from United but from football, seeking his new world and his new life in the pet shop business.

* * *

Stalybridge is one of those small towns on the fringe of Manchester that like to cling to a notion of independence. The locals tell you they will never consider themselves part of a metropolitan sprawl but will always live in a secluded corner of Cheshire. As if to underline their devolutionary zeal, they have a football team, who play in the Vauxhall Conference, called Celtic. There is a comfortable, self-sufficient rather than affluent feel to the town centre and part of the main street has succumbed to the compulsion for pedestrianism.

Down on the left-hand side, beyond every other familiar frontage of a shopping centre, is the focal point of John Aston junior's working world. Pets World. The first thing that strikes you, considering his aversion to United, is that the lettering is white on a red background. The window beneath is a kaleidoscope of colours, crammed with dog baskets and mattresses presumably designed for sundry furry creatures. The second thing that strikes you about the place is that there are no furry creatures. 'Foods and accessories,' the lady assistant explains. It does actually say that outside!

The shop is of modest dimensions, yet every conceivable form of furry creature comfort, entertainment and sustenance seems to be available here. Now if Benfica had afforded Aston so little space in '68 it might have been a different story. The narrow path between the boxes and toys leads to a back room and stacks of cages and pens.

This is probably as far removed from United and football as you can get. It is almost inconceivable it is run by the star of a European Cup final, the man we see in the mind's eye skipping over another despairing challenge and haring for the line. It is an almost anonymous little shop in an almost anonymous little town centre. That is perhaps appropriate, after all. Certainly it would appear to suit John Aston junior just fine.

Some years after United's European Cup win he talked of the 'strange night' that completed the reincarnation and fulfilment post-Munich. He consented also to give his recollections of the match and its significance to *The Independent* newspaper:

It was a particularly good night for me because there were a lot of world-class players on the pitch whose reputations preceded them. I was a bit of an unknown quantity. I think only Brian Kidd was younger than me. People say it was the best game I had for United and I think I'd probably agree. I'm not being immodest, but if they'd had a man-of-the-match award I think I would have won it. The game went very quickly. I remember half-time coming and thinking we'd only been playing for about 15 minutes. The atmosphere was tremendous.

It was the only time I ever played at Wembley. I was a Manchester lad and I'd always supported the team. I was about ten when Munich happened, so by 1968 it was half a lifetime away to me. It was only when I was older I realised how close they were to each other. My father played for United so I had the pleasure of knowing quite a few of the United side, especially Mark Jones and Tommy Taylor. I think if that team had lived they would have won the European Cup.

Now, as the 30th anniversary approaches and as United renew their pursuit of that giant trophy, Aston feels no desire or obligation to talk about the club or the cause. Indeed, he is openly and unapologetically hostile to the invitation. It is as if time has reopened rather than healed old wounds. It is as if he welcomes the opportunity to cleanse himself of the stains of hypocrisy and to be honest to himself, his father and the world. He will have no more truck with phoney magnanimity and threadbare platitudes. This is a man speaking his mind and heart.

I'm not interested in football any more and I'm not interested in Manchester United any more. It was all a long time ago, anyway. I played till I was 33 but I've not seen a game for, oh, I bet it's 15 years. I never go these days and I've no interest in going. I just wouldn't watch a game any more. Nothing against the club, but at the same time I just don't want to talk about it any more. That's the past, another life as far as I'm concerned.

I've said it all in the past and gone along with it. That's what people want to hear. They want to hear nice things said about Manchester United and about Matt Busby. They want you to say, 'What a great club, what a great manager, what a great night.' That's all they want to hear, the nice things. But they're all clichés, all sound-bites, and I don't want to say them any more. I'm not bothered about any of it any more.

Life goes on and I've got a new life here. I prefer to look forwards rather than backwards. I've got a business to run and no time for dwelling on the past. It's so long ago I can hardly remember it anyway. It seems like a different life, and that suits me.

The bitterness towards United is obvious and many would perhaps consider it understandable, but surely that should not sour the taste and satisfaction of the occasion and his contribution to United's success?

Of course it was a special occasion for me and I'm proud to have been a part of it, and to have played the part I did in the final. But that's my feeling and it's a private feeling. I don't see why it should be of interest to anyone else. I'm not a famous person. I'm an ordinary bloke getting on with his life and his business. That's all there is to it and that's all I want.

I look at some of the old sports stars doing the rounds these days, the likes of Fred Trueman, recalling stories from way back in their after-dinner speeches and so on, and, quite frankly, I find it slightly pathetic. I don't want to get into any of that. I think it's all a waste of time.

And so he recoils to his own preferred world, his business and his family. It is reported a third generation of Astons, Mark, made such a big impression as a midfield player he fully justified his selection for the English Universities side. It is difficult to imagine that did not reawaken John Aston junior's interest in football.

# SUBSTITUTE: JIMMY RIMMER

Born: Southport, 10-2-48
Debut: v Fulham (h), 15-4-68
United career: Football League – 34 appearances, 0 goals;
FA Cup – 3, 0; Football League Cup – 6, 0; Europe – 2 (1), 0.
Total – 45 (1), 0.

The man who did not play because of injury springs readily to mind. The image of Denis Law watching the final through a haze of inebriety from his hospital bed is almost as vivid as George Best's shimmy round the goalkeeper to score that crucial second goal. But the man who sat on the bench? Not so easy. In fact, it may surprise many who remember the final that substitutes existed at the time. Aficionados, however, will have the answer to a popular football trivia question: which English player won European Cup winner's medals with two different clubs yet played only 11 minutes of a final? Jimmy Rimmer is that man.

Substitute goalkeepers only were permitted in 1968 and Rimmer sat on the sidelines at Wembley, waiting and hoping in vain for the chance to make an appearance. Fourteen years later he was in the starting line-up for Aston Villa against Bayern Munich in Rotterdam but soon gave way to the recurrence of an injury, and Nigel Spink, his understudy, became the star of another English success. Rimmer's medals, you sense, do not fully compensate.

Many consider Rimmer was equally unlucky to be released by United. Had he been born a year or two earlier, Busby might not have felt the need to sign Alex Stepney. Had he been born a year or two later he would have been the natural successor. Rimmer grew up quickly in United's nursery but had limited opportunity to claim a first-team place. By the 1973–74 season Tommy Docherty considered him surplus to requirements and, after a loan spell with Swansea, he moved to Arsenal.

He established himself as a regular in the side and did so again following his transfer to Villa in 1977. His consistent excellence earned him a full England cap – thereby matching Stepney's international achievement – and left a trail of 'I told you so's' all the way back to Old Trafford.

Rimmer played out his Football League career at Swansea, where he settled, and switched to coaching after an encore in Malta. A decade on, he lost his job and wandered in the wilderness until he received an unlikely offer he could not refuse: to help guide China through their World Cup qualifying campaign. He was off the bench like a shot.

* * *

Sunday evening at a hotel in Blackheath and Jimmy Rimmer is grateful for the chance to catch up with a couple of old pals. Still more appreciated will be the coming weekend at home, a short sojourn to be enjoyed after the Chinese uproot their English training camp. Then he is on the road across Asia and, he hopes, back to Europe for the World Cup finals in France. Beyond that, perhaps even the glow of the limelight in his own country. Rimmer's role with the Chinese squad has recharged his spirits and reawakened an ambition that took him to United in the '60s and through the junior ranks. He recalls,

> Everything started really well for me when I went there. Everyone was saying what a good prospect I was and I got a lot of encouragement. I played my way through the various teams and at 17 I was a regular in the reserves. That was at a time when they had the likes of Dave Gaskell, Harry Gregg and Pat Dunne, all highly rated keepers. The competition was very strong but I seemed to get promoted up the order and I was very happy. Even in the reserves. I was still very young and keepers always mature later than outfield players.

It was a lively environment. While the Holy Trinity and other revered figures maintained their sacred status, and with it an inevitable distance, the tyros gathered on the cathedral steps with due respect, but also a sense of fun, a mood of optimism and an appetite for adventure. Rimmer found a soul-mate in an even younger player who would make an indelible mark on the European Cup final.

That was a great time to be at the club because they won the Championship twice, all the great players were there and, of course, Matt Busby was there. There was a real excitement about the place and you felt proud to be part of the club, even if you were a young reserve. The senior players were all fine with me – Bobby Charlton, Denis Law, Nobby Stiles, all of them. But the younger lads naturally stuck together more and I always got on well with Brian Kidd, who of course also went to Arsenal.

He had a terrific talent, a tremendous shot, and when he got his chance in the first team he grabbed it. When I travelled with the first team I tended to stick with Kiddo and he was always good for a laugh. He was good fun and always up to something. I remember once when he was all cool and sophisticated, ordering steak tartare. When it arrived he wanted the chef to cook it! After it was explained to him this was how it was supposed to be, he decided he'd better just ask for an ordinary steak. Typical Kiddo.

But he did brilliantly, and to be in the European Cup final team on his 19th birthday was amazing, really. Then he went and topped it all by scoring. John Aston was another of the lads I mixed with, and it was good to see him have such a great game in the final. It showed that even at the biggest club in the land there was a chance for lads coming through the ranks. I was pleased to be part of the final squad. I felt time was on my side and was confident I had a future at United.

So Rimmer sat out the match in near anonymity and completed the first part of his trivia question. He now admits, however, he watched the unfolding drama, and Stepney's full part in it, with churning emotions. He shared the anxieties and the tensions, then the elation as United mugged Benfica with those three goals in the first period of extra- time. He even had his winner's medal at the end of it all. And yet . . .

I remember sitting on the bench and going through it all with the rest of them. I had just a plain jersey. No number on the back of it. Jimmy Murphy and Jack Crompton were there, and Sir Matt. Sometimes he sat up in the stand but at Wembley he was down on the bench with the others. I was delighted, just like everybody else, that we came through it all, the ups and downs, and won it. I knew how much it

meant to the club and especially to Sir Matt. And my medal
was just the same as all the other players'.

But in a way I felt a bit of an outsider that night. I've got
to be honest: I would have given anything to have gone on.
Just for a minute. Even 30 seconds. So I could have said I
actually played in United's European Cup-winning side. I
didn't want to wish Alex any harm but I would have loved to
have been on the pitch, especially as it was at Wembley.
When it got to 4–1 it was all over. I could have gone on then.
Just for a bit, to be part of it. But that sort of thing didn't
happen then and I had to just sit there.

Rimmer had been cast as the 'forgotten man' and somehow he could
never quite break free of the part. He played for the first team in 20 League
matches during 1970–71, yet made only a handful of appearances in the
three seasons before and after. And then another young goalkeeper came
into the picture. Rimmer was no longer in the frame.

Sir Matt thought I should have stayed at the club and told
Tommy Docherty he shouldn't sell me. Harry Gregg always
recommended me and reckoned I was the biggest goalkeeping
talent at the club. But Tommy Doc thought otherwise. Paddy
Roche was coming through and I had to go. No disrespect to
Paddy, but look what happened afterwards. Even Tommy
Doc admitted later that he got that wrong. I know I made one
or two mistakes as well, but you have to allow for that with a
young keeper. Sir Matt thought I was reaching the right age
to be given a chance and a run in the first team. At a club like
United there are always going to be young players who don't
get a chance and have to move on. It can be hard, but that's
the way it is.

In a way I should thank Tommy Doc for selling me to
Arsenal. I'd moved from one massive club to another and got
regular first-team football. Then I moved to another great
club in Villa, and there we went all the way to the European
Cup. So I had a tremendous career, at different clubs, in
different parts of the country, and enjoyed a lot of success. I
also played for my country, so I could hardly have done more.
It's just that I'll always wonder what might have happened if
I'd stayed at United. It's only natural. You don't want to look
back and you always say there's no point, but even so . . .

Setting the second part of the trivia question did nothing to assuage him.

> We'd had a great run through to the final at Villa and I'd
> played in the other games, but then I got injured in the last
> League game. It was on the Friday night, funnily enough
> against Swansea. I went up for a ball with Bob Latchford, fell
> over backwards and hurt my neck. Tony Barton, the
> manager, wanted me to play and I had injections, as we did
> then, and it was decided we should give it a go. It didn't
> work. After 11 minutes I had to come off and on went Nigel
> Spink. It seems I was just fated as far as European Cup finals
> were concerned, but it makes a good trivia question. I
> suppose it's a claim to fame.

If Rimmer left the grand stage bearing the scars of frustration, he was to eke out a lasting satisfaction from the fringe theatre of the European game. At Swansea he played his last matches in Britain and turned to coaching with the club.

> I had ten years with them, coaching the youth and reserve
> teams, and produced a lot of players for them. Eight or nine
> of them became first-team regulars and a number of others
> moved on to become first-team players with other clubs. I
> think I can feel proud of what we achieved over those years,
> and it's a good feeling knowing you've put something back
> into the game by bringing through these young lads. And
> then I got the sack. When football is all you've done and all
> you've known from 15 to 50 and you are suddenly told you're
> no longer wanted, it comes as a terrible blow. I was out of the
> game for six months, apart from doing a bit of scouting.

It is the Tony Dunne scenario all over again: wandering the grounds and boardrooms under the dubious cover of 'scouting' duties, with half an eye on somebody else's job. Like Dunne, Rimmer wanted to feel better about himself. A solution was offered by Ted Buxton, long-time friend, aide and confidant of Terry Venables.

> I had realised after talking to friends that there was no point
> feeling sorry for myself, moping around and waiting for the
> phone to ring. I'd got to start ringing around to let people
> know I was eager and available for work. You can be

forgotten all too quickly in this game and I didn't intend to let that happen to me. So I put out some feelers. Then Ted rang me and said there was a job in China. He's the technical advisor and they wanted a coach. So I became their first English coach.

His brief, ostensibly, was to work on the goalkeepers – two of them giants at 6ft 4in and 6ft 5in – but he has gradually extended his sphere of influence, to the apparent approval of his employers and charges.

I love it. One or two of the players and members of staff speak English, so communication is not proving a problem, and I've never come across anyone so disciplined and dedicated. The squad were together, away from their homes and families, for four and a half months earlier this year. We've got this stint in England, and then we're back to the World Cup qualifiers for another couple of months. They're more than happy to work and train long hours – ten till twelve, four till six and then another hour in the evening. They desperately want to do well and they are technically brilliant – different class. On top of it all the money is good. I've made more in the last year than in five years with Swansea.

Much as he has warmed to the challenge and his new work colleagues, this spell back in the old country has rekindled a desire to make an impact here.

It has been enjoyable for me and a good experience for the players. We've got games with teams at Nottingham Forest, Crystal Palace, Chelsea, Charlton and Arsenal, behind closed doors. The Chinese don't like to play friendlies in public. All these clubs have been co-operative, as have Charlton and Greenwich University, allowing us to use their training facilities. I've got to admit I'd like another chance to show what I can do over here. We're happy living in Swansea but I'll move for the work. Maybe if I get China to the World Cup finals for the first time in their history, I'll get noticed and be offered a job.

And no longer be the forgotten man? China, alas, did not qualify.

# THE ONE MISSING: DENIS LAW

Born: Aberdeen, 24-2-40
Debut: v West Bromwich Albion (h), 18-8-62
United career: Football League – 305 (4) appearances, 171 goals;
FA Cup – 44 (2), 34; Football League Cup – 11, 3; Europe – 33, 28.
Total – 393 (6), 236.

They crowned him King and the statistics above should provide sufficient explanation. But they do not. They reveal nothing of his charisma, his aura, his sheer presence. They give no inkling of the lightning reflexes, his phenomenal aerial ability, his agility and powers of improvisation, or the posturing of the supreme showman. The goals were despatched with a flourish and audacity as well as astonishing regularity. The moment he trotted on to the pitch, his blond mane flopping in time with his short, light steps, shirt out, the cuffs of his sleeves gripped in his fists, a sense of excited expectation seized his subjects. Denis Law generated enough electricity to light a small town.

He hit Old Trafford like a high-voltage bolt, that instant, dramatic impact jolting club and supporters into new life and a state of optimism. Bobby Charlton had carried the weight of the crusade since Munich and the burden had taken its toll. The arrival of George Best was still a year away. Law was the catalyst for the revival, even if his new team-mates required the best part of a season to effect the chemical reaction. Victory in the European Cup final completed the process, but Law was not at Wembley to share the glorious conclusion. As we have heard, he was there in 'spirit', laid up in hospital because of his lingering knee trouble.

He might well have reflected, in a trough of self-pity, that he never wanted to be a footballer in the first place. The son of an Aberdeen trawlerman, he had no intention of following in his father's wet footsteps, either, a sample of life at sea convincing him he should stay on dry land. His boyhood ambition was to be a draughtsman, no meagre aspiration considering his background. He was brought up in a council tenement block, the youngest of seven children. A little money had to go a long way. He was 14 before he had his first pair of proper shoes. His first pair of new boots, like other luxuries such as socks, had to be hidden when his father was home from sea. However tough times may be, mothers will always spoil their sons.

Football was the escape, yet even when, at the age of 15, he was invited to Huddersfield Town for trials he harboured no serious thoughts of making a career in the game. One glance at the kid down from Scotland suggested he was wise not to dream. He was frail, pale, of modest height and wore corrective glasses because of a squint in his right eye. All of which goes to prove first impressions can be deceptive.

An operation cured the squint, rendered the glasses redundant and gave the young Aberdonian a different perspective on his life. The new-found confidence was reflected in his football and others recognised an uncommon talent. He was only 16 and playing in Huddersfield's youth team when the club were offered £10,000 for his services. The bid, which was rejected, had been made by Manchester United's Matt Busby. Law was still 16 when he made his League debut, so establishing a club record. Two years later he had his first full international cap – a post-war record – and scored, albeit fortuitously, in the 3–0 win against Wales. Scotland's manager at the time was Matt Busby.

Law went on to score 30 goals in 55 appearances for his country and was acknowledged as one of the great exponents of the global game. He played, and scored, for the Rest of the World side against England at Wembley in 1963, a match which celebrated the centenary of the FA. The following year he became only the second British player, after Sir Stanley Matthews, to be voted European Footballer of the Year.

His domestic career did eventually take him from Huddersfield to Manchester, though not directly to United. In 1960 he was transferred to City for £55,000. His new team proved a letdown, but he confirmed an extraordinary instinct for scoring goals and became the subject of another trivia classic. He scored seven goals in an FA Cup tie and ended up on the losing side. He had scored all City's goals as they led 6–2 at Luton when the match was abandoned because of a waterlogged pitch. He scored again in the rearranged tie, which City lost 3–1.

In the summer of 1961 he joined the bounty-hunters headed for Italy and became the first Briton to be involved in a £100,000 transfer. He signed for Torino, whose entire side had perished in a plane crash in 1949.

Even with Joe Baker, another Scot, for company, Law could not come to terms with the suppressed version of the game accepted as the norm in Italy, or the constant attention of the media. He had occasion to confide in an old admirer that he yearned to return to England. On 12 July 1962, and after lengthy and tedious negotiations, Matt Busby had his man. Law became a Manchester United player for a British record fee of £116,000.

He scored his first League goal for the club within seven minutes against West Bromwich Albion – and the making of a King had begun. His goals kept a floundering United out of the Second Division and a characteristic piece of opportunism to beat Gordon Banks put the team on course for their 1963 FA Cup final victory against Leicester City. His influence and appeal reached a peak in the mid-'60s, coinciding with United's Championship successes.

Harnessing this dynamic force, however, came at a price. The overspill of energy regularly landed the Scot in trouble with referees – so regularly, in fact, it became a slightly embarrassing joke that he timed his annual explosion of temper and subsequent suspension conveniently for the Christmas holiday footballers were not supposed to have. He explained candidly that when kicked or punched, he kicked and punched back. Recurring knee problems blighted his later years and deprived him of what would have been his biggest match, the European Cup final.

He survived two transfer listings by United – the first in a famous stand-off with Busby over wages, the second when everyone seemingly ignored it – before he was finally released in 1973. He returned to City for his encore season and, with his final act in League football, back-heeled the goal which effectively consigned United to the Second Division. He ended his playing days in more joyous circumstances, with Scotland at the World Cup finals in Germany. He came back to Maine Road to be told they could offer him only reserve-team football. This was not the way to go. Strutting the game's grandest stage was. He'd done that; he'd done just about everything. This was the time to quit.

The father of five was never drawn to the idea of adopting his own football family as a manager and drifted instead into the TV and radio punditary business. Considering his aversion to the media throughout his playing career, this development was viewed with contempt by some of his new colleagues, but the name and the personality represented an undeniably attractive proposition. Although his broadcasting work has diminished in recent years, he has a vibrant after-dinner routine and loyal subjects who will forever regard him as the King.

\* \* \*

A light drizzle speckles the panoramic window of the clubhouse and Denis Law grimaces. He checks his watch and paces the lounge again. Still no sign of his playing partner but then, given the conditions out there, he is not unduly concerned about waiting in here, especially if he can organise a warm drink. The beverage ordered, he nestles into an easy chair.

Shay Brennan was surprised to hear Law was playing golf again, and the Scot nods. 'Yes, after 20 years, and I'm enjoying it. I love the game and played quite a lot when I was younger. I had to give it up because of the old knee trouble. But, touch wood,' he says, leaning forward to tap the table, 'I've had no problems. I'm playing off 18. Mind you, I'm a bit of a fair-weather player. Can't say I'm too enthusiastic about playing when it's cold and wet.'

He glances over his shoulder towards the window. The rain appears to have all but ceased, clearing the view across a gentle, green Cheshire landscape. Law is encouraged to stand and take a closer look. The stance is eerily familiar. At the age of 57 he could still be the King. Still lean, straight. Sharp features beneath a full thatch of hair. The face is lined but the expressions are alert. The electrical supply is still switched on. Here, however, he has uncovered a quiet haven and can play golf in relative anonymity. Providing, that is, his playing partner turns up.

'Typical Crerand,' he says with exaggerated dismay. 'Late as usual.'

Almost before the words have tumbled, a phone rings. Guess who?

'Aye, it's Pat. He's at the hospital. His daughter's just had a baby. He'll probably be an hour or so yet.'

Outside, a pale sun is reflecting from the damp practice green and one or two more members are dragging trollies from their cars.

'That's better. I think I'll go and hit a few balls till grandad gets here.'

Law and Crerand are and always were kindred spirits. They joined United within seven months of each other. More specifically, they joined Matt Busby and his new family. They responded to the Scottish bond and, although they were more volatile than their boss, he valued their fervour. He convinced Law, as he would convince Crerand, they were coming in at ground level of something big. Law had played under Bill Shankly at Huddersfield and although he, too, was a very different character from Busby, their roots and football principles were the same. Both managers hailed from the Scottish coalfields; both believed in a beautifully simple game played by committed men, as Law recalls.

> I think it was always said that people from Scotland, like people from the North-East, would battle for you. Managers looked for that in players. Busby had lost half his team at

Munich and I was happy to come back from Italy to play
with the likes of Bobby Charlton. It was a dream come true
for me. Then, a year later, George Best came into the team
and the next five years or so were great years at the club.

Although I didn't enjoy the football in Italy – it was very
defensive, very negative – there's no doubt I came back a
better player. After a season of being really tightly marked I
had a much sharper awareness and learned how to find space
for myself. So when I came back to England, where forwards
had more time and space anyway, I found it much easier to
score goals. It's a much better game in Italy now and I loved
everything away from the football: the food, the people,
everything. Today I'd probably enjoy playing over there. But
not then. It was awful.

Such was Law's determination to leave Italy he refused a lucrative move
to Torino's neighbours, Juventus. He was encouraged by Busby's reciprocal
resolve and inspired by the ethos the manager – and his assistant, Jimmy
Murphy – imbued at Old Trafford. Law had stood on the Scoreboard End
the night United played their first match after the crash, the FA Cup tie
against Sheffield Wednesday, and was moved by the emotion of the
occasion. With Busby still seriously ill in Munich, Murphy was in
temporary charge. Law would discover that Busby 'treated his players like
human beings' and that Murphy would have no truck with cheats.

Playing with Charlton (interestingly, Law felt the England hero was more
effective as a winger than a midfield player), then Crerand and then Best,
he was able to exploit the sharper awarenesss he had added to his game. The
direct supply or the rebounds ensured rich and often easy pickings for a
player capable of flying, jack-knife headers and acrobatic scissor kicks.

We had so many great players and the way we played, always
going forward, there were always plenty of chances. Bobby
could knock in those 30-yard goals with that terrific shot of
his, but I used to get a lot of my goals from the shots the
goalkeeper saved but couldn't hold. When Bobby lined up to
shoot I'd move in on the keeper because I knew there was a
good chance he'd drop it, and often he did. I picked up the
scraps. I couldn't shoot like Bobby. The six-yard box was my
area. Anything further than the penalty spot was a bit too far
for me.

Self-deprecating? Of course. A hint of old rivalry? Very likely. Law, like Charlton, maintains they are embraced in genuine camaraderie, but the Scot must have pondered, as he lay in his hospital bed, that he should have been raising aloft the European Cup. He had been the captain. Now the honour was Charlton's. Law would also express the view that Best sometimes held on to the ball too long and would reveal that some players resented the publicity the Irishman attracted. They were all human. Including the King.

But Law knew his value to the team. Busby effectively confirmed it when he insisted Law had to play in the decisive League match at home to Arsenal on Monday, 26 April 1965, despite having half a dozen stitches in his knee. He scored twice in the 3–1 win while Leeds drew 3–3 at Birmingham, a combination of results which ensured the Championship was United's.

The following year Law decided it was time his value was appropriately recognised and 'tried it on' with Busby. He asked for more money and threatened to leave if the club did not comply. Busby put him on the transfer list and summoned him from Aberdeen to Old Trafford. Law, who had no desire to join another club, was forced to make a public climb-down and read out a prepared statement of apology. Behind the scenes, however, Busby had given him a rise, although not the signing-on fee Law had also requested. A compromise had been struck and, in the eyes of the outside world and the other players, the pay structure had not been broken to accommodate the wishes of one individual. Busby and Law were happy.

Law continued to repay United with his goals – celebrated with his trademark salute, a ramrod right arm thrust into the air – but at increasing cost to himself. The stitches, strappings and painkilling injections could not keep him going indefinitely and, after United's Championship victory in 1967, 'the old knee trouble' proved more difficult to patch up. He made only 23 League appearances in the 1967–68 season and mustered a mere seven goals. He scored twice in his three European Cup games before bowing to the inevitable. He failed a fitness test on the morning of the return leg against Real Madrid. He sat in the dug-out as his team-mates eked out an improbable passage to the final and solemnly accepted he could have no part at Wembley.

He elected to forego a trip to the final as a spectator and instead sought to cure his knee problem. Three days before the biggest match in United's history, Law was admitted to St Joseph's Hospital, Whalley Range, Manchester, for an operation. The surgeon removed a one-and-a-half piece of cartilage and with it a load off the player's mind. Law had arranged for friends to join him at his bedside to watch the match, but had not bargained for the enthusiasm of the nuns.

One of the sisters came in that morning – I couldn't believe it – at six o'clock in the morning and she had this huge rosette. I wanted to see that at six o'clock in the morning like I wanted a hole in the head! So the celebrations started well, well before the game.

I was dying for the lads to do it for Matt. That was what mattered. It was very nerve-racking, particularly when Eusebio broke through a few minutes from time. I thought, 'That's it, we're never going to win this thing,' but somehow either Alex Stepney saved his shot or it hit him. I think Eusebio saw the headlines because he tried to blast it. If he could have his day again I'm sure he would side-foot it. If Jimmy Greaves had been on the end of that chance we would have lost. But we deserved to win because we went at them throughout.

After the game the lads phoned me up in a drunken haze while I was having a few beers in the ward with some pals. I think I was the only one in bed that night! At one stage the TV cameras came in but they wouldn't take any shots of me because, as they put it, I was too 'emotionally disturbed'. The next day Sir Matt and the players came by the hospital with the Cup. A lovely gesture.

Law's version of the aborted television interview corresponds roughly with David Coleman's. His assessment of United's, and more specifically Busby's, achievement is unequivocal.

When you think that Matt nearly died at Munich and then, ten years later, had created another great side and won the European Cup, it is incredible. He had taken English football into Europe, way back in the '50s, and it was fitting Manchester United should become the first English team to win the European Cup. The Cup-Winners' Cup and UEFA Cup are good trophies, but the main one is the European Cup.

Law was able to play a more regular part in United's 1968–69 campaign and scored 30 goals from 43 games, but when the match officials refused to rule he had turned the ball over Milan's line in the Old Trafford leg of their semi-final, his hopes of a European Cup final appearance had gone. His hopes of playing on with United into the 1973–74 season were dashed by

Docherty, and he went back to Maine Road. And then came *that* goal.

> The ball came into the box, a few minutes to go, and I just
> back-heeled it in. I hadn't got a clue where the goal was, but it
> went in. It was a fluke, really.

Fluke or not, United were on their way to the Second Division and even a
pitch invasion could not save the former champions of Europe from their
wretched fate. Law's countenance was as glum as any Stretford Ender's. There
was no ramrod salute of the right arm, no self-satisfied grin, no celebratory
jig. Just a funereal march away from the scene of the treachery, his head
bowed in sorrow. 'I have seldom been as depressed as I was that weekend,' he
admits.

Making the Scotland World Cup squad revived his spirits and playing in
the match against Zaire provided an appropriate finale. He had realised a
lifetime's ambition. A season in City's reserves was highly unlikely to top that
and so, on August Bank Holiday, 1974, Law announced his retirement.
Management did not appeal to him and it was only when his playing days
became memories that he began to appreciate fully the life he had left behind.

> Management is a different ball game. You need a hard streak
> in you to do the job. You've got to be good and cruel, and if
> you've not got it you'll be out. If you had your time as a player
> again you'd probably enjoy it a bit more. When you retire you
> miss the lads more than anything. It took me three years to get
> over it. Mind you, it wasn't so much of a family when someone
> had to get a round in!

The radio work has also dwindled and again Law is self-deprecating. 'Past
my sell-by date,' he says. His enduring popularity with dinner audiences and
fast-food supporters would indicate this is not so. His enthusiasm for United
past and present bridges the generation gap.

> It would be apt for United to win the European Cup again 30
> years after the first win and 40 years after the Munich tragedy.
> The old players would be delighted for the club and the fans.
> I was fortunate to play under two great Scottish managers in
> Bill Shankly and Sir Matt, and I'm sure that if Alex Ferguson
> wins the European Cup he will be regarded in the same
> mould. Like Matt's team in the '60s, Fergie's team plays
> exciting, entertaining football.

# PART IV

# REALITY . . . AND NEW DREAMS

Sir Matt Busby's European champions returned to domestic football an even more prestigious scalp. Their achievement had earned the respect and admiration of the English game but now it was back to the day job and they were put through the mill. The injured Aston was replaced by Willie Morgan, signed from Burnley, and although some of the old swagger was occasionally evident – they annihilated Queens Park Rangers 8–1 – their League form was ominously erratic. They finished the First Division campaign 11th, their lowest position for six years.

This season, however, offered a new challenge, even beyond the boundaries of the European game. United's success at Wembley had booked them a meeting with their South American counterparts, Estudiantes of Argentina, over two legs for the World Club Championship and, despite the savagery that had marred Celtic's encounter with Racing Club the year before, Busby and his adventurers embarked on this journey into the unknown.

Any foreboding was totally justified. Hostility on and off the field soured the entire experience. On arrival in Buenos Aires for the first leg, United were soon made aware Argentina were not amused at being called 'animals' by Sir Alf Ramsey during the 1966 World Cup. The Argentine media and public, in turn, denounced Stiles as the 'Assassin'. The United party were given armed guards, even at Mass. On the field of play they were afforded no such protection. Charlton had to have stitches in a gashed shin and Stiles had a cut and swollen eye after being butted and punched. To add almost inevitable insult to injury, he was sent off for a characteristic gesture.

In the circumstances, United were content to be returning home trailing only 1–0. That confidence was shaken when Estudiantes plundered a goal just five minutes into the night at Old Trafford. They were in command and knew it, stifling, containing and frustrating United's every manoeuvre. The cynicism was less overt, but eventually it caused Best to snap, the Irishman's retaliatory punch resulting in his dismissal. Morgan turned in Crerand's free-kick three minutes from the end, but a play-off, and intercontinental supremacy, proved beyond them.

Consolation might have been retrieved on the more familiar fields of Europe, in defence of their trophy. They loosened up with a 10–2 aggregate defeat of Waterford, Law announcing his recovery from surgery with seven of the goals. Another two from the Scot and one by Kidd appeared to have seen off Anderlecht but United required a goal from Carlo Sartori in the away leg to squeeze through 4–3 on aggregate. Progress against Rapid Vienna was more comfortable, United following up another 3–0 home win (two for Best, one for Morgan) with a goalless draw in Austria.

United had sustained their remarkable record of consistency in the competition, reaching their fifth semi-final in five attempts. A second consecutive final loomed larger in their sights as they came through the first half-hour of their match against Milan at the San Siro unscathed. More encouraging still was the withdrawal, through injury, of the sublime Gianni Rivera. But goals either side of half-time, by Sormani and Hamrin, swung the balance of power. It might have been worse, especially after the dismissal of the tempestuous young full-back John Fitzpatrick.

Back at Old Trafford the faithful remained convinced the cause was not hopeless. A lone voice from the 63,000 called out, 'Andiamo vincere, Rocco.' Whether or not Milan's coach heard that vote of confidence, the Italians did indeed go on to win the tie on aggregate. Charlton's goal, fashioned by Best 20 minutes from the end, was all United could eke from Milan's stubborn resistance. They claimed another, insisting Law had put the ball over the line, but the officials were unmoved. United were out, their exasperation compounded by the knowledge Ajax would be no match for the winners of this semi-final. Their judgement was sound, Milan winning the final 4–1. They also won the World Club Championship – against Estudiantes.

It was a sad and poignant night for another reason. Sir Matt Busby, creator and inspiration of all that Manchester United stood for, was stepping down. To be more precise, he was stepping up, to general manager, and from 1 June 1969 Wilf McGuinness, one of the family, a man who understood the dream and felt for the crusade, would take over team affairs with the title of chief coach. Being called manager at this stage might have been too much pressure for a 31-year-old promoted from youth-team coach, Busby reasoned. He was told he had the job for three years and Sir Matt would be there to help, counsel and generally take the administrative and political weight off his shoulders.

McGuinness, his promising international and club playing career truncated by injury, had no problem with the general arrangement. He was a bouncy, bumptious Mancunian. He had worked with the England squad during the 1966 World Cup. He was brimming with enthusiasm and ideas. New ideas. Tactics. Strategies. He believed United had to adapt to an evolving game by harnessing their traditional flair rather than giving it free rein. And if he didn't get what he wanted from established players, he would replace them. Even if their names were Charlton and Law. The senior players were his contemporaries, his friends. But if he had to be tough and bruise a few egos, then so be it.

McGuinness improved United's League position that 1969–70 season to eighth and they reached the semi-finals of the League Cup and FA Cup. It was, to use more recent football parlance, 'something to build on', and McGuinness was rewarded with the title of manager. Shay Brennan, McGuinness's best man, was released as part of the restructuring. He saw Rimmer as the long-term goalkeeper. Fresh faces were introduced, and he still had Best shredding defences and capable of rescuing the team single-handedly. Best could not, alas, rescue McGuinness. Two days after Christmas, the manager was sacked.

United had again reached the semi-final of the League Cup under McGuinness and again lost, but it was their indifferent showing in the League which concerned Busby and the board. That and the stories of discontent among the senior players. For all that cocky exterior, McGuinness had a fragile soul, and to be shunned this way by his club, and by Busby, shattered him. Busby took temporary charge, and the team stabilised and finished the season eighth. Again. The club would resume the search for his successor, this time outside the family.

McGuinness was offered his old job but found Bill Foulkes in the way and instead accepted an invitation from Aris Salonica, in Greece. His hair went white, then went altogether. Coming to terms with baldness was the easy part. Over the years, however, he learned to live with the emotional scars. He had a short spell with a second Greek club, Panachaiki Patras, before returning to England. He worked with York, Hull and Bury, ultimately as physiotherapist.

Today McGuinness deploys his ready chatter and regenerated enthusiasm on the after-dinner circuit and local radio. He lives with his wife, Beryl, in a large Victorian house in a quiet neighbourhood where Altrincham becomes Timperley. At the age of 60, he is as jovial, friendly and candid as the image he has always projected. 'I've not changed – I'm still bald.'

He was another Collyhurst Catholic, although his family moved up Rochdale Road to Blackley and he went to Mount Carmel School. 'Bernard Manning went there as well.' A school for comedians, presumably. Like

Manning, he had roots in the other camp. His father was a City fan. But McGuinness maintains, 'In those days we wanted all our teams to do well. I was a Manchester lad and supported all the teams in the area. I still do.' He jumped at the chance of playing for United.

I joined in the same week, Coronation Week, 1953, as Bobby. I was in the team before Bobby. As a 17-year-old I was understudy to Duncan Edwards and got a Championship medal in 1956. I shot up very quickly after the accident. Within six months of being a reserve at United I was playing for England, at the age of 20. I played twice for the national team. I felt that even if Duncan Edwards had still been around I could have got in the side because he was that great he could play anywhere.

I had a great belief in myself. I think everybody does, but I was noisier than others. Cockier. Roger Byrne clipped me more than once for standing my ground. I missed only one of the European trips before Belgrade and was on the list for that match, but I twisted my knee and was carried off in the reserve game on the Saturday before. It was diagnosed as a torn cartilage and my name was crossed off the list.

I was in Manchester city centre that Thursday with a friend from the *News Chronicle*. There was a placard and this guy was shouting, 'United plane crashes on runway.' We thought they'd bumped something, never for a minute that it was serious. We went round to the *News Chron* offices and somebody said, 'There's been fatalities.' I couldn't believe it. We were in a state of shock. At first we just heard the names of survivors – Bobby, Dennis Viollet, Bill Foulkes, Harry Gregg. And we're saying, 'What about all the others?' It was late at night when that news came through.

When I got home that evening my mum and dad knew about it and my mum said, 'Come on, we're going to church.' They were having a novena at Mount Carmel and I'll always remember praying there, in tears, hoping all the names would come through, that they'd survived. I was praying and promising I'll never do this or that again if my friends can be alive. But then when we got back home, late at night, I knew my friends had died.

The next morning I went down and into the dressing room. One or two reserve players were there and Jimmy came in and just said, 'See you Monday.' There were private tears. We were just stunned. Gordon Clayton and I went to see Eddie Colman's parents and girlfriend. We didn't know what to say. I think Gordon and I went to every funeral. We were the representatives because we were injured.

McGuinness recovered from that injury but suffered a more serious setback the following year. 'I broke my leg and there were complications.' He rolls up his trouser leg to reveal what looks like the surface of the moon.

I had a bone graft and Matt Busby said there was a job for me here. I could train, keep fit and if ever I felt I could make it back, go for it. That's what I did. The lads used to laugh at me, limping round the ground. It was pretty awful, really. But I was only 22 when I broke my leg. Nowadays I probably would have got back.

I was a coach with England Youth from 1964 and in 1966 worked with Alf Ramsey's World Cup squad. I felt good in training and matched some of them, so I thought if I could do that I could get in United's team. So the next season I made a comeback and played 30-odd Central League games, but was never quite there. I was sub at Leicester and Paddy had a bad match, and I was saying, 'Come on, Paddy, get off.' But he didn't. I never got a game but I told them I made them play that well they won the Championship in 1967. I decided it was time to concentrate on the coaching, where I had something to offer.

I thought Matt would go on a lot longer, and I was hoping he would. Then I thought I'd be in with a chance of working beneath him. But not when he announced it, not really. The odd flash and dream that you might be in with a chance goes across your mind, I must admit. If you're the type of person I am you believe anything's possible. I thought they might get a big name from outside, and usually they bring in their own staff. But, in fairness to Matt Busby, he was very loyal to his staff. Everybody had been there a long time – maybe too long, some people say.

Then I had a little whisper, from the Irish scout, Billy Behan, who'd been talking to Matt, that I was in with a shout, and I told a few people to get a bet on. And I think the day before, the word was, 'You'd better come in with a tie on tomorrow, there's an announcement.' I thought, bloody hell, I could be in here. Whether it was over-confidence I don't know, but I wasn't a bit nervous, because he'd still be here, which I was glad about. As for the rest of the staff, like Johnny Aston and Jack Crompton, I didn't think it was for them. So I thought, that'll do.

He called me in before the press conference and said all the team duties were mine, the coaching and the training, and that he'd act as general manager. But the team was mine; I'd pick it. There were a few grey areas but I thought we'd sort them out later. This was great. Really it would have been better if we'd dotted the i's and crossed the t's. There were certain players I mentioned I'd have liked – such as Mick Mills, Colin Todd and Malcolm Macdonald – and if we had got them it might have helped. I went to watch Macdonald playing for Luton at Mansfield and stood on the popular side. Sir Matt and Jimmy Murphy went in disguise to watch him somewhere and said, 'Yes, you're right.' He did all the negotiating but said Macdonald had an option with Liverpool. Then, blow me, he went to Newcastle. If I'd been more experienced and really at it I might have done something about it. I mean, we let them have four of our players in that period, including Don Givens and Jimmy Ryan, good players, and we should have forced the issue.

But did he try to force the issue too vehemently with his players, his old pals?

Not really. I wanted to be fair. I tried to do it the Matt Busby way, in many ways. Tactically I might have tried to bring in things they may have thought weren't for them. But Matt Busby did tactics. He was the first with the tactical board, no matter what they say about playing off the cuff. His final words were always, 'Go out and play and enjoy yourselves.' But on a Friday he'd have a team talk. He went round every player of the opposition. I followed those sort of lines.

But I also learned from Alf. I remember a goal Denis Law scored from a free-kick played behind the wall after he ran over the ball. Well, I got that from England Youth and told the lads, before I became manager. I told them to try things. I came with ideas. Sometimes when you're at one club you get blinkers on. Yes, I know you can over-coach and that wasn't Manchester United's way, but dealing with young players and the World Cup-winning team you pick up other ideas which are good ideas. They could have helped.

Another was what we called 'restart'. Some of the players said 'restart?' and I explained it was when the referee blew his whistle for a throw-in, corner, whatever, and you work on it to retain the ball or work a goalscoring position from it. We could have enhanced ourselves, I felt, with some of those ideas but based on the United way of playing. I think some of the lads appreciated that. Where it went wrong was through misunderstandings, and stories that were presented or interpreted the wrong way. I look back and say, yes, that happened, but it didn't happen anything like the story that has come out.

There were stories that Bobby resented me. He didn't resent me one bit. I was a bit annoyed at Alex Stepney for putting it out that I made Bobby do press-ups in the rain. That was a light-hearted thing and it wasn't in the rain. Look, I'd grown up with lads like Bobby and Shay Brennan. Then little Nobby came on the scene. 'Happy', we called him. Well, we called him a lot of things, but he was a great lad, a Collyhurst lad. And Brian Kidd. I thought I was friends with them all. I fell out, sure I did, with certain people. You do that. But the club's the main thing and personalities mean very little when it comes down to it. We were United.

Anyway, Nobby and Shay were fun-loving lads and the other lads joined in. If they lost at cards they'd carry people's bags, call people 'sir'. Little fun things. I grew up with that. Another rule was that anyone caught with his hands in his tracksuit pockets during training does ten press-ups. This particular day Bobby had something on in town and got changed into his suit before the usual team talk. So he joined us on the pitch at the Cliff for that and Shay and Nobby went behind him, pointing. He'd got his hands in his pockets. I said, 'Bobby, I'm sorry, they've caught you. Ten press-ups.' Well, Bobby wasn't going to laugh at it, but he bent down, in his suit, did his ten press-ups and that was it. Do you think he would have been standing out there if it had been raining? That annoyed me. It was rubbish.

The day I got the sack Kiddo blasted off at the others – 'You've done this, you've done that.' He told them they'd let me down. Young Kiddo, Collyhurst lad. He was one of my favourites for the future. He felt there was a reason to do that. I don't know if anybody was talking behind my back. I knew some of the lads played golf with Sir Matt and discussed things. Why not? He was the general manager. He had so much faith in me to give me the job and I had so much faith in him because I thought the world of him. We all did. So I could see no problem. I didn't see it as going behind my back. I honestly believed he would see it in the right way.

I never really found out why it happened. Perhaps it was those grey areas, too many of them, and me being inexperienced. Of course, I was learning, and of course I made mistakes. Even the most experienced do. It's part of the learning process. So these things didn't worry me and that's why I was hurt when it finally happened. Because I felt we were going through together, and that hurt. And I was bitter. I felt that if I'd had my three years, not just 18 months, I would have been that much better. I spent two hours trying to make him change his mind.

In hindsight, it did come too soon for me. It would have been far better if he'd brought me on a lot slower, rather than letting me pick the team. But he wanted out, really. I didn't realise how much it had taken out of him. Especially Munich, of course. And yet coming back showed how strong he was. And, don't forget, he was in his sixties.

At the time I didn't think the job was that big. People say the pressure of managing caused my hair to fall out. It wasn't that at all. I went white and then lost my hair after I left United and went to Greece. I put it down to leaving United, not worrying. I was very hurt and wanted to hurt back. I felt badly let down. I never hated Matt. I just wanted him to feel like I felt. That's why I wanted them to think I was going to tell my story to the papers. You do things like that. To me it was the end of the world.

I went for the whisky in the boardroom and there was none in. There usually was. On Sundays we had meetings of the staff – Jack, Johnny, myself. Like they did before Munich – Matt, Jimmy, Bert and Ted. That was another blow. Ted died before I got the job. You need people like that. We'd have a chat, a couple of whiskies, then off home. So that day I was drinking sherry and Jack came in. I'd rung him and said it was all over. Jack was kind. I banged my head against a pillar, I was that hurt. When they went down I thought, 'Serves you right.' They'd had two others after me and still hadn't put it right, so it wasn't only me.

Matt was a hard act to follow. It wasn't that he interfered. I felt I was nearly there. We did well in the cups. But they couldn't keep it up in the League and the youth policy had stopped. Some players were getting old, some had injuries. They were creaking. When I dropped Bobby and Denis you'd have thought I'd dropped the atom bomb. But Matt Busby had done it. I learned the lesson, though, that you don't drop people unless you've got somebody better to replace them. Bestie was brilliant for me, most of the time. People say Matt should have done this or that with him, but he played a lot of games for the club and I'll never knock him.

The reason I still love United is because of all the enjoyment I've had, especially in my playing days. I loved those people. I loved the Busby Babes. We were all together. And I wouldn't have been anything without Jimmy Murphy. He made us believe. It was the combination of Matt and Jimmy that made it work. And all the unknown people at United, behind the scenes, who helped. I owed them all so much, not only Matt Busby and Jimmy Murphy.

But that night at Wembley, in '68, we all knew what we were doing it for. Because he *was* Manchester United. To me, anyway. It wasn't the directors or whatever else. It was Matt Busby. I knew he was thinking of the lads who died at Munich, and the ones who were injured. I thought, this great man, he's thinking it's for them, and I'm thinking it's for him. He's Manchester United. And this really is Matt Busby. I was very emotional that evening. I never stopped shouting during the match. It's all right thinking it's your destiny, but you've still got to win it. And it was magnificent.

It's better to remember the good things first. Forget the bad things. My son, Paul, runs the School of Excellence there but I would have the same feelings now if he didn't. It was my life. Alex Ferguson brought the 1990 FA Cup-winning side over to Bury for my testimonial, at no charge. I was at

Bury for 11 years as coach, trainer, physio and cat-feeder. I was limping away and couldn't carry on. We got 8,000. It was great.

And now it's great for me to see the present team, like it is for Bobby, because we went through it all from 1953. It's tremendous to watch these kids today put together the kind of moves that bring back all the memories. Bobby says the same. I have tears in my eyes because we are back to the Babes.

I believe Alex Ferguson's side will win the European Cup in the near future. Alex is different in many ways from Matt Busby. You can see when Alex is angry; you couldn't be sure with Matt. He could smile warmly, then rip you apart. But the end product is the same, and now, for me, Alex is Manchester United, as Matt was. Alex has proved himself as time has gone on. Perhaps if I'd had time to develop . . .

* * *

While Busby steadied the ship in the second half of the 1970–71 season, completing his record stint as manager of one club, the search was on to find his next successor. Don Revie and Dave Sexton were among those mooted, but the concerted move was for Jock Stein, the man who had made Celtic champions of Europe a year before Busby's triumph. Crerand, a common confidant, approached Stein, who then met Busby, and the deal seemed done. Until Stein turned down the job, explaining his wife did not wish to leave Glasgow.

When Sexton also dropped out of the running and nothing developed on the Revie front, United turned to Frank O'Farrell. The Irishman's astute stewardship of Leicester had impressed Old Trafford. He also carried himself with dignity. And he was a Catholic. Busby assured him there would be no interference from him, that he was bound for the boardroom. O'Farrell, with his No. 2 Malcolm Musgrove in tow, accepted.

O'Farrell's United blazed into the 1971–72 season. By the turn of the year they were five points clear at the top of the First Division. Best was superb. But if three consecutive draws hadn't provided evidence the flame was flickering, seven successive defeats were conclusive. Now the true sentiments came out. O'Farrell believed the old guard were past it; they regarded him as a distant, introverted stranger, tucked away in his eyrie. Best, disillusioned by it all, was into disappearing mode. United finished yet another Championship eighth best.

The club responded to O'Farrell's demands for new players. Martin Buchan was a good investment and injury cut down the luckless Ian Moore. Wyn Davies was an inexpensive flutter, but Ted MacDougall, signed from Bournemouth for £200,000, was a more damning gamble. He was simply out of his depth. Many inside and outside the club reached the same verdict on the manager. A humiliating 5–0 defeat at Crystal Palace on 16 December 1972 left United second bottom of the First Division. Behind the scenes at Selhurst Park, O'Farrell's successor was being primed. Three days later O'Farrell, along with Musgrove and Aston senior, were sacked. United announced that Best was out also.

Tommy Docherty had been a particularly interested spectator at the Palace match and his presence was remarkably convenient for United. Busby had been taken by his management of Chelsea and Scotland. He appeared to have the strength of character and purpose deemed necessary at Old Trafford. He was bumptious and outspoken, a rogue even, the antithesis of O'Farrell. But look where nice, quiet men get you! Law and Morgan, who worked with the Doc on the international scene, backed Busby's judgement. Docherty, duly released by the Scottish FA, was walking through the door at Old Trafford almost before it had slammed behind O'Farrell.

That door would rarely be closed over the ensuing months, such was the frenzy of comings and goings. With Paddy Crerand as his assistant, Docherty feverishly went about the task of resuscitating the ailing giant. George Graham, Alex Forsyth, Jim Holton, Mick Martin and Lou Macari came in. In a less conspicuous deal, he lined up a young Irishman called Gerry Daly. MacDougall went to West Ham.

Docherty now had to consider what roles Charlton and Law might play in his plans. Charlton took the matter out of his hands and retired at the end of the season, making his final appearance for United at Chelsea. Law was dismayed by a statement he would be given a free transfer. He claimed Docherty reneged on an agreement there would be no announcement until the player's testimonial, scheduled for early the following season. But Docherty was restless to pursue his renaissance. He had steered the club away from relegation – they finished 18th – and now he believed the only way was up.

Best made a last, ill-fated attempt at a comeback to reinforce the new crusade, and Law and Dunne appreciated his contribution to their testimonials. But perhaps symptomatic of United's state of health was their resorting to Stepney as penalty-taker. At one stage of the season his two successful conversions made him joint top-scorer. Docherty signed Stewart Houston and Jim McCalliog, and introduced Brian Greenhoff, yet could not resist the spectre of relegation this time. The reality of United's ignominy was numbing, the irony of Law's part in the last act Shakespearean. They finished the season 21st, the position they had occupied when Docherty was appointed.

The club could not countenance further managerial upheaval and gleaned some consolation from a restoration of traditional footballing values in the closing matches. That optimism and trust were not misplaced. Docherty's dervishes rampaged through the Second Division. He had a new centre-forward, Stuart Pearson, and then bought a right-winger from Tranmere called Steve Coppell. The tempo and enthusiasm of the team were set by the midfield men, Daly and Sammy McIlroy, the player cast as the last Busby Babe. They returned to the First Division as champions.

That momentum, sustained with the recruitment of a left-winger, Gordon Hill, and picked up again after Stepney reclaimed his place from the hapless Paddy Roche, carried them to third place in the League and to the FA Cup final. Defeat at the hands of Second Division Southampton at Wembley tarnished the recovery, but did not inhibit it or the ebullient manager. The club were back in Europe for the first time since 1969.

United overcame Ajax in the first round of the UEFA Cup, only to be eclipsed by Juventus. They were also more vulnerable in the League and tailed off in sixth place. In the FA Cup, however, they were not to be denied, defeating champions Liverpool 2–1 in the final with goals by Pearson and Jimmy Greenhoff, brother of Brian, who added guile to Docherty's vivacious team. Jimmy Nicholl and Arthur Albiston had emerged as the full-backs, and Stepney had garnished his career with another Wembley success. Docherty now recalls,

> When I took the job they were obviously in decline, otherwise they wouldn't have come for a new manager. I saw that game at Palace and could see the state of the thing. The '68 team had grown old together and the team now needed not one or two players but seven or eight. There was very little youth policy and I felt a lot of players weren't interested in how they were playing as much as how long they were playing. I could see what Frank O'Farrell was trying to do but was unable to do. So when I got the job I thought, if I don't get rid of some of them, they'll get rid of me – the way they got rid of Frank O'Farrell.
>
> I always felt it was my destiny to manage Manchester United. I don't know why, it was just in my bones. I knew Matt very well. He was manager when I played for Scotland.

After the Munich crash Jimmy Murphy tried to sign me for Old Trafford, but Preston wouldn't let me go to Manchester United. In fact, I'd been invited for trials at United after finishing my National Service. Had I accepted I might have been in the crash. With all these things, I just felt I was destined to go there some day, in some capacity.

The players I got rid of had been great players. Bobby helped me by saying he was thinking of retiring. Eventually I would have had to tell him his days had gone, and I'm grateful he spared me that. It's difficult to tell the supporters their favourite is leaving. Same with Denis Law. They idolised him. But I knew Denis had gone. I'd known him a long time. I captained Scotland when he got his first cap. I took him under my wing. He and Dave Mackay and I were great pals, which made it much harder. But I wasn't running the club for Tommy Docherty or Denis Law, I was running it for Manchester United, and I told Denis to his face he was cheating. Matt was against it. He was very fond of his old players, which was understandable. But they had to go.

I agreed to have Paddy as my assistant because I thought it would please Matt. Worst decision I've ever made in my life! I should have got the sack for that. Socially, first-class, but the most disorganised person you've ever met in your life! About a year later I told the board I'd made a mistake. Matt was obviously in favour of Paddy but Big Louis and the rest never really were, and they decided for him to step down. Paddy had daggers drawn for me after that. There are stories saying I stitched him up, but I didn't have to – he stitched himself up.

It was Matt and Paddy who brought George back. Matt asked me what I thought and I said the way we were going we'd be glad for anything. Crerand said he could get in touch with him and I thought, 'There's a surprise.' I had a chat with George and he looked all right. Paddy arranged a place for him to train in the afternoons. Fair dos, he worked hard, and he was still only 27. He should have been at his peak – and that's what annoyed me about him. He deprived so many kids of seeing arguably the best in the world.

Anyway, he got himself in decent condition and played a few games, the last one at QPR. But you could see the fear in his eyes before games. He could beat people, piece of cake, but couldn't leave them for dead. The pace had gone. Whether the blood clot was bothering him I don't know, but he was moaning and groaning, and, of course, people were out to make a name for themselves against him. They'd say, 'Bestie's back, I'll show him.'

He was picked to play in the Cup tie against Plymouth. Pre-match meal was 11.30 for 12. No sign of George. I was told at 2.30 he'd arrived. He was stoned. I said, 'George, come back on Monday and I'll talk to you. You're in no condition to play today.' We had to change the team-sheet to hand in to the referee. He didn't come in on the Monday and I never saw him for a long time after that.

I fell out with Stepney and Morgan after leaving them out. They thought it was personal. It wasn't. I had to make these decisions for the good of the club. Wilf didn't have a chance. He was a player with them all and a lot of players undermined him. I felt sorry for Frank because he tried to make the break. We were players together at Preston and he was godfather to my son. Lovely man. But we fell out when I took the job and I said if I hadn't, somebody else would have. When Frank left, John Aston got the sack as well, and there was a deal done to keep his mouth shut. I assumed Jimmy Murphy was still there, and Jack Crompton. I brought them back to bring back all that experience.

Matt wasn't too pleased about Jimmy coming back. Something went wrong there. I believe when Frank arrived, Jimmy left with a payment that was meagre and Jimmy was disappointed Matt didn't look after him the way he felt Matt should have. When I got Jimmy back he was very emotional. I brought him back for scouting. And decisions. He found Coppell and Hill. He'd say sign him or don't sign him. I didn't see Coppell before he came here – £30,000, plus £15,000 after 50 matches. After two games we sent Tranmere the extra money.

Jimmy Murphy was different class. He didn't get half the credit he deserved. What upsets me about Manchester United is how little is spoken about the man. In my opinion he was as great as Busby. Matt was wonderful, but he wouldn't have been half the man without Jimmy, and vice versa.

Jimmy Murphy died on 14 November 1989, aged 79. Docherty continues,

> I never felt under pressure to follow Matt. I just wanted to improve the team. One of the mistakes I made the year we went down was going too defensive. Matt said, 'Tom, it's none of my business, but if we're going down let's go down with a bit of style.' He was right, and we had a bit of a flurry.
>
> I don't agree with those who think it was a good thing we went down. I'd like to have struggled a couple of years and stayed in the division. It's a blemish on your personal reputation. When we got back up and did well I didn't really think we were heading for the Championship. We didn't have the steel. We weren't strong enough at the back. We were more of a Cup side. Great to watch, but not quite there for the Championship.
>
> They were always careful with money at United. Lots of times we should have gone into the market and they wouldn't, which was disappointing. They are the biggest club in the world and everyone wants to play for them. I would have got the players. Peter Shilton would have come but they wouldn't pay the wages. Our players were on £300 a week. Shilton wanted £400.
>
> To this day I don't really know the reason for my sacking. I've heard lots of stories. Heard it was the directors' wives, heard it was some of the players' wives. I personally think if Matt had said 'he stays', I'd have stayed. I didn't socialise with Matt so much and consequently I think I cut myself off. I heard that Laurie knew about other things that had gone on at the club and said that if I didn't get the sack he'd spill the beans.
>
> I'd like to think I could have got United to where they are with Fergie's resources. Dave Sexton got more money to spend than I got, Ron got more and Fergie has had more again. I think the present team is potentially better than the '68 team. They've got class players. Schmeichel is the best in the world. Keane is outstanding. You don't need some of his antics off the pitch. But you need a dirty bugger in the middle of the park, yes. I would have made Keane captain. My favourite is Scholes. Great player. But Law, Best, Charlton – now you're talking about a different breed

altogether. There's nothing like that in the side today. If Law played today they'd definitely win the European Cup. If Denis had played against Dortmund he would have had a hat-trick. Maybe four, maybe five.

\* \* \*

After the roller-coaster ride with Docherty, United opted for the boating lake. They entrusted Dave Sexton with the oars. A good man, widely respected in the game. And quiet. And wary. And discreet. And a Catholic of the kind O'Farrell was. As Docherty ruefully observes, the club did support Sexton with a substantially bigger budget. He had earned recognition at Chelsea and Queens Park Rangers with more modest means, but now exercised his financial muscle to bring in Gordon McQueen, Joe Jordan, Ray Wilkins and Garry Birtles for £2.75m. And still United could not find their panacea.

They were knocked out of the Cup-Winners' Cup in the second round by Porto and finished tenth in the League in 1977–78. They improved by only one position the following season but reached the FA Cup final and lost 3–2 to Arsenal in a thrilling climax. Gary Bailey had become the regular goalkeeper and in 1979–80 Sexton had the foundation for a Championship challenge. They were runners-up. A year on, however, they were back in an ominously familiar spot, eighth, having failed to clear the first hurdle in the UEFA Cup. A run of seven wins from the last seven matches was a mite unfortunate from the board's point of view. They had already decided Sexton must go.

The directors – and many critics and supporters – felt United had lost their sparkle, that they had become downbeat in the image and likeness of their boss. They needed a lift, a fresh vitality. So they went back to the other end of the managerial spectrum, to an expansive personality. Big in every sense. Ron Atkinson was the man they believed would fit the bill. He revelled in the role of the flamboyant manager-star. Anonymity was not in his vocabulary, although he was no less a football man than any of his predecessors. He was not, however, a Catholic, but suggested, 'I could be converted!' Witty, too.

Fun was back on the agenda at Old Trafford, yet not at the expense of business. Atkinson paid £1m for Frank Stapleton and a British record transfer fee of £1.5m to sign Bryan Robson from his former club, West Bromwich Albion. Few shared Atkinson's conviction it was money well spent, but soon Robson would be captain of club and country and acknowledged as the most influential player of his generation. The

Dutchman Arnold Muhren complemented Robson's midfield power with his subtlety. Paul McGrath combined both qualities at the heart of the defence, the emergence of a young striker called Mark Hughes persuaded Atkinson he should not shell out more cash for Peter Beardsley, Norman Whiteside was a first-team substitute at 16, and Jesper Olsen and Gordon Strachan relit the torch for wingers. These were some of the key figures in Atkinson's evolving team.

They delivered results with style. United won the FA Cup in 1983 and 1985 and were regular contenders in Europe again, defeating Barcelona before losing to Juventus in the Cup-Winners' Cup semi-finals in 1984. They opened the 1985–86 First Division campaign with ten consecutive wins. Their first title in 19 years beckoned. And then the style and the results waned. Injuries to Robson palpably weakened the side but other reasons were sought, and by the end of the season sections of the gallery were calling for Atkinson's head.

Extrovert though he was, he could not bring himself to court the fans, and they never warmed to him the way they had to Docherty. He complained the crowd had to be stoked up by the team, that they lacked passion. Like Docherty, he left home for another woman, and although Maggie Harrison – now Mrs Atkinson – was unrelated to anyone at the club, the inevitable publicity was not well received in some quarters. Perhaps more relevant were stories of indiscipline and excessive drinking among the players. Whatever their cumulative effect, a dismal start to 1986–87 sucked him into the abyss. The Championship – and a return to the European Cup – had disappeared from United's view and Atkinson paid with his job. He now says,

> When I went there the first statement I made was that I wanted to make them a major European club again, which we did. We got into Europe every year, and I think that from 1969 to when I joined them they had got there only three times. It was a hell of a night when we beat Barcelona 3–0 at Old Trafford to go through on aggregate, but I have to say we were a bit fortunate in that match. The one I look back on was the semi, which we lost 3–2 on aggregate against possibly the greatest Juventus side ever, with seven or eight of the Italian team that went on to win the World Cup in 1986. The following year we were the first team to win at Dundee United in a European game.
>
> We had quality players, no question about that, and I thought the Championship was within our capabilities.

People used to go on about the fact that United had not won the League for 15 years or whatever it was, but I'd say don't blame me for that. I've been here only two. I think the present team are very good and must have a chance of the European Cup.

Atkinson looked on from a variety of posts, in England and the Continent, as his successor survived inauspicious early years of tenure to create a team with such prospects. He had the satisfaction of denying United the League Cup in two finals, with Sheffield Wednesday and then with Aston Villa, but wryly digested the irony that the club's faith and patience in Alex Ferguson were eventually rewarded.

Many observers believed the man who made Aberdeen dare to take on and conquer the Old Firm had been the object of United's attention for some time before Atkinson was removed. Ferguson was renowned as tough, as a disciplinarian, and as a winner. He had taken the Cup-Winners' Cup to that far-flung corner of Britain. Here was the man to get the Old Trafford house in order. He in turn considered himself the man to shift the English seat of power from Merseyside. New players arrived in waves: Brian McClair, Steve Bruce, Mark Hughes (retrieved from Barcelona); then Mike Phelan, Neil Webb, Gary Pallister (for a record £2.3m fee), Paul Ince and Danny Wallace. Paul McGrath and Norman Whiteside departed. But more than three years into the job, Ferguson had made scant impression on the game south of the border.

'You maybe analyse more when you are in that situation, and deep down you worry,' he says. 'I'm no different from anyone else. I felt we were going the right way, but what I needed was a bit of luck. I had that with Mark Robins's goal and the FA Cup win against Forest. Eventually winning the Cup against Palace helped the players overcome a lot of doubts about whether they were good enough to play for Manchester United.'

United followed up that success by winning the Cup-Winners' Cup in 1991, their first European triumph since 1968, defeating Barcelona 2–1 in the final at Rotterdam. They mopped up the obscure 'Super Cup' but now the clamour was for the Championship, and Ferguson, aided by his new assistant Brian Kidd, steered United to the brink of the title after winning the 1992 League Cup. Ferguson blamed a fixture congestion in the final week for their capitulation; critics contended the manager's anxieties had been transmitted to the players. Either way, Leeds United, whose players included Gordon Strachan and a Frenchman, Eric Cantona, edged in front to become champions.

The jury is similarly split on Ferguson's signing of a new striker in

November 1992: inspiration or desperation? Beyond dispute is that Cantona, at £1.2m, proved one of the club's greatest investments. United won their first title – in the shape of the inaugural Premier League Championship – for 26 years at a canter. Among those who acclaimed the champions at Old Trafford was the president, Sir Matt Busby. Smiling, applauding and doubtless reminiscing.

As Ferguson says, 'Winning the League for the first time with United was definitely the high point, because that was the catalyst. That settled everyone down. The supporters lost their anxiety.'

So, too, perhaps did Ferguson. He might also say Cantona was the catalyst. Here was a man apart (who else would have contrived that kung-fu assault or the subsequent philosophical drivel?) and yet adored within the team and in the stands as a cult-figure-cum-messiah. He was the most venerated player at Old Trafford since the Holy Trinity. His football was almost spiritual, his goals as crucial as they were divine. And around him Ferguson assembled worthy disciples: Peter Schmeichel, Denis Irwin, Roy Keane (the natural successor to Robson) and Andrei Kanchelskis. Equally important was the influx from the junior ranks: Ryan Giggs and then Gary and Phil Neville, Nicky Butt, David Beckham and Paul Scholes, enabling Ferguson to maintain his domination of the domestic game.

Sir Matt Busby was not among those who acclaimed United's League and FA Cup double-winners of 1994. He died, at the age of 84, on 20 January 1994. The outpouring of grief, the carpet of flowers and red and white favours, and the tributes from around the world testified to his legacy and stature. Although some, as we have heard, would defer, most subscribe to the view that this was also fitting recognition of his humanity. And most suspected he was smiling and applauding approvingly from his celestial vantage point as his club embraced their maiden double.

His momentous European Cup achievement, however, had not been emulated and, much as Ferguson was conscious of a potential 'albatross', he could not camouflage his ultimate ambition. A new generation of players and supporters had hooked on to the old dream. United made an uneasy return to the grand stage, nudging past Kispest-Honved of Hungary but losing to Galatasaray on the away-goals rule. They beat the same Turks 4–0 a year later but that was not enough to keep them in the Champions League. A 4–0 defeat in Barcelona effectively put paid to that. United were still out of their depth in this company. English football's five-year exile following the Heysel tragedy was a factor, as was the three-foreigner rule, restricting the manager's options and disrupting the team pattern.

Ferguson's side, deprived of Cantona's brilliance as a consequence of events at Selhurst Park and frustrated at the last by the profligacy of Andy

Cole, their record £7m signing, yielded their Championship to Blackburn Rovers and the FA Cup to Everton. Although Schmeichel's heroic late goal saved United's unbeaten home record in Europe, it could not spare them a first-round exit to Rotor Volgograd in the UEFA Cup. Salvation to the greater good was at hand. Cantona was restored to active duty and his propensity for conjuring vital goals brought the title back to Old Trafford. Against Liverpool, it also reclaimed the FA Cup and completed an historic second double.

The remaining challenge for Cantona, as well as United, was the European Cup. Neither he nor Schmeichel could prolong that proud, 40-year run at home. That it should be ended by a fluke goal and a modest Fenerbahce team rendered it all the more galling. United were beaten 1–0 on five occasions, twice by Juventus, twice by their semi-final conquerors, Borussia Dortmund (yes, that team again). Despite their 4–0 obliteration of Porto in the home leg of their quarter-final, a deficiency in front of goal proved their undoing against Dortmund. Had they been able to sign Alan Shearer . . . Hypothetical now. Another Championship, United's fourth in five seasons, revived most hearts, but not Cantona's. His influence had diminished and he decided his remarkable four and a half years at Old Trafford were over. The thespian manqué was off to find a new *Théâtre des Rêves*.

Ferguson was accompanied for the formal announcement of Cantona's retirement from football not by the player but by Martin Edwards, the club chairman and chief executive. Edwards appears for signings and other such public rituals yet rarely looks comfortable in the glare of the media. Unlike some of his counterparts, he prefers to cede publicity to his manager and players, stay indoors and keep his own counsel. Adverse reports in the past regarding club and private matters have made him retreat still further into his lair. But then he has always advocated the right of the manager to manage. He has pledged his managers moral and financial support, and got on with the next stage of building United's business empire.

Edwards became chairman at the age of 34 in succession to his father, Louis, who died in February 1980 after television allegations about his business affairs. Edwards junior's reputation took a buffeting over the aborted sell-out deals with Robert Maxwell and Michael Knighton before he floated United on the stock exchange. He has been perceived as a money man rather than a football man. He rejects that notion, insisting his motivation has always been the prosperity, on and off the field, of the club, just as his father's was. Big Louis was sometimes portrayed as a comic figure, as Busby's stooge, but his son believes he played a defining role in the development of the Manchester United we see today.

Edwards, sitting in his unextravagant office, says,

> The European Cup was the highlight of my father's involvement with United. He was made a director the day after the crash and he'd seen it through to '68. Although he didn't become chairman till 1965, when Harold Hardman died, he had effectively been the leading light for some time because Harold Hardman had been ill. He was a great friend of Matt's, so he would have got a lot of pleasure out of Matt's winning it. Together they had driven the club after Munich, culminating in that great win at Wembley. I was with the party that night and I think in his own way it meant as much to father as it did to Matt.
>
> It's very difficult for a son to talk about his father, but I have no illusion as to how he did build the club up after Munich. It needed a strong personality and he put the club on a very sound financial footing. He was very instrumental in building the old North Stand for the World Cup in 1966 and that stand was a model for everybody else. We were the first club to introduce boxes, and all that helped fund the side of the '60s. Before Munich, United weren't big buyers, but a lot of the players who helped build up the club were bought in the early '60s.
>
> There are differences between my father and me in terms of personality, but we are very alike in that we have both allowed the manager to manage. I think the job of chairman, and chief executive, is one of support. You have to balance the development of the stadium with the development of the team. There's no point having a magnificent stadium if you can't fill it. And I think if we moved from here it would be over my dead body.

Ferguson's declared ambition is for Old Trafford, which now has a three-tier North Stand and an all-seated capacity of 55,300, eventually to house 80,000. Planning and financial considerations present problems, although Edwards has stoked up the debate on the reintroduction of standing areas both to accommodate more customers and enhance the atmosphere. It was an uncharacteristic venture into the media spotlight.

> Some chairmen like publicity. It's down to the individual. I don't seek publicity. I'm happy if I'm not in print, but also

because it tends to mean everything is going reasonably well. If the board decides something's wrong with the business and that the manager has to go, then clearly it's the chairman who has to do the dirty work. I've had to do it twice. The first time, with Dave, was probably harder because I'd been chairman for only a year and we'd finished the season with seven wins on the trot. But I felt we'd gone backwards, and we needed a change. People were voting with their feet.

With Ron it was slightly easier. Although we'd finished the previous season fourth, our form in the second half of the season was actually relegation form. That continued into the start of the next season and I think we were in 19th place or something. It was nothing to do with personal matters.

It took Alex time but the circumstances were different. We took into consideration that he was new to the English game. Coming down from Scotland it was difficult. I don't think Alex knew the players quite as well as he thought he knew them. He inherited a team he wanted to change. He brought in a lot of new players and we knew it was going to take time to bed them in. Plus we knew how hard he was working behind the scenes on youth development and the structure of the club. Not many clubs would have been as patient, but that 'non-decision', if you like, was as important as any decision we've made. I take pride in that.

We know we made the right decision because of the success we've had since. Now we're having those great European nights again and I'd love us to win the European Cup again, but you've got to be careful you don't get too hung up on it, otherwise it becomes a millstone. A bit like the League became. The European Cup will be a bonus. Now that we're not restricted by that ridiculous three-foreigner rule which forced us to drop key players, we have no excuses and can be judged for the team we are. Our youngsters have gained experience in Europe and with England, and if we're going to achieve the big one that's all going to help.

The '60s team was great, and I don't think we had anything in the '70s and '80s to compare with it, but the '90s team does, and in a very big way. I think the double-winning side of '94, in every way, was as good as the '60s team. For me the '94 side was better than the '96 side, although that side is still growing. But I've been watching United regularly since 1958 and I think, man for man, the '94 side was the best I've ever seen. Charlton, Law and Best were absolutely exceptional, but the quality, in depth, of the '94 side was even greater. Think about it. Schmeichel, Parker and Irwin at full-back, Bruce and Pallister together, Keane and Ince, Kanchelskis and Giggs wide, Hughes and Cantona at their peaks up front. And remember, that team nearly did the treble.

The success of the team and the company, now valued at more than £400m, is indisputable. But what about the image of United as a gargantuan manifestation of greed? An image he has possibly perpetuated through his negotiations to sell control of the club? And by cold-shouldering old players?

The Robert Maxwell thing never got off the ground. He rang me up and said he wanted to make an offer and we fixed a date. We agreed it should be kept quiet, then he announced it to the world and in the end it was all about nothing. Michael Knighton said he would buy my share, make a general offer to other shareholders, but also provide £10m to fund the redevelopment of the Stretford End. We hadn't got the cash to do that, which is why I don't regret agreeing the sale. Unfortunately his backers withdrew and it got very messy.

I don't accept that we don't make former players welcome. Does Shay Brennan have a problem? Does Pat Crerand have a problem? Does Denis Law have a problem? They don't. But having said that, you can't make allowances for every old player at every game. If they want to come on a selective basis, fine. We welcome them. But these are the difficulties we have.

Of course I am concerned about our image. But a lot of things about Manchester United get blown up out of all proportion. At one time United was everybody's second favourite team, and when we became successful and probably commercial, that changed. Now you either love United or you hate them, and I don't think we're everybody's second favourite team any more. It's the nature of this country. In America if you are successful you are a hero. We get a lot more stick for doing exactly the same thing that everybody else does. Every club would like to be as commercially successful as United.

There will come a time when I know it's right for me to step aside. I'm not one of those who believes you can go on forever, and in business things change, attitudes change, systems change. You need new ideas coming in. If I step aside as chief executive and the club want to retain me in some capacity, perhaps as chairman or a role with a watching brief, then I would be delighted to stay. I've given too much of my life to United to outstay my welcome. The club is more important than me.

Ferguson also stressed the club was more important than any individual as he resumed the European Cup campaign in 1997–98 without Cantona, the soul of his team. A self-inflicted knee-ligament injury to Keane tore the heart out of the team as well. But Ferguson had bought Teddy Sheringham to play in Cantona's role, and Henning Berg to reinforce the defence. He looked to Ole Gunnar Solskjaer and Ronny Johnsen to confirm the promise of their first year, Karel Poborsky and Jordi Cruyff to improve, and Cole to rediscover a semblance of the form that made him a goalscoring sensation at Newcastle. And, of course, he had his kids, growing, developing, oozing the self-belief of their forebears.

The lesson of Best, an entirely new phenomenon in the game of the '60s, had forewarned and forearmed Ferguson. He had not been caught unawares and would not allow his young players to be exposed to the temptations and pitfalls of the outside world. In a sense Cantona, too, protected and nurtured them. His departure released them like doves to glorious flight. And now United looked an even stronger team, neither dependent on nor in awe of any individual.

Goals from Irwin, Berg and Cole away to the Slovakians FC Kosice instantly smoothed United's European path. Next up, at Old Trafford, were Juventus, who had beaten them twice in the previous Champions League but had lost in the final to Dortmund. United were reliving the nightmare when Alessandro del Piero floated beyond the grasp of their defence to score after just 23 seconds. Deep into that first half Ferguson's side could still not get to grips with the Italians. But gradually Sheringham imposed himself and when he leapt to head the equaliser the course of the contest changed. Didier Deschamps's dismissal left United important extra space, but by then their football was irresistible. Scholes's composed finish and Giggs's rocket, launched from a narrow angle, had the stadium in a state of frenzied exultation.

This was the kind of emotion-charged night Ferguson and Schmeichel implored of their fans, the kind of night Atkinson yearned for, the kind of night that hypnotised Charlton and Stiles. The people stood *en masse* behind the goals in defiance and in timeless honour of the cause. This is no bonus. This is everything.

Zinedine Zidane's converted late free-kick irritated rather than threatened United and Juventus did not misinterpret the message already delivered.

Another delightful execution by Scholes and Irwin's emphatic penalty emphasised the ascendancy in a 2–1 win against Feyenoord at Old Trafford. Cole became the club's first player to score a hat-trick in the European Cup since Denis Law against Waterford in 1968 as United defeated the Dutch again, in Rotterdam, 3–1. They were the only team in the competition with maximum points from four matches and had virtually guaranteed passage to the quarter-finals. A 3–0 home win against Kosice confirmed the booking, and although a 1–0 away defeat to Juventus allowed the Italians on board as one of the two best runner-up teams, United anticipated a springtime trip to Monaco with justified optimism

The dream was alive again.